# GIANTS OF SCIENCE

# GIANTS OF SCIENCE

Philip Cane

*Illustrated by*

Samuel Nisenson

First Published in India 2017
**Reprinted 2020**

ISBN 978–93–83723–22–5



*Published by*
**LG PUBLISHERS DISTRIBUTORS**
49, Street No. 14, Pratap Nagar
Mayur Vihar Phase I, Delhi 110091
lgpdist@gmail.com

*Printed at*
Sapra Brothers, Noida

# *Table of Contents*

## PYTHAGORAS

The Pythagorean theorem is probably more widely known than any comparably profound mathematical idea. This theorem was, as far as is known, first used by the Egyptians. They used it without having any mathematical proof that the idea was correct. Pythagoras is credited with being the first to show precise proof of this wonderful mathematical idea.

Pythagoras' theorem, which is a cornerstone of all technology, proved that the sum of the squares on the shorter two sides of a right triangle is equal to the square on the hypotenuse. (A right triangle has one angle of 90 degrees, a "right" angle.)

One of the important right triangles in the history of measurement is the one that has one side 3 units long and the other side 4 units long. The hypotenuse, or side opposite the right angle, is 5 units long. The squares on the sides, as can been seen from the drawings, contain 9 small squares and 16 small squares. The square on the hypotenuse contains 25 small squares. This shows that 3 x 3 plus 4 x 4 equals 5 x 5. The theorem is also true for every other right triangle. This geometric problem has been so interesting to mathematicians that there have been over one hundred different proofs of the Pythagorean theorem, including an original proof by President Garfield.

Pythagoras was born about 582 B.C., a native of Samos, Greece. Nothing is known of his personal life. He probably traveled through the Mediterranean, visiting the Egyptian centers of learning. In 529 B.C. he was driven from Greece to Southern Italy by the tyrant king, Polycrates. With his followers, he founded a kind of religious brotherhood devoted to mathematics as well as religion and philosophy. The members of the Pythagorean group were all aristocrats and were sworn to secrecy. As a result, the brotherhood was looked upon with suspicion by the common people.

Pythagoras and his followers believed that the human soul is immortal and returns to earth again and again, in different people. He believed that animals and men are related and that a human soul might be born into an animal. This, he taught, could be avoided if man lived a pure life. As a result, discipline in the society was very severe; self-discipline, purity, temperance and obedience were watchwords.

The Pythagoreans gave Copernicus the first inkling that the sun was at the center of the universe. Pythagoras believed that the paths of the planets must be circular. The circle, he argued, is the most perfect path. The earth, the stars, the planets, and the universe as a whole were spherical, he argued, because the sphere is the most perfect solid figure.

In addition to astronomers and mathematicians the brotherhood had biologists and anatomists. They discovered the optic nerves and the Eustachian tubes.

The Pythagoreans brought their mathematical science into music. A musical note is a pure sound that is pleasing to the ear. Certain pitches, when played together, are pleasing, while other combinations are jarring. Pythagoras discovered that simultaneous notes produced by strings that had lengths in simple ratios one to the other were harmonious. For example, if one string is twice as long as another (and both the same thickness and stretched to the same tightness) the sounds would be pleasing. This is true, too, if the lengths are 2 units and 3 units or 4 units and 3 units. In musical terms, 2 to 1 represents the octave; 3 to 2 the perfect fifth; 4 to 3 the perfect fourth. Musicians know these combinations of tones as the purest.

Two hundred years later, the learned Aristotle said of the Pythagoreans, "They applied themselves to the study of mathematics and were the first to advance that science. Having been brought up in it, they thought its principles must be the principles of all existing things."

Present day scientists are still trying to reduce the universe to the certainties of mathematical formulas.

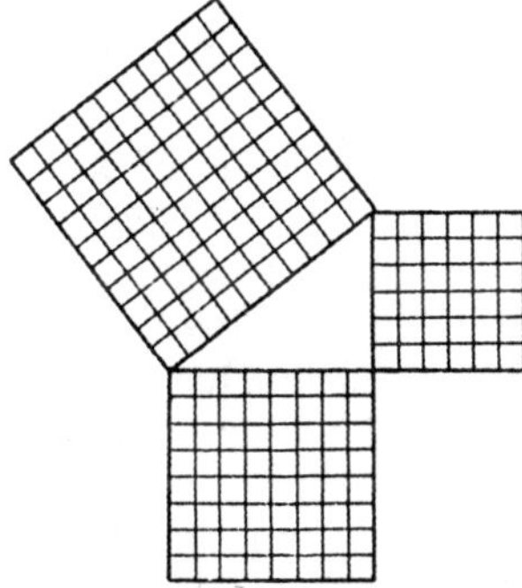

*The Pythagorean Theorem: The square on the hypotenuse equals the sum on the other two sides. 36 plus 64 equals 100.*

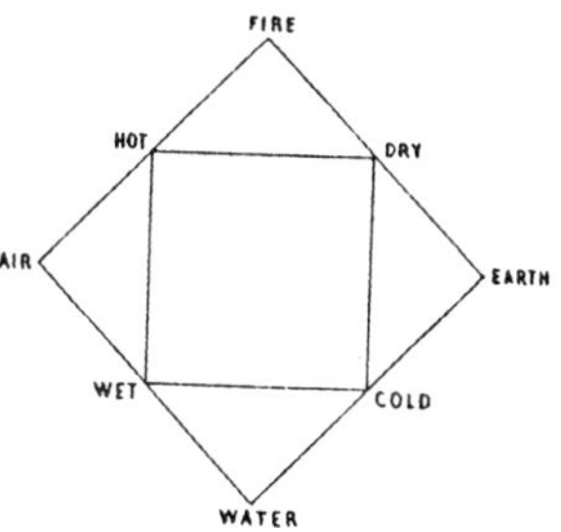


*The four elements and the four qualities according to the teachings of Pythagoras.*

## EUCLID

"Anyone who was not transported by this book in youth was not born to be a theoretical searcher." It is, to this day, studied by high school students, more than two thousand years after it was written. "This book" that Albert Einstein was referring to was the *Elements* of Euclid. It has been translated into every known language. The first edition in English appeared in the year 1570. The English translation was made from a Latin translation of an Arabic translation from the original Greek. The book was written about 300 B.C.

Euclid of Alexandria was a Greek mathematician and teacher. Practically nothing is known of his personal life. No records have been uncovered to tell us the date or even place of his birth. About all we know is that he taught mathematics at the Royal School at Alexandria, Egypt, and that he wrote a book that has probably sold more copies than any other book outside of the Bible.

Euclid is rightly called the father of geometry. He assembled all the known geometrical ideas, all the apparently unrelated pieces of information that had grown up as a result of practical need, into a related, understandable, beautifully developed system. He arranged the material, supplied the steps that led one mathematical proof into the next, supplied missing proofs and theorems and wound up with a pre-eminent demonstration of man's ability to think.

Egypt has been called the "Gift of the Nile," because ancient Egypt owed much of its greatness to the Nile River. Agriculture was made possible because the Nile, in overflowing its banks each year, covered the fields with black fertile mud brought down from the distant mountains of Africa. The floods brought problems along with the wealth. Landmarks were wiped out, the Nile changed its bed each year and the boundaries of property were vague. If taxes were to be collected on the land, the area of a man's property had to be known.

Geometry (the word originally meant land measuring) was developed to fill this practical need. The Egyptians apparently did not pay too much attention to the theoretical basis of the geometry they used so long as it gave them reasonably good results. In fact some of their geometry was inaccurate. All irregular areas were computed by dividing the land into a number of triangles and then figuring the areas of the triangles. Many an Egyptian overpaid on his taxes because the surveyor used the accepted but wrong formulas in calculating the area of the triangle.

The Egyptians knew how to construct a right angle by a method still used to lay out a playing field, or the foundation for a barn, when a surveyor's transit is not available. They used a rope triangle with sides that were three, four and five units long. When the rope is stretched with the knots at the corners, the angle between the three-unit and the four-unit side will be a right angle. The Egyptian surveyors were called rope stretchers.

Thales, a Greek mathematician, learned about the Egyptian geometry methods and wondered why they worked. This questioning was the first step in building geometry as a science. Thales in his search to satisfy his curiosity introduced the idea of deducing facts only from known principles and then following these thoughts as far as they would lead. He didn't forget, though, that geometry was a practical science and could be used in navigation and astronomy as well as in land measures and pyramid construction.

The next step in the development was the work done by Pythagorus and his followers. They separated geometry from all its practical applications and were interested only in finding logical proofs about geometric facts. And they further developed the method of reasoning that has stood the test of time, not only in geometry but in all areas where man uses his mind. This great method is called deductive reasoning.

Deductive reasoning tries to find an answer to a problem by making use only of facts that have been previously agreed upon. Practically every detective story turns out to be an example of deductive reasoning, but science is the greatest detective story of all. Arthur Conan Doyle has his fictional detective Sherlock Holmes say, "From a drop of water, a logician could infer the possibility of an Atlantic Ocean or a Niagara Falls without having seen or heard of one or the other. So all life is a great chain, the nature of which is known whenever we are shown a single link of it. Like all other arts, the Science of Deduction and Analysis is one which can only be acquired by long and patient study."

Euclid collected all the works of Thales and Pythagorus, and Plato and the Greeks and Egyptians that had gone before. Euclid's great contribution was not the solution of new problems in geometry; it was the ordering of all the methods known into a system in which known facts could be combined to discover new ideas and prove them. Starting with simple definitions called axioms, Euclid combined them into statements called theorems which are proved by logic.

Plato understood the importance of geometry. Geometry was the entrance exam to his Academy. He said, "Let no man ignorant of geometry enter my doors."

Abraham Lincoln agreed on its importance too. At the age of forty he studied Euclid, not for the mathematics, but as training in reasoning.

The study of mechanics, sound, light, navigation,

atomics, biology, medicine, all branches of science and technology depend on the teachings of Euclid. Science will continue to use deductive reasoning as it goes on to greater discoveries.

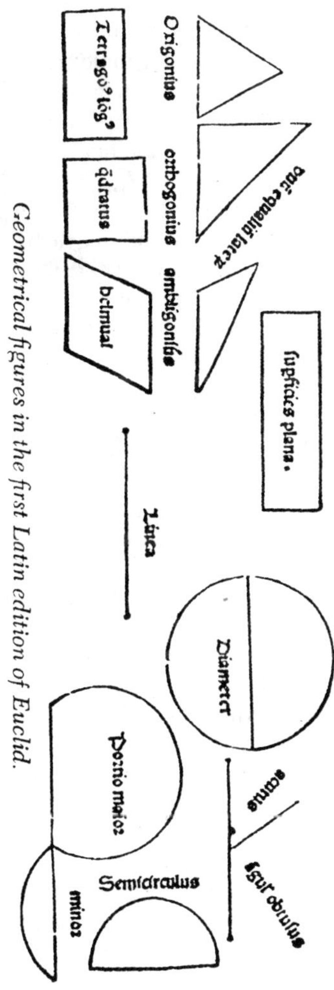


*Geometrical figures in the first Latin edition of Euclid.*

## HIPPOCRATES

"I swear that I will carry out this oath. I will use treatment to help the sick according to my ability and judgment, never with a view to wrong-doing, to none will I give a deadly drug, even when asked to do so. Into whatsoever houses I enter, I will enter to help the sick. Whatsoever I shall see or hear in the course of my profession, if it should not be published, I will never divulge it."

These ideas are contained in the oath taken, to this day, by graduating medical students. The full statement, known as the Hippocratic Oath, is based on the teaching of the great Greek physician Hippocrates.

As is the case with many of the ancient Greeks whom we know through their writings, very little is recorded of the personal life of Hippocrates. It is recorded that he was born on the Greek Island of Cos, in about 460 B.C. The temple of Aesculapius was located on this island and Hippocrates' father may have been a temple priest.

There are some who say that Hippocrates never lived, and that his seventy medical treatises are the work of a group of men. However, Plato, the outstanding Greek historian and philosopher, speaks of Hippocrates as an individual. Plato said that Hippocrates traveled widely, teaching medicine as he went from place to place. Hippocrates' school on the island of Cos was probably a successor to that established in the sixth century B.C. by the Greek mathematician Thales. The school instructed its students in the proper personal relationships between doctor and patient as well as in the principles of medicine.

Until the advent of Hippocrates, the practice of medicine was in the hands of the priests of Aesculapius, the Greek and Roman god of healing. Aesculapius, according to legend, was so skilled a physician that he was supposed to be able to bring the dead back to life.

Illness was thought to be a result of the displeasure of the gods toward man, therefore the way back to health was thought to be through offerings to the gods. Sick people, came (if they were able) to the Temple of Aesculapius to seek the assistance of the priests in gaining favor with the gods. Many patients went home cured as a result of the natural healing powers of the body. The temple priests occasionally provided ointments and medications, which may or may not have had something to do with the recovery of the more fortunate patients.

We can well imagine that Hippocrates must have been looked upon with some suspicion, since he denied the powers of gods to heal, but he was clever enough not to oppose completely the popular feeling about the gods. An early version of the Hippocratic oath starts "I swear by Apollo the Physician, by Aesculapius, by Health, by Panacea and by all the gods and goddesses. . . ." But Hippocrates believed only in the facts as ascertained by observation and experiment. He tried to overcome superstition as regards disease and its cure.

The abilities of Hippocrates were heralded throughout the civilized world. Artaxerxes, the Persian King, offered his limitless treasure if he would quell an epidemic that was destroying the Persian armies. Since Persia was then at war with Greece, Hippocrates turned down the treasure, replying that honor forbade assistance to his country's enemies. There is a famous painting showing this incident; it hangs in the Medical School of Paris.

The teachings of Hippocrates, as detailed in his medical treatises, were rediscovered during the Middle Ages. Unfortunately the books were accepted as being finally and completely true and accurate, and as the ultimate word in medical theory. While there is much in his writings that may still be useful today, this slavish acceptance of Hippocrates held back medical progress for hundreds of years. Galen, about 200 A.D. disagreed with Hippocrates on many points, but that didn't shake faith in the absolute infallibility of Hippocrates. The French still say, "Galen says yes, Hippocrates says no," to indicate contradictory aspects of any moot question. This is not the only instance in history where slavish acceptance of even a good doctrine has held back progress. Science must always be ready to re-examine its past.

Hippocrates considered the study of anatomy to be the most important aspect of medical study. Later the study of anatomy was ignored and was not revived until Vesalius practiced it in the early fifteen hundreds. By that time surgery was in the hands of the barbers.

During the reign of Henry VIII of England (1509-1547), a law was passed forbidding barbers from doing

*Treating the sick in ancient Greece.*

any surgery except bloodletting or tooth pulling. At the same time, surgeons were forbidden to give shaves. The barber pole still commemorates the barber's surgical history. The white stripes represent the bandages, the red stripes represent the blood.

The Hippocratic oath separates the duties of the doctor and the surgeon – "I will not use the knife . . . but I will give place to such as are expert therein." Hippocrates placed the surgeon on a higher pedestal than the doctor, even as we often do today.

Hippocrates is the father of modern medicine. He looked for the explanation of diseases in the world about him and not in the whims of the gods. He taught that the physician must observe the patient carefully and record the symptoms of disease. In this way he could build up a record to show how the patient might be cured. He set forth procedures for observation of the patient. The appearance of the patient's eyes and skin, the temperature of the body, the appetite and waste elimination aspects. He insisted on day-by-day notes and kept a medical chart of the patient's progress. He was conscious of the effects of climate and the change of seasons on the various illnesses, such as the fact that we have more colds in the winter. It was his attention to this matter that linked up to the idea of

*Ancient Greek physicians in the laboratory.*

astronomy and medicine–since astronomy was important in the determination of the various seasons–and so for centuries medical students studied astronomy for no very good reason.

Hippocrates was conscious of the status of the physician and the necessity of building up confidence in the medical man. He advised the doctor to tell the patient what the course of the disease would be, for if the doctor forecast accurately, "He will be the more believed to understand the cases, so that men will confidently entrust themselves to him for treatment."

Many of the things Hippocrates recorded sound very up-to-date, for instance:

> People who are naturally very fat are likely to die earlier than those who are naturally slender.
>
> Older people require less food than young people.
>
> Eat more in the winter and less in the summer.
>
> Lean people can take small amounts of food, but this should be fat; fat persons may take much food, but it should be lean.
>
> Worry, fatigue, and chills – wine drunk with equal proportions of water soon removes these complaints.

## ARISTOTLE

"If I had my way," declared Roger Bacon, "I should burn all the books of Aristotle, for the study of them can lead to a loss of time, produce error, and increase ignorance."

This extraordinary statement by an outstanding scientific thinker, critical as it sounds, is in reality a magnificent tribute to the influence and importance of this early Greek scientist-philosopher.

Aristotle was born in 384 B.C. in the town of Stagira at the northern end of the Aegean sea. His father was an educated and influential man, the court physician to the grandfather of Alexander the Great. His early education was obtained at home and his father provided him with an extensive background in the Natural Sciences.

In 367 B.C., at the age of seventeen, he went to Athens which was a center of learning. In Athens he studied under Plato, the great philosopher of the time. Here he showed independence of mind and spirit, taking what he felt was useful in Plato's thinking, but disagreeing with, and extending Plato's philosophy when he felt the need to do so.

Aristotle soon became recognized as an outstanding

teacher. He was called to Macedonia to tutor the fourteen-year-old Alexander. Alexander, who became Alexander the Great, never forgot his teacher and later provided him with funds to continue scientific studies and research.

It is estimated that Aristotle produced somewhere between four hundred and a thousand books. There is some question as to whether he produced the books alone or whether he simply collected the writings of fellow scientists and philosophers. The writings are so extensive and cover such a wide field of activities that it seems hardly possible that one man could have produced them.

It is known that Aristotle had one of the earliest teams for scientific research. About 1,000 men traveled throughout Greece and Asia collecting specimens of sea and land life and making reports to Aristotle of their findings.

It is in the fields of biology and zoology that Aristotle made the most lasting of his scientific contributions. In this activity Aristotle displayed a remarkable understanding of scientific method as we recognize it today. He spent much time at the waterfront collecting and examining the sea life about him, and his observations about animals of all kinds are extraordinarily good.

Some of his findings, once thought to be absurd, have been found to be perfectly accurate. He recognized the ladder of nature: the way living beings may be classified by their complexity. He recognized the functional perfection of the creatures about him – realized how they are fitted to the conditions of their lives. Aristotle was, early in civilization, a forerunner of that great band of scientists who recognize that there is system and order in the world – that things are not haphazard.

A basic method of science is observation and experiment in the laboratory and in the world about us. Aristotle and his research team performed beautifully in this way in the field of biology. There was a gap of some 1,500 years before Albertus Magnus took up Aristotle's work and enlarged upon it. Magnus, too, made original observations upon which he based his extensions and criticisms.

Aristotle did not confine his biology to externals, but was the first person to make dissections of animals. He uncovered some of the differences in internal structure. Here again he was a forerunner of modern biological methods.

H. G. Wells in *The Outline of History* said about Aristotle: "He anticipates Bacon and the modern scientific movement in his realization of the importance of ordered knowledge. He set himself to the task of gathering together and setting down knowledge. He was the first natural historian. Other men before him had speculated about the nature of things, but he, with every young man he could win over to the task, set himself to classify and compare things."

Why then did Bacon want to avoid the study of Aristotle? Because Aristotle, who was so careful in his biology was woefully wrong in his physics. The scientific method he used so well in biology was misused or ignored in the study of astronomy and physics. The influence of Aristotle was extraordinary for 1,500 years: his writings began to take on the aspects of articles of faith and were accepted as being true simply because Aristotle had written them.

Here are some of the ideas Aristotle advanced. He supposed that all the properties of all things on earth could be accounted for in terms of whether they were hot or cold, wet or dry in varying amounts. Changes in these qualities could be explained by supposing four elements: water, air, fire, and earth. Many things could be explained on this basis. For instance if a log is put on a fire, *water* will ooze out of the wood, *air* (smoke) comes out, *fire* will appear from the log, and *earth* (ashes) will be left. The heavens were made of another element, which did not change. Thus the universe was made up of five elements.

The heavens were in outer space; fire went up, earth went down, water went above earth, air went above water but below fire. The four elements of the earth went up or down; the Heavenly element traveled in a circular motion. The circle was a perfect figure and therefore obviously the correct motion for the perfect element.

In 1609 when Kepler found that the planets moved in elliptical paths he had difficulty convincing himself that this was true because of the long history of Aristotle's heavenly element.

Since the time of Galileo it is well known that, neglecting air resistance, heavy and light objects fall at the same rate. Aristotle, however, made some inadequate observations and came to the wrong conclusion. He saw that a stone falls faster than a leaf – which it does – and he concluded that the heavier body falls faster than the lighter body. For example he argued that a two-pound weight will fall twice as fast as a one-pound weight. But he didn't try it; he was satisfied that it was logical and therefore true.

In about the year 1585 a Dutch mathematician dropped two balls made of lead out of a window. One ball weighed ten times the other. They were dropped onto a wooden platform thirty feet below the window. There was one sound as they hit, proof that both weights hit at the same time.

Aristotle was a great man of science. The tragedy was that he was too great. The lesser minds that followed him accepted his errors along with his achievements and sought to find in his writings the answers to all problems for all time.

## ARCHIMEDES

The ability to observe what happens, to understand what is observed, and to use the information to discover new ideas is the mark of the scientist. Archimedes took a bath and came out, not only clean, but with an important idea – now called "specific gravity."

Archimedes was born about 287 B.C. at Syracuse, Sicily. He was the son of a Greek astronomer, Pheidias. Archimedes studied at the famous school of mathematics in Alexandria, the center of learning in the later Greek world. He was a student of Cenon of Samos, the noted mathematician of the day, a follower of the famed Euclid.

Archimedes spent his life in philosophical and mathematical studies. To the Greeks of his day, manual labor was considered degrading, and they looked upon experimentation with distaste. Many scholars believe, however, that Archimedes must have performed actual physical experiments before he was able to formulate his mathematically exact conclusions. Archimedes did not describe the experiments, but he wrote up his conclusions as though they resulted from purely mental theorizing. From other writings, however, we find out that he had made many practical applications of his findings.

The story is that he arrived at the idea of specific gravity – still called Archimedes' Principle – while in the bathtub. King Hiero II had ordered a new crown and had supplied the crownmaker with a quantity of gold. The finished crown weighed the same as the gold, but the suspicious King thought that some silver had been mixed in with the gold, to the illegal profit of the crownmaker.

It was already known that different materials had different weights: A cube of gold weighed more than the same size cube of silver. A simple solution, then, was to melt down the crown, cast it into a cube and weigh it. If it weighed less than the same size cube of gold, the crownmaker had mixed in some silver and had taken the King's gold. But this "simple" solution would destroy the crown. The problem was to check the quantity of gold in the crown without destroying the crown. The King asked Archimedes to look into the matter.

And so we come to the celebrated bath. As Archimedes settled himself in the bathtub the level of the water rose, of course. The more of his body that was under water, the higher the water rose. Archimedes realized that this was a fine way to measure an irregular volume. Archimedes filled a container with water and carefully suspended the suspected crown in the water. He caught the water that spilled out – the overflow must be the same volume as the crown. Now it was a simple job: obtain a volume of gold equal to the volume of the water and check its weight against the weight of the crown.

The greedy goldsmith was found guilty and was execut-

ed. But more important, scientists and engineers have since compared the weight of a volume of material with an equal volume of water and called the result Specific Gravity.

The specific gravity of gold is about 20, which means that a pint of gold would weigh twenty pounds, since a pint of water weighs about one pound. A pint of silver would weigh only about ten pounds.

Closely related to the measurement of the gold crown is the matter of buoyancy. Possibly Archimedes noticed that the bath water seemed to hold him up, that he tended to float, or he may have noted that some materials such as wood, do not sink in water. He wondered whether the water had any buoyant effect on objects that sank. He studied the problem and came up with the idea that "a body immersed in a fluid is buoyed up with a force equal to the weight of the fluid that it displaces."

This means that if a block of iron weighs, let us say, eight pounds, it will take up a certain amount of space. It will, if placed in a filled tank, displace a certain amount of water. In this case about one pound. If we weigh the block of iron while it is in the water it will seem to weigh seven pounds. The seven pounds results from its original eight pounds less the one pound of water it displaces. It has been buoyed or lifted by the amount equal to the weight of the water it pushed aside.

The reason we can float and swim is because our bodies weigh just about the same amount as the water we displace. Thus in water we weigh practically nothing. That is why it is much easier to float when we are completely under the surface, head and all, than if we try to keep our heads out. A piece of wood, or a boat, does not float entirely on top of the water, but must sink just deep enough to displace an amount of water equal to the weight of the wood or the boat. As a ship is loaded with cargo it sinks deeper and deeper into the water, since it must displace more water in order to equal the weight of the ship. Thus we speak of the displacement of the ship. A modern passenger liner may displace 80,000 tons of water; in other words, it weighs 80,000 tons. Submarines – including the atomic sub – depend on Archimedes' Principle.

Archimedes is credited with inventing a device for lifting water. This is still called the Archimedean screw. It consists of a large spiral screw fitted snugly inside a cylindrical case. As the screw is turned, the water is pushed along as shown in the illustration. This same principle has been used for handling wheat, and the screw drive is used in automatic stokers for bringing coal to a furnace and for removing the ashes. The same idea is found in most every home – look at the meat grinder a housewife uses and see how the screw drives the meat along.

Archimedes developed and demonstrated the mathematics behind the use of the lever. By méans of this simple device man has been able to multiply the force available in his own hands to enable him to move very large loads. To emphasize his point Archimedes declared, "Give me a place to stand, and I will move the earth." The law of the lever can be understood from the diagrams.

The force needed at one end of the lever to move a load at the other end of the lever depends on the distances to the pivot. For instance a weight of 1,000 pounds can be moved with a force of 100 pounds if the distance from the moving force to the pivot is ten times the distance from the weight to the pivot.

Look at the see-saw in the park. A light child at one end, but far away from the crossbar, can balance a heavier child at the other end, providing he is closer to the crossbar.

Archimedes contributed to pure as well as applied mathematics. One of the problems that has never been

solved is that of "squaring the circle." This really means to find the *exact* area of a circle. Mathematicians have given us a very close idea. They tell us that the area of the circle is equal to $\pi R^2$, where $\pi$ (pi) has the *approximate* value of 3.1416. This number has never been determined exactly, even with the use of modern giant electronic calculators, but Archimedes calculated the value of $\pi$ with remarkable accuracy, at between 3.1408 and 3.1429. He also did a great amount of work in what is called analytic geometry, especially in the properties of sections of spheres and of cones. A spiral, called the Spiral of Archimedes, is still studied by every student of calculus.

Archimedes was particularly proud of his work with the sphere and cylinder. He worked out the formulas for the surface area and the volume of the sphere, as well as the formulas for the cylinder into which the sphere would exactly fit. Archimedes showed that the sphere is the most efficient solid figure. You will see water tanks in the form

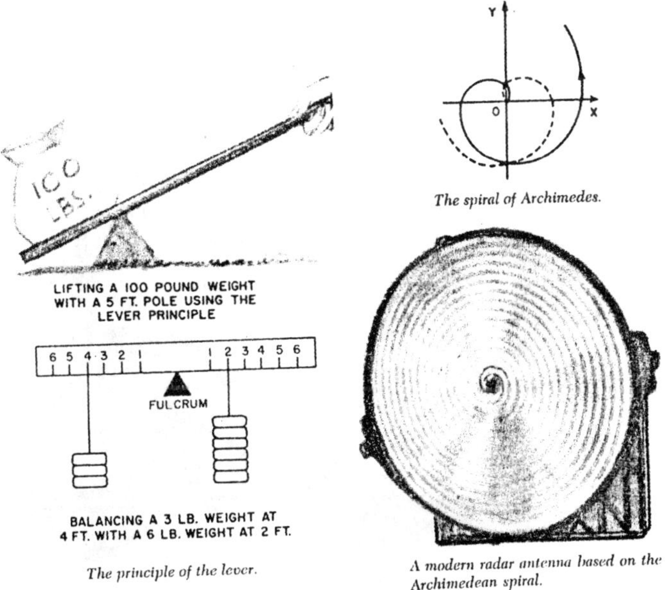


*The spiral of Archimedes.*

*The principle of the lever.*

*A modern radar antenna based on the Archimedean spiral.*

of a big ball. These hold the most water, using the least amount of material for their construction.

Archimedes turned his talents to the machinery of war, as did many scientists in the history of civilization. His knowledge of levers was used in the construction of catapults. History records that it was Archimedes' catapults that "wounded the enemy at every range" and turned the tide in favor of the Greeks during the defense of Syracuse in 215 B.C. Polybus, the historian said, "So true it is that one man and one intellect, properly qualified for the particular undertaking, is a host in itself." In modern times we see that this is still true; it was only a small band of atomic scientists who produced the terrible atomic weapons.

Several years later, Syracuse was captured by Marcellus, the Roman general. He had given orders that Archimedes be spared and his home left untouched. Something went wrong and Archimedes fell victim to the sword of a Roman soldier. The Romans buried him with honors and marked his tomb with his favorite symbols, a sphere and a cylinder.

Archimedes was a giant, a scientist and mathematician of extraordinary greatness – "one man and one intellect – a host in itself."

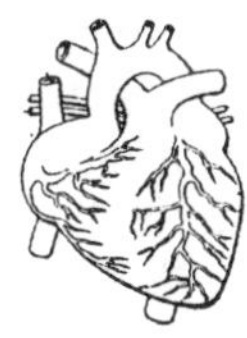

## GALEN

"[I will] trust none of those . . . statements until I have tested them for myself insofar as it has been possible for me to put them to the test. So if anyone after me becomes, like me, fond of work and zealous for truth let him not conclude hastily from two or three cases. For often he will be enlightened through long experience as I have been."

These are the words of the physician Galen, who is in the front rank of the medical giants of history and who is called the father of anatomy. His monumental encyclopedia of medicine *Anatomical Exercises* was the cornerstone and final authority of the medical profession for almost fifteen hundred years. His words seem to us all more remarkable because they embody modern scientific method of experimentation and the multiple testing of results.

Galen was born in A.D. 129 at Pergamum in Asia Minor. Asia Minor is the peninsula located between the Black Sea and the Mediterranean. It is separated from Greece by the Aegean Sea. This peninsula, in modern times, is mainly occupied by Turkey. Asia Minor was one of the most prosperous regions in the civilized world during Galen's lifetime. The Roman Empire held sway and ruled this civilized country wisely and well.

Galen's father was from Greece and was well educated. He was well versed in arithmetic, geometry, and astronomy; he was a mathematician as well as an architect. Galen's father was a great positive influence on his life. It was from him that Galen formed his own scientific attitudes. His father advised, "Magnify truth alone, hear and judge all, follow no one sect or party." His mother's influence was great too: from her he learned patience, to control his temper and to consider well before he spoke. Her influence was by bad example; she was a terrible shrew and he determined not to follow her example.

Up to his fourteenth year, as was the custom of the time, he was taught at home. He was then sent to attend lectures at the various schools which taught the precepts of the famous Greek philosophers. When Galen was seventeen, it was decided that he should study medicine. Surprisingly enough, this happy choice of a profession was decided upon as a result of a dream. In those days general belief in dreams was very strong and was accepted even by such educated people and clear thinkers as Galen and his father.

Galen studied medicine under the leaders of the profession. He studied in Pergamum, at Smyrna, and at Corinth. His studies were in all subjects of the times: geometry, astronomy, music, and language, as well as medicine.

He studied until he was twenty-nine – a long time for those days – and then returned to Pergamum to practice medicine. Galen was very successful as a physician and was called to Rome to act as the official doctor for the gladiators. Although the Romans loved the bloody exhibitions of gladiatorial combat – exhibitions of men fighting with knives to destroy each other – they curiously objected to dissections of human bodies. Galen used his position to make anatomical studies.

Galen made extensive studies in anatomy and physiology. Twenty volumes, each containing more than a thousand pages, have survived. Unable because of the laws to make complete studies of humans, he studied the structure of apes to fill in gaps in his knowledge, and based his treatises on his careful observations.

He made a study of the heart, describing the muscle layers and the valves. He came close to the principle of blood circulation but guessed wrongly that the blood oozed from the right chamber of the heart, through the dividing wall. He identified the main blood channels, but failed to determine the regular route to and from the heart. He thought that the veins and arteries carried the blood in some irregular fashion, in directions to and from the heart.

Galen came very close to modern knowledge with respect to the nervous system. He realized that all the nerves report to the brain, either directly or through the spinal cord. He performed experiments on animals by cutting the spinal cord at various levels and observed the resulting loss of control of the various functions of the animal. He correctly predicted the effect of cutting the phrenic nerve. This is the nerve that controls the movement of the diaphragm in breathing.

Galen recognized the value of the pulse rate in determining the condition of the patient, and at the same time realized that the pulse would also respond to emotional stresses. He anticipated the genetic theories of Mendel by observing that children frequently resemble their grandparents more closely than their parents. He recognized that the body perspires all over, even if we can't see it happen.

The work of Galen was considered infallible by medical men for more than fifteen centuries. Doctors who questioned his authority were likely to lose their reputation. This in spite of the fact that Galen himself advised that statements be put to test.

In the sixteenth century, Andreas Vesalius, a Belgian doctor, who conducted anatomical investigations on human bodies, tried to shake Galen's authority. But it was not until William Harvey, in the following century, published his experiments on the circulation of the blood that Galen's influence on medicine was shaken. In Vesalius' time, if an anatomical investigation indicated that Galen's work was in error, the authorities in the field would say that the human body must have changed since Galen's time. Galen could not have been wrong.

Galen would not have countenanced this slavish adherence to his works – he himself said, "The surest judge of all will be experience alone."

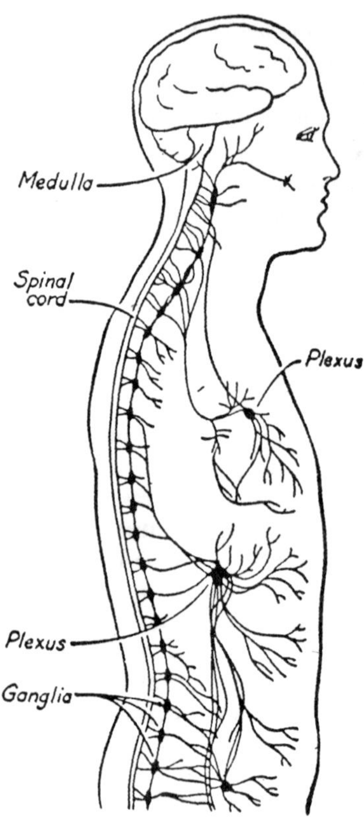


*The nervous system.*

## LEONARDO DA VINCI

On a hilltop in Florence, a handsome golden-haired young man released some birds – probably swallows – from a cage. He watched them intently as they winged their way through the air, now flying, now soaring. As he watched the birds fly, Leonardo da Vinci made notes of his observations.

He observed the birds because he was convinced that the same principles of flight would hold true for men as well as for birds. He took notes in mirror writing to keep his observations secret. Many people in Italy already thought him quite mad, and Leonardo did not want to add fuel to their fire. Man fly! indeed that's impossible.

Leonardo da Vinci is considered by many historians to have been the greatest experimental scientist of his age and is acknowledged to have been one of the greatest artists of all time. He is probably best known as the painter of the "Last Supper" and the "Mona Lisa." In addition to his many world-famous paintings he left us more than 5,000 closely written and beautifully illustrated pages detailing his observations and outlining inventions of all kinds. His writing was all done in mirror image to maintain secrecy. Leonardo da Vinci was an inventor, civil engineer, military engineer, astronomer, geologist, anatomist, as well as a pioneer aeronaut. He was not merely versatile; he was outstanding in every field. It was through his art that he became interested in science and his scientific studies probably helped make him a great artist.

Leonardo was born in the village of Vinci, near Florence, Italy, in 1452. He was the son of a village official and of a servant girl in the village inn. He spent his early years in the home of his grandparents.

The schoolboy Leonardo showed his genius early by solving difficult mathematical problems. At the same time he displayed a notable talent for painting. At sixteen he was apprenticed to the artist Andrea del Verrochio. Under this tutelage he learned to work with wood, marble, and metal. Verrochio, impressed with Leonardo's abilities urged him to study the Latin and Greek classics, philosophy, mathematics, and anatomy. These studies, Verrochio maintained, were necessary if Leonardo were to become a truly able artist.

Leonardo completed his apprenticeship at the age of twenty-six and was admitted into the Artists' Guild. He was now free to obtain his own patrons. As a result of a novel musical instrument – a lute in the shape of a horse's head in which the teeth served to select the tones – Leonardo attracted the attention of Duke Ludovico Sforza, the then ruler of Milan.

The various kingdoms of Italy were in constant strife with each other and Leonardo da Vinci turned his attention to the design of military equipment. While in the employ of the duke he also made plans for the design of new cities to replace the plague-ridden towns of his time. He realized the importance and value of a municipal sewer system. He offered many projects for consideration, but none seems to have been accepted. The only thing he produced for the duke was the painting "The Last Supper" which was ordered by the duke for presentation to the Refectory of Santa Maria.

While at Milan he became interested in anatomy. He

sought out the famous doctors of the age and arranged to witness dissections. Exceptional anatomical drawings were the result of his interest in this phase of scientific activity.

The Duke Ludovico Sforza was captured and imprisoned by the king of France, and Leonardo lost his supporting patron. At this juncture he went to Venice to offer his military inventions to the authorities. He had planned a diving suit and a submarine. These devices are among the few that were not fully explained in his notebooks. He said he did not divulge his methods of construction because he was afraid of "the evil nature of men who would use it as a means of murder at the bottom of the sea."

For a brief period, Leonard was employed as a cartographer by Cesare Borgia. Borgia, a despot, planned to conquer all of Italy and engaged Leonardo to make maps of Tuscany and Umbria. These maps are based on surveys and measurements Leonardo made himself.

In 1500, in his late fifties, Leonardo returned to his native Florence where he remained for six years. During this period he painted the famous "Mona Lisa," whose provocative smile still provides mystification and enjoy-

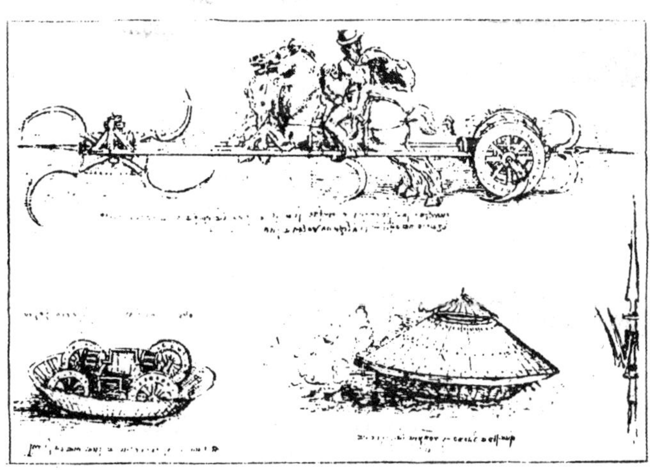

*Leonardo's drawings for war machines.*

ment to the thousands of people who view it at the Louvre Museum in Paris, France.

Other great artists of the time, including Raphael and Michelangelo, were busy painting in the Vatican and its Sistine Chapel. Leonardo went to Rome, but was unable to obtain a commission. He was in some disfavor because of his anatomical studies and drawings. As a result of this unhappy condition he left Italy, never to return. He spent the few remaining years of his life in the employ of the French king.

Leonardo da Vinci the artist has been well documented. His paintings remain, to this day, wonderful expressions of genius. Leonardo da Vinci the scientist-inventor is difficult to define. He was a man ahead of himself. His conceptions, all feasible, were so far ahead of contemporary thinking that he could get little if any support for them. Part of his difficulty was his penchant for accepting many commissions and then failing to deliver, because of lack of time and concentration.

His inventions are interesting and varied. His machine gun was a forerunner of the American Gatling gun used in the Spanish-American War. Leonardo's gun consisted of many barrels mounted on a triangular support. While one group of guns was fired, a second group was being loaded and the third group was allowed to cool. His military tank consisted of a mobile enclosure in which there are breech-loaded cannon. The tank had four independently mounted wheels and could be turned in any direction. The motive power was provided by manpower. This was before any mechanical power, other than water or wind power, had been developed.

In addition to his submarine and diving bell which have been mentioned before, he invented a double-hull ship. If the outer hull was penetrated by enemy gunfire the ship would still stay affoat.

In what would be called instrumentation in today's scientific age, Leonardo was equally active. He designed an anemometer, which is a device to measure the speed of the wind. This consisted of a vane which was pivoted in such a way that the wind could swing the vane. The angle of swing is a measure of the force of the wind.

Leonardo's clock was the first to indicate both hours and minutes. This clock was weight driven and escapement controlled.

The modern automobile contains an odometer. That is the device that tells how far the automobile has traveled. It works because it counts the number of revolutions made by the wheels and through gears and cables changes this information into miles. Leonardo da Vinci didn't have an automobile, but he needed to make measurements of distances for his mapping project. He designed an odometer for the purpose, a wheelbarrow-like device which the operator pushed along the road. As the wheel turned, it drove gears which ended in a dial that showed how far the wheelbarrow had moved.

Leonardo invented many mechanisms that are in use in similar forms today. These have been refined to make use of modern materials such as steel instead of wood, but the principles were developed by Leonardo da Vinci. He made a device not unlike an automobile jack for lifting weights. His model of a variable speed drive, used gearlike wheels of different diameters, meshing selectively with a cone drive. His roller bearings were away ahead of his time. He constructed a differential, which in principle is used in the rear end of the automobile today, permitting one wheel to turn faster than the other as the automobile is driven around a curve.

The machine tool industry would find that their screw-cutting machines and file-cutting machines are not too different in practice from those designed by Leonardo da Vinci.

Hydraulics was of especial interest to Leonardo. He designed a pump which used the power of the stream to raise water. A paddle-wheel in the running stream drove a large cog wheel which in turn operated piston pumps to raise the water. The entire structure was over seventy feet high. He was interested in other aspects of water: he studied the shapes of fish and his observations resulted in a streamlined design for a ship. The problems of irrigation and of navigation came into his field of endeavor and he made large plans to divert rivers for these purposes.

About 1490 Leonardo designed a flying machine. This machine (it never flew) was to be operated entirely by manpower. The flyer was supposed to flap the huge wings by moving his feet. He also designed a kind of helicopter, which consisted of a large screw thread. This was to be spring driven, but did not work. The power available was much too small. He built a linen-covered wooden frame in the form of a pyramid. This early parachute was tried out from a tower and was successful in slowing down the descent of a weight.

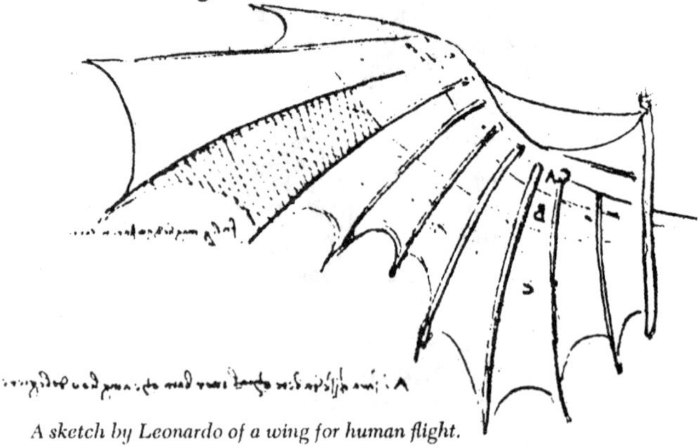

*A sketch by Leonardo of a wing for human flight.*

Leonardo da Vinci was an extraordinary botanist. His drawings and writings show that he was aware of positive and negative heliotropism – the tendency of some plants to turn toward the sun, while others turn away from it. He noted that some roots turn into the earth, others tend to grow to the surface; this is called positive and negative geotropism. He noted the rings in the trees and their relation to the age of the tree, and his drawings of flowers show that he understood that male and female plant life exists.

He collaborated with a physician in the study of anatomy. His drawings show a profound understanding of the anatomical structure of man. His drawings of the skull show for the first time the openings in the forehead and in the jaws – medical men call them the frontal and maxillary sinuses. His drawings are the first that accurately present the double curvature of the spine. For the first time too the position of the unborn baby in the mother is shown with accuracy. His drawings and descriptions of the heart are extraordinarily accurate: the chambers, the valves, the total structure are pictured.

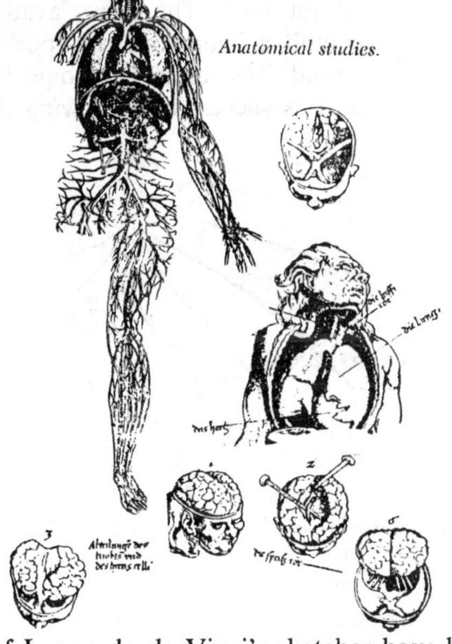

*Anatomical studies.*

Many of Leonardo da Vinci's sketches have been made into working models. Occasionally there are exhibitions of these devices. A notable collection is owned by The International Business Machine Corporation whose founder Thomas J. Watson has said:

> Invention is one of the greatest arts. In its broadest sense it embraces all of the arts. Leonardo da Vinci, interpreted through his paintings, studies, scientific investigations and inventions, brings before us a worthy example of a man exercising to the fullest extent his capacities to think, feel and create in service of his fellow-men.

NICOLAUS COPERNICUS

"Does the sun move?" "What time does the sun rise?" "Look at the beautiful sunset." Popular language confirms what our senses tell us – the sun moves.

Of course we know that popular language and our senses are wrong, for it is *not* the sun that moves; it is the earth. For many centuries, however, the astronomers believed that it was the earth that stood still while the heavens revolved about the earth as a center.

In about A.D. 150 Ptolemy, a famous Egyptian astronomer, worked out a system that could predict the future positions of the planets fairly well, but since he assumed that the earth was at the center, he could not account fully for the apparent wandering of the planets. (The word planet meant "wanderer" in Greek.)

About four centuries earlier a Greek astronomer, Aristarchus of Samos, had advanced the theory that the sun was at the center of the universe. But this was so strange an idea that Aristarchus' system was ignored.

It was not until about 1540 that Nicolaus Copernicus, a Polish astronomer, mathematician, scientist, physician, priest, and statesman, realized that the apparently complex motions of the planets could be readily explained by holding the sun still while the earth and planets moved in orbits about that dazzling star. It took 150 years more for the world to accept this notion – a notion that goes counter to our senses.

Nicolaus Copernicus was born on February 19, 1473, in the town of Torun in Poland. He was the youngest of the two sons and two daughters of Nicholas Koppernigk and Barbara Waczenrode. (Nicolaus Copernicus is the Latin spelling of Nicholas Koppernigk.) His father and mother were members of leading families of the town. Torun was a prosperous trade center and Nicolaus' father was not only a wealthy merchant but a magistrate and civic leader. When Nicolaus was ten years old his father died, and it was decided that the children be adopted by their uncle, Lucas Waczenrode, a priest.

Under the influence of Uncle Lucas, who was a scholar and who had become a bishop, Nicolaus decided to follow a career in the Church. He set about getting an education that would enable him to succeed in that ambition.

When he was eighteen, Nicolaus entered the university at Cracow, Poland. Cracow was the capital of Poland, a city known throughout Europe for its wealth and culture. The university at Cracow attracted students from many foreign lands – from Germany, Hungary, Italy, Switzerland, Sweden. These students used Latin as the common language; indeed, all learned books were writen in Latin, and all educated men were required to master that language. The student Nicolaus attended courses that encompassed philosophy, astronomy, geometry, and geography.

The study of astronomy was of great significance at this time. Sea commerce was developing rapidly, ships were becoming larger and were traveling farther and farther from shore. When Copernicus was nineteen, Columbus had traveled across the ocean and discovered America. The art of navigation was dependent upon specially calculated astronomical tables. There was also a definite need to set up an accurate calendar, so that church holy days could be properly celebrated.

The education of Copernicus might seem strange to us. He traveled from Cracow University to the law school at Bologna, Italy. From Bologna he continued his studies at the University of Padua. He finally received a Doctor of Laws degree from the University of Ferrara in 1503. Students traveled from university to university in those days.

Nicolaus went home to Poland, but not to stay. He convinced his uncle that the study of medicine would be valuable in the service of the church. Apparently there were no financial problems because Nicolaus, now age thirty, returned to Padua to the medical school.

The study of medicine was, in those years, closely allied to the study of astronomy. There was supposed to be a mystic connection between the organs of the body and the signs of the Zodiac. The Zodiac was the name given to the area in the heavens where the sun and the major planets seem to move. This area is divided into twelve parts of 30 degrees each, and each part is represented by a separate symbol, called a sign of the Zodiac. The sun moves into a different zone approximately each month; the planets move erratically through the Zodiac. To this day people who call themselves astrologers, will undertake to "tell fortunes" based on the pattern of sun and planets on your birthday.

At some point during his years of study Nicolaus had received an appointment as a canon of the church at Frauenberg. This appointment was due as much to his bishop uncle's influence as to Copernicus' own ability. He was, however, well prepared for the position. He had received training in theology and philosophy and had traveled extensively in Italy, the center of the church. He had received a doctorate in church law and had studied medicine. He knew Greek as well as Latin and had read many of the philosophical, mathematical, and scientific classics of Greece and Rome.

At the age of thirty-three Copernicus, finished with schooling, returned to Poland to take care of his now aged and ailing uncle, the Bishop Waczenrode. He had ample opportunity to continue the studies and observations that were to result in a new explanation of the mechanism of the universe. Upon the death of his uncle, Copernicus returned to his post at Frauenberg to begin his long-delayed service as canon of the cathedral. He established himself in one of the turrets of the defensive wall which enclosed the cathedral. This turret still stands and is known as Copernicus Tower; it was his observatory.

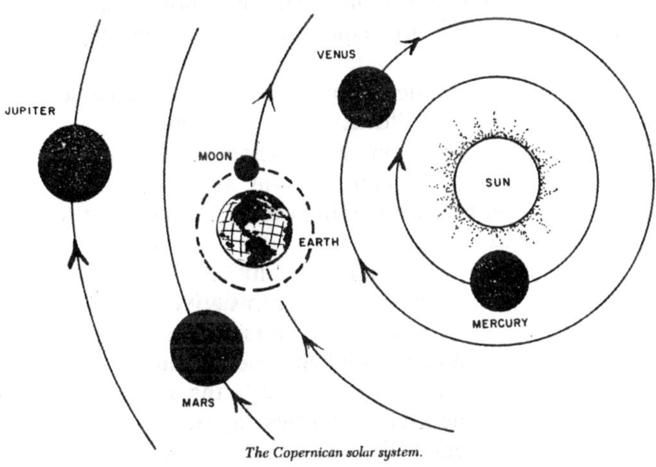


*The Copernican solar system.*

Copernicus took, as being accurate, the astronomical measurements which had come down to him from the Greeks and the Arabs. He thought, however, that new measurements might be useful, because there was an idea current that slow changes might be going on in the heavens. Copernicus had poor instruments and his measurements were no more precise than those the Greeks had made 1,500 years before. It was not as a result of his measurements, but rather as a result of his mathematical and philosophical formulations of the theory of the universe that the world marks him as a giant. Later astronomers, Tycho Brahe and Johannes Kepler, had to make corrections of his predictions, but Copernicus had made the beginning.

In the spring of 1539 a twenty-five year old German scholar, George Joachim Rheticus, came to visit Copernicus. Rheticus, a genius in his own right, had been appointed professor of mathematics at the University of Wittenberg when he was but twenty-two. He was welcomed by the aging Copernicus. Rheticus spent more than two years with Copernicus, studying his theories and manuscripts. It was Rheticus who urged Copernicus to publish his great findings, and it was to Rheticus, in Germany, that the manuscript was sent for printing. The book is called *De Revolutionibus Orbium Coelestium* now usually shortened to "Revolutions."

Unhappily the printed copy of his work, a work which ranks with Newton's "Principia" as a product of scientific genius, was seen by a Copernicus who was no longer lucid. He was near death, suffering from apoplexy and brain hemorrhage, no longer of sound mind, when the first copy was brought to him.

A brief mention of what "Revolutions" contains gives only a small idea of the greatness of its author. Copernicus set up a general picture of the universe with the sun at the center and the earth revolving, as a planet, about the sun. He explained the reasons for the seasons. He pointed out that we do not see the stars in the same celestial position in Italy as in Egypt, and indeed we cannot see stars from the Northern Hemisphere that we can see from the Southern Hemisphere. When a light is put on the tip of a mast, it appears to observers to drop gradually as the ship goes out to sea. Finally the light disappears, seeming to sink into the water. He used these arguments to prove that the earth is a sphere.

Copernicus discussed the apparently erratic motions of the planets, sometimes moving forward sometimes backwards and, in between, standing still. He showed how the motions were quite regular if the sun is considered the center of movement of the planets.

His mathematics told him, following Ptolemy's ideas, that the irregularities of the planetary motions must be based on movement in one circle or a combination of circles, since only by assuming circles could the motions repeat themselves. He showed that the earth need not be in the center of the universe to have it seem to be in the center, provided the heavens had enormous sizes compared to the distance between the earth and the actual center. We can see what he meant if we draw a circle twelve inches in diameter and then place a dot one-sixteenth of an inch from the center. The dot would still seem to be in the center of the circle.

Copernicus gave detailed accounts of the motions of the earth, the moon, and the planets. He provided diagrams showing the course of each planet and deduced tables that predicted the motion and position of the planets relative to the earth. His predictions, based on his not too accurate observations were later corrected by Kepler who showed that the orbits of the planets were slightly elliptical. The predictions were sufficiently accurate, however, to enable a new, more precise calendar, the Gregorian Calendar, to be devised.

Copernicus, in company with many great men of his age, did not confine his talents to his scientific endeavors. Poland was split up into many small separate states; there was no dependable money system. Higher and higher prices plagued the people as a result of the many small wars constantly being fought. Copernicus was aware that if both good and bad money were in use, the good money would be hidden by the people, who would spend only the bad money. Many years later this idea was made into a principle of economics called Gresham's Law.

Copernicus wrote a book suggesting that all the Polish states have the same coins, that they be of guaranteed weight, and that all old coins be turned in to the government. The opposition of the profiteers was too great, and these suggestions were not acted upon. It is interesting to note that Sir Isaac Newton was called upon to solve a similar problem for the British Government, and he made virtually the same suggestions, which were adopted to the advantage of Britain.

Copernicus was not the first man to arrive at the theory that this was a sun-centered universe. But the Greek astronomer, Aristarchus of Samos, who had guessed the truth centuries earlier did not prove his theory with the facts. It was left to Copernicus, 1,800 years later, to impress his theory on the mind of mankind. Copernicus described his own theory beautifully. He said: "In the midst of all dwells the Sun. For who could set this luminary in another or better place in this most glorious temple, than whence he can at one and the same time brighten the whole."

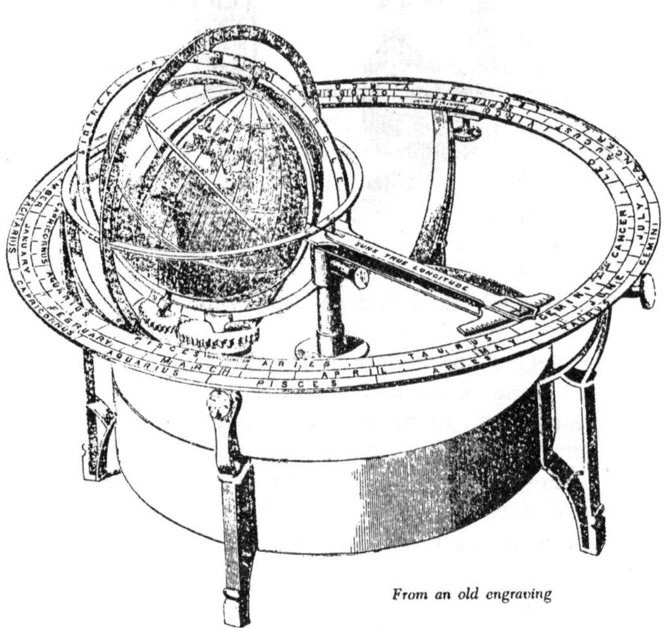


*From an old engraving*

*A globe designed to exhibit the motions of the earth.*

*From a drawing by Van Calcar.*

## ANDREAS VESALIUS

"I am aware how little authority my efforts will carry by reason of my youth, and how little I will be sheltered from the attacks of those who have not applied themselves to anatomy." Thus the twenty-eight-year-old Andreas Vesalius requested protection of the Emperor Charles V. Vesalius was about to publish seven books which he called *De Humani Corporis Fabrica*, "On the Structure of the Human Body."

Vesalius knew he was in for criticism of his book; he was about to attack medical practice and medical education and he was to cast great doubt on the infallibility of Galen. Galen had stood as the cornerstone of anatomical education and practice for about 1,300 years. It is no wonder that the young man hesitated to publish his finding without calling on Charles V for protection.

Andreas Vesalius was born in Brussels in the year 1514. His father had been appointed apothecary to Emperor Charles V. Among his forebears – he was of German descent – were many physicians. As a youth he must have been a nuisance to his family; his main hobby and amusement was the dissection of animals, birds, and mice. With this family background and his own absorbed interest it was foreordained that he should study medicine. He attended the University of Louvain and the medical school of the University of Paris. He completed his medical studies at the University of Padua, where he was appointed to the faculty as professor of surgery and anatomy. He remained there until 1543, teaching, studying and preparing his great work. With the publication of the book, the storm broke and Vesalius was forced out of his position at Padua. He became court physician to Charles V of Spain. He did no further work on anatomy, but remained in the court as physician to Philip II, the son of Charles V.

Andreas Vesalius first awoke to the problem of medical education while he was a student at Paris. Anatomy is, of course, an important branch of medical knowledge and it would seem almost impossible to teach it without showing the parts of the body. This may seem to be distasteful, but it is only by such study that physicians and scientists can advance their knowledge of the human body and thus be able to heal the sick. Even today many people and many religions look with great disfavor upon the dissection of human bodies. When Vesalius first studied anatomy, his professor seated himself on a chair and read passages from the anatomist Galen. Galen died in the year 200 A.D. and had written his accounts of human anatomy on the basis of his dissections of barbary apes. While the professor read his time-honored notes, an assistant pointed out the parts described by the professor. In the event that the passage from Galen did not match the specimen under inspection, it was hastily explained that the human body had changed in structure. Nobody would disagree with Galen; he was the authority! This in spite of the fact that Galen frequently disagreed with himself.

Vesalius was dissatisfied with this type of instruction. He recalled his own early dissections of animals and birds and determined to learn human anatomy in the same way. A problem was that of obtaining bodies for dissection. This was solved by body snatching (a practice that remains in the horror movies of the present day) which lead to grave robbing and possibly worse. But he never permitted anyone to perform the dissections for him; he realized that he would have to see for himself. The anatomy courses he taught were well attended; his students were required to make their own dissections, not simply to stand around and watch. His book, he declared, was a guide and was not to be used as a substitute for the firsthand study of the human body.

He criticized the doctors of his day. He wrote, "Then, when all the rest gradually gave up the unpleasant duties of their profession, without, however, giving up any claim to money or honor, they quickly fell away from the standard of the doctors of old." Methods of diet, he said, were left to nurses; compoundings drugs was left to the apothecaries; and surgery was left to the barbers. Nothing was left to the doctors. He made a plea for the return of the doctor to all the aspects of healing.

The *Fabrica,* Vesalius' book, owes much of its greatness to its illustrator, Jan Stephen van Calcar, a Flemish painter. Van Calcar was a student of the famous Titian. The drawings are still among the most accurate and natural representations of human anatomy in existence.

Andreas Vesalius died in 1564, a victim of ceaseless criticism of his methods and results.

*From a drawing by Van Calcar.*

Vesalius is important because he was the first to lead the way back to actual investigation of human anatomy, a practice that is standard in the medical schools of today.

## GALILEO

"I Galileo Galilei, son of the late Vincenzio Galilei, of Florence, aged 70 years, being brought to judgment . . . abandon the false opinion which maintains that the Sun is the center and immovable, and I will not hold, defend, or teach the said false doctrine in any manner."

Thus, did this aged and ailing mathematician, scientist, astronomer, and experimental genius pretend to accede to the prosecutors who decided by decree that the earth was the center of the universe. Galileo, possibly the best known scientist in the history of the world was forced, upon pain of death, to publicly recant scientific truths he had discovered and developed.

In his active life he had destroyed many of the "truths" of Aristotle and had set up the basis for Newton's developments. He is often called the founder of modern experimental scientific method, although equipment had not yet been developed to make really accurate measurements.

Galileo was born in 1564, the same year as William Shakespeare, to the wife of a wool merchant in Pisa, Italy. His father was a member of the nobility of the region but was not financially able to maintain his position in society. He attempted to support his family by means of composing music, but was forced into trade. As a child Galileo showed unusual abilities. He was very talented musically and played the lute and the organ. He was interested in art and gained local attention for his excellent paintings. And he was very good with his hands making toys and gadgets.

Pisa is in the Italian State of Tuscany which was an early center of art and learning, and Galileo was exposed to this cultural atmosphere in his home and in the city about him. Encouraged by his father to become a doctor, Galileo entered the University of Pisa to study medicine.

While at the University, at the age of twenty, he made his first scientific discovery. The story goes that he watched the chandelier swing from the roof of the cathedral at Pisa. He timed the swings, using his pulse beat as a "clock" and found that the swings were regular. After carrying out some experiments, he decided that a pendulum of a particular length takes the same time to make the same number of swings regardless of the size of the swing.

He put his discovery to practical use by suggesting that the pulse rate of medical patients be measured by using a pendulum. Although he designed a pendulum clock, it does not appear to have been built. Some time later Christian Huygens constructed an accurate clock using the pendulum as the timing control.

In 1585 Galileo, having run out of money, was unable to continue as a student at the university. He continued to study on his own, but shifted his attention to mathematics. It was at this time, too, that he began to be openly critical of some of the "laws of motion," as set down by Aristotle.

His work came to the attention of the Grand Duke of Tuscany, who traditionally took care of outstanding artists and intellectuals. The Grand Duke created a position for him at the University of Pisa, setting him up as a professor of mathematics. The twenty-five-year-old Galileo was not popular with the other professors. He was young, he did not have a university degree, and he dared to question the science of Aristotle.

Aristotle had observed a leaf and a stone fall to the

ground and had come to the general conclusion that a light body falls more slowly than a heavy one. Truly a leaf does fall more slowly than a stone but this is due to air resistance, a factor ignored by Aristotle. Galileo doubted that Aristotle's conclusion was true if weights heavy enough to neglect air resistance were involved.

The story – perhaps it is legend – is that Galileo dropped two balls of unequal weight from the famous Leaning Tower of Pisa. Gathered about was the entire faculty of the university. The unequal weights hit the ground at the same time. Galileo was right and Aristotle was wrong, but the professors were not all convinced.

Whether this story is true or not, we know that Galileo carried out a considerable investigation of the problems associated with falling bodies, scientific work that went far beyond the idea of just dropping weights from a tower. The problem was to be able to find out how long it took a body to fall a given distance. There were no accurate clocks, let alone stop watches or the electronic timing devices of the present day and it takes only a little more than three seconds for a weight to fall from the Tower of Pisa to the ground.

You can see the problem that faced Galileo. He had to devise a method that would not depend on timing a direct

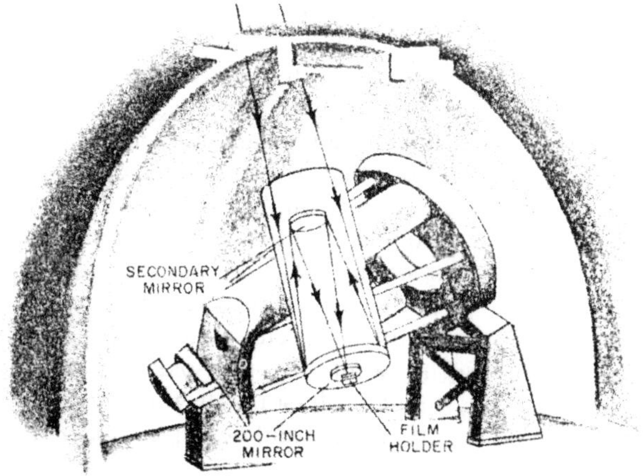


*Cutaway view of the giant reflecting telescope on Mount Palomar.*

fall. Galileo made a straight beam, about twenty-two feet long, and cut a groove in the beam. By tilting the beam, he could get a ball to roll down the groove. He timed the motion with a kind of water clock that operated by letting water drip out of a hole into a catch bucket. The weight of water would tell him the time. He let the ball run the whole distance, then half, then a quarter and so on. He made hundreds of measurements at various angles of tilt. He used his mastery of mathematics to summarize the result that the distance covered by the ball increased with the square of the time. If at the end of one second the ball rolled five feet down the slope, at the end of two seconds it will have rolled *two times two* times five feet, or twenty feet, at the end of three seconds it will have rolled *three times three* times five feet, or forty-five feet.

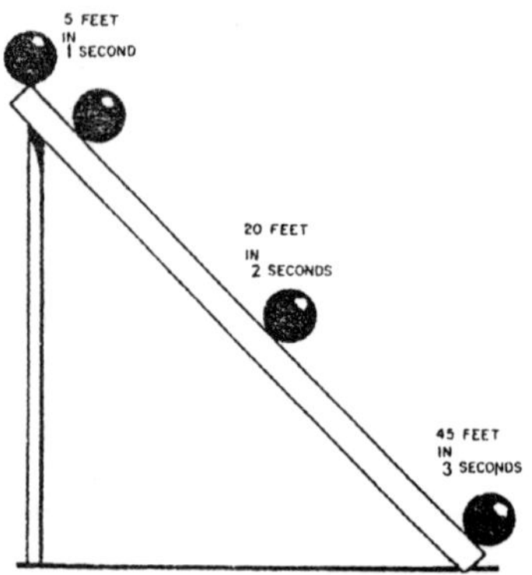


*Galileo's experiment on gravity.*

Galileo followed this with another interesting experiment. He made two grooved slopes, connected together at the bottom with a smooth curve so that a ball could roll down one slope and up the other. As near as he could tell (and he must have made a very smooth slope and a very smooth ball) the ball rose up to an equal height. He imagined a smooth plane sloping slightly downward: a ball would accelerate, that is, pick up speed. If the plane sloped upward a ball would decelerate, that is, lose speed. Therefore, he said, if the plane were level and perfectly smooth and we started a ball moving it would go on forever. This action is called inertia and it is theoretically true. Newton used this idea in his "Principia" later on, refined it and expressed it as the first law of motion.

Now Galileo used two ideas to solve an important military problem. There was the need to predict the path of a cannon ball. Galileo solved this problem by imagining that a cannon ball moved forward horizontally at an unchanged speed, and at the same time it fell to the ground in accordance with the law he had discovered by rolling balls down the inclined plane. He discovered that the path is a parabola, a curve of a particular shape that had been known to the ancient Greek mathematicians. The accuracy of gunfire was increased greatly as a result of his work.

The scholarly world was still embroiled in disagreement over Copernicus' statement that the earth, not the sun, was moving. Galileo showed that you cannot use the fact that the object dropped from the tower falls directly beneath it to prove that the earth does not move. When an object is dropped from the mast of a moving ship, it falls to the deck alongside the mast. This, Galileo explained, was similar to what happens when an object is dropped from a tower onto the ground.

We cannot tell the difference between standing still and moving without changing speed, except by watching something on the outside. Notice next time you are in an automobile waiting for the light to change, if the care next to you rolls forward you think you are going back, unless you can see the buildings stand still. Thus Galileo argued, in support of Copernicus, that the earth could be moving, even if our senses told us it was standing still.

Although his theories were correct, and he proved them by experiments and demonstrations, Galileo was dismissed from his position at the University of Pisa in 1591. He had aroused the suspicion of his colleagues by his constant attacks on the dearly held, but erroneous physical theories of Aristotle. However, a year later, Galileo was appointed professor of mathematics at the University of Padua. He had earned widespread fame for his experimental and mathematical developments. Students came from all over Europe to study under him.

At Padua he became interested in astronomy. He heard of the invention of the telescope and set about to build one, grinding his own lenses. Galileo turned his telescope skyward and came up with many startling discoveries. He concluded that the surface of the moon was not perfectly smooth, but, like the earth, was covered with mountains and valleys. He measured the heights of the mountains on the moon. Galileo observed that the planets were not like the stars, but were more like the moon, illuminated from the outside. He observed that the stars were "blazes of light, shooting out the beams on all sides and very sparkling."

He made obseravtions of the Milky Way, in which he found myriads of stars. Galileo discovered four of Jupiter's many moons. He observed the dark part of our moon and concluded that the earth reflects the light of sun as do all the other planets. If the earth were observed through a telescope located on the moon, it would have phases too. Inhabitants of the moon might say, "There's a full earth out tonight." His discoveries brought him new fame and with the fame came the abuse of the "learned ones" who still refused to give up the idea that the earth was not at the center of the universe.

Galileo, at odds with the theories of Aristotle sometimes used much the same methods as the early Greek thinker. He, like Aristotle, worked out much of his physics by reasoning. He made, as did Einstein three centuries later, "thought experiments." A thought experiment is one that is imagined and where the results are imagined. The level plane experiment described before was a thought experiment. However, Galileo also used actual experiments to confirm his reasoning.

Galileo spent his later years writing *Dialogues on Two New Sciences* which summarized his work on motion, acceleration and gravity. This book was published in 1636. In 1632 he had published *A Dialogue on the Two Principal Systems of the World* which was a brilliant explanation and extension of the Copernican system of astronomy, correctly describing the sun as the center about which the earth and the planets rotate. It was these works which brought him into difficulty with the authorities and which he was forced to deny. But it was these books which the world remembers.

Galileo died in 1642. He was a giant on whose shoulders Newton stood to see further.

## JOHANNES KEPLER

"It may well wait a century for a reader, as God has waited six thousand years for an observer."

Johannes Kepler, in this fashion, announced his discovery of the laws of planetary motion. He knew that his explanation of the motions of the planets, published in 1618, would be unpopular and would be considered anti-religious. Kepler agreed with Copernicus that the sun was at the center of the universe and that the earth traveled around the sun. This correct theory was in disfavor.

But in addition, Kepler advanced another theory: *the planets,* he found, *did not move about the sun in perfect circles.* This theory, too, was bound to be unpopular. For centuries the circle was considered the perfect figure, divinely given and therefore the only path in which heavenly bodies could be expected to travel.

So Johannes Kepler introduced his writings expecting that it would take mankind another century to agree with his explanation. Kepler's laws were so well developed that they stood the test of two hundred years before minor inaccuracies were observed.

Johannes Kepler was born in Weil, a town in southern Germany in the year 1571. He had a severe case of smallpox when he was only four years old. This left him with poor eyesight and with crippled hands.

His father was a soldier of fortune and his mother was an innkeeper's daughter.

Although handicapped by an often drunken father, a not quite mentally balanced mother, as well as by impaired eyesight, physical weakness, and crippled hands, Johannes was a good student from his early school days. The ministry was selected for him as a career and he attended a seminary to study theology.

He obtained a scholarship to the University of Tübingen, where he was introduced to the study of the Copernican ideas about the movement of the planet about the sun. The fascination of science and mathematics was too great and he gave up the idea of becoming a minister. When he was twenty-three he accepted an invitation to become Professor of Astronomy at the University of Graz.

Kepler married a wealthy young lady and seemed set for the rest of his career when religious disturbances made it impossible for him, a Protestant, to remain at Graz.

Surprisingly enough this man of science still had some association with astrology. He kept a daily record of his own life events, alongside of the positions of the stars and the planets. He, of course, denied that he had any belief in astrology, but he was undoubtedly influenced by all the superstitions of the past. Along with his remarkable and correct mathematical studies of the movements of the planets he erroneously attempted to weave in the idea of

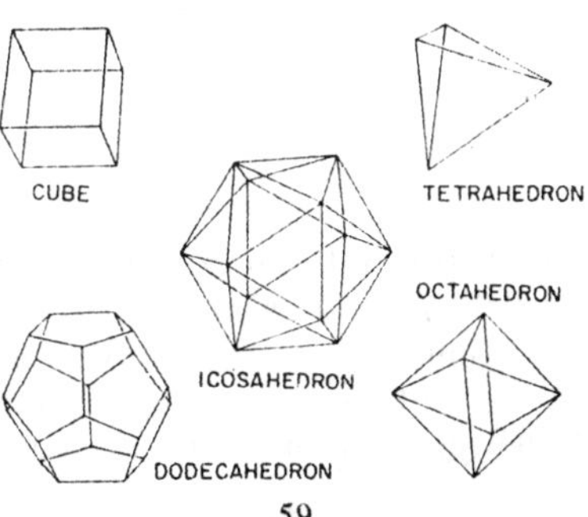

the "perfect" solids, the cube, the tetrahedron, the octahedron, the dodecahedron, and the icosahedron. This was a throwback to the ancient Greek philosophers who tried to explain the makeup of the universe on the basis of "perfect" figures.

Kepler left Graz and joined the exiled Danish astronomer Tycho Brahe at Prague. Brahe was in opposition to Copernicus. He decided that the laws of God and the principles of physics were violated by the idea that the sun was at the center of the universe. Accordingly, he set out to try to prove that the earth was the center. Brahe had made many thousands of very accurate observations and is remembered for the listing of stars which he published in 1592. It may be that he soon convinced himself that he was wrong, because he did accept Kepler as his assistant and as his successor, in spite of the fact that Kepler believed in the sun as the center of the universe.

Upon the death of Tycho Brahe in 1601, Kepler continued the astronomical observations, and under his leadership 228 additional stars were carefully studied. The analysis of Brahe's data brought Kepler to the laws of planetary motion which Newton explained by gravity and which have lasted to this day. These same laws govern the basic motions of the man-made satellites.

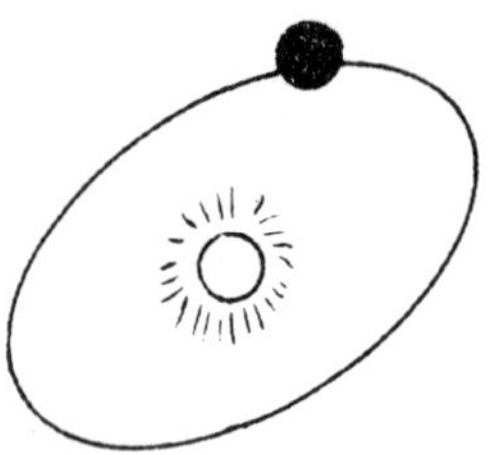

Kepler not only discovered that the planets move about the sun in oval paths, but he also noticed that each planet changes speed as it moves about its orbit. As the oval path brings the planet closer to the sun, the planet picks up speed. Kepler worked out the time it takes a planet to travel around the sun. The planets which are close to the sun take less time than those that are at a greater distance away.

He made exact mathematical calculations to show how this worked out for each planet. We may wonder at the accuracy of the observations when we realize that the path of the earth about the sun is very close to a circle. If we think of an ellipse 100 feet across in one direction and 99½ feet across the other way we can get some idea of how close the path of the earth is to a circle. No wonder it took so long to destroy the idea of the circle as the perfect path.

Kepler made contributions to related areas in science. Studies in vision and optics developed some important ideas about the refraction of light. He suggested the principle of the astronomical telescope. His mathematics led him to the brink of calculus, and he had important ideas about gravity and the tides of the oceans.

Johannes Kepler died in 1630, twelve years before the birth of Isaac Newton, who was to construct his own great work with at least one foot on the shoulder of this giant of a scientist.

## WILLIAM HARVEY

"The greatest news from the country is of a huge pack of witches. It is suspected that they had a hand in raising the great storm at sea."

This was a message of importance in the year 1634. People still believed in witches. Dr. William Harvey, physician to the king, was ordered to examine these "witches." To his credit, they were acquitted on the basis of his examination and report.

However, Dr. William Harvey is not included among the giants of science because he spent his time contradicting the witch nonsense of his era, but because he is the discoverer of the circulation of the blood. Harvey's seventy-eight-page treatise *Anatomical Dissertation Concerning the Motion of the Heart and Blood in Animals* published in 1628 constituted a major scientific breakthrough, after which knowledge of living functions advanced steadily and continuously.

William Harvey was born in Folkestone, England, on All Fools' Day in 1578. He was the son of Thomas Harvey, a wealthy merchant who served as an alderman and later as the mayor of the town. William was part of a large family – ten children in all, three daughters and seven sons. The family was prosperous, healthy and happy.

In 1588 the ten-year-old William entered Kings School, Canterbury. This was the same year that saw the Spanish Armada destroyed by the British Navy. When he was fifteen, William entered Cains College in Cambridge. This college was lucky to receive the bodies of two criminals to dissect and study. Harvey's interest in medical study was aroused.

From Cambridge, he went to the famous institution at Padua, the center of medical and scientific learning made famous by Galileo and Vesalius. Unfortunately, the influence of Vesalius had waned, his great work on human anatomy was ignored and Harvey was taught according to the centuries-old authority of Galen. Harvey was unhappy, but he did not express his doubts out loud until he received his medical degree. He returned to London and received a license to practice medicine. At the same time he was admitted to the College of Physicians at Cambridge University.

Three years later he became a Fellow of the College and was appointed a physician at St. Bartholomew's Hospital. He lectured on the theory of medicine. Competent and self-assured, the rather small, dark-skinned Harvey quickly established a reputation as leader in the profession.

William Harvey was attached to King Charles I as court physician. He led a rather stormy life, as King Charles fought a losing battle with parliament and with Oliver Cromwell. Fortunately, Harvey settled down to research at Oxford in 1642 and was no longer associated with Charles I when Charles was beheaded in 1649.

What did Harvey do that gives him his high place in the history of medicine? And how did he do it?

He had studied living animals. He opened up the chest cavity and observed the beating of the heart directly. He saw that the heart moved and then was motionless, that this motion and rest were repeated over and over again. Harvey took the heart of the living animal in his hand and noted that it alternately became hard and then soft, just as the muscle of the arm becomes hard when we "make a muscle." He saw that when it became hard it also became smaller in volume and when soft it was larger. The color of the heart changed, too. When hard and small it was paler than when soft and large. After many observations on many animals, William Harvey came to this conclusion: The heart is a hollow muscle; when the muscle acts the space inside gets smaller and squeezes out the blood – that's why it gets pale. When the muscle relaxes, blood flows into the larger cavity and the heart gets redder. The heart is therefore a pump.

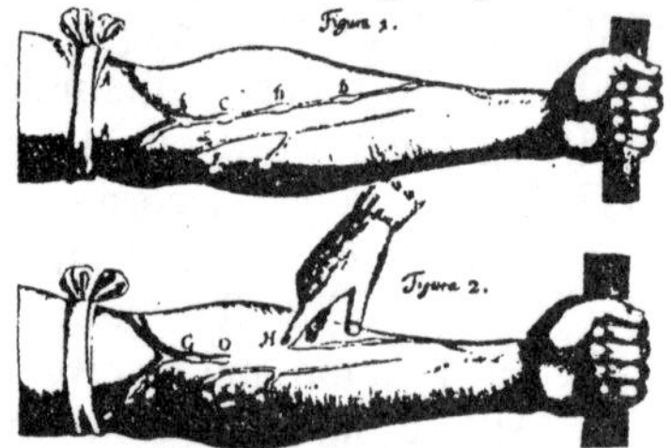

*An illustration from the original edition of Harvey's book, showing the veins of the forearm.*

Having established this important fact he followed the path of the blood through the body. He noticed that the arteries pulsate at the moment the heart contracts, and if an artery is punctured the blood comes out in spurts. And by blocking the arteries at various points he came to the conclusion that the arteries did not produce this pulsation, but that it was due entirely to the action of the heart.

Now he began to be concerned about the quantity of blood being transmitted through the arteries. He estimated that the heart pumped two ounces of blood on each stroke and that there were seventy-two strokes per minute. A quick calculation told him that the heart pumps more than a gallon of blood a minute or – incredibly – more than 1,500 gallons a day! "How," asked Harvey, "could this be possible?" And he answered his own question: This is only possible if the *blood moves in a circle,* that is, if it starts at the heart, is pumped through the body and goes back to the heart. *The blood,* he concluded, *must circulate.*

Dr. Harvey examined the structure of the body again and made some more experiments. He carefully examined the veins and the arteries and discovered that they were one-way passages. These passages are equipped with flaps that act like valves. The valves in the arteries permit the flow away from the heart, while the valves in the veins permit blood flow only toward the heart. He proved the action of these valves by experimenting on animals. He opened a vein and introduced a probe into it. The probe readily went toward the heart but would not move when pushed in the opposite direction; the valves interfered.

More and more experiments and careful rechecking, and soon he was able to map the flow of blood through the heart and arteries into the veins and back to the heart. And everywhere on the trip Harvey found valves, specially designed to enable the blood to flow in the one direction.

We hear nowadays of marvelous operations which repair damage to the heart, of plastic valves and plastic tubes, of pumps that keep the blood going through the body while surgeons operate – marvels of modern medicine.

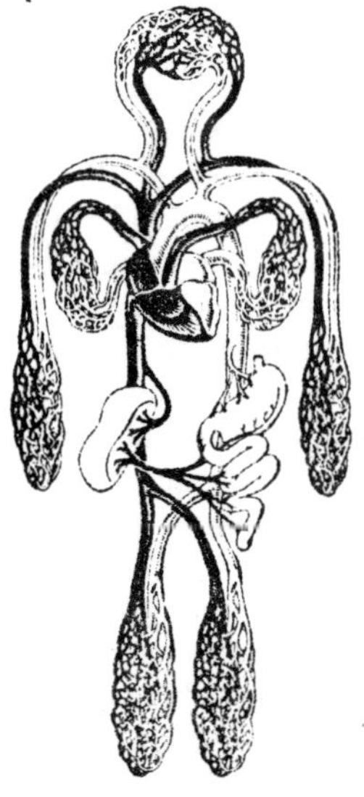

*A diagram of the circulatory system of the body.*

But the most learned surgeon of modern times would be helpless without the aid of that magnificent medical experimenter William Harvey.

## EVANGELISTA TORRICELLI

Try this – but over the sink, please. Fill a tumbler about three-quarters full of water. Drape a handkerchief loosely over the mouth of the tumbler letting it touch the water. Tie a piece of string tightly around the handkerchief to hold it to the water tumbler. Now turn the tumbler upside down – rapidly.

"Nature," declared Aristotle, "abhors a vacuum." And in spite of modern inventions and all kinds of advanced machinery, Aristotle may have been right; perhaps there is no such thing as a perfect vacuum. A few molecules always seem to survive man's attempt to clear a space of all gases. But these few molecules weren't what bothered Galileo when he discussed a pump problem with one of his students, Evangelista Torricelli. The problem of an approximate vacuum, let alone a perfect vacuum, hadn't been solved.

Torricelli, physicist and mathematician, was born on October 15, 1608, at Faenza, in northern Italy. He did so well at the Jesuit College of Faenza that at sixteen his uncle, a priest, sent him to Rome to study the sciences under Benedetti Castelli. Castelli, a pupil of Galileo, was a professor of mathematics at the Collegio di Sapienza. Torricelli's first essay, *On Projectiles,* was sent to Galileo by Castelli. Galileo was very much impressed by the young student's mathematical and analytical abilities. Torricelli, however, did not meet Galileo until three months before the master's death. Those three months in 1641, Torricelli spent with the now-blind Galileo, as his helper and assistant.

Galileo had first interested Torricelli in the problem of creating a vacuum. The pump makers of the Grand Duke of Tuscany had tried to raise water to a height of 40 feet by means of a suction pump, but found 32 feet to be the limit of the rise. Galileo suggested that Torricelli investigate the problem.

Two year later – now mathematician to the Grand Duke of Tuscany and professor of mathematics at the Florentine Academy – Torricelli demonstrated his now classic experiment. Perhaps more important, he explained the reasons for his results.

Fortunately glass making was a highly developed art and industry in Italy. Torricelli was able to obtain glass tubes which were almost four feet long. One end of each tube was closed. Torricelli filled a tube to the brim with mercury. He held his finger over the open end of the glass, inverted the tube and placed it into a bowl partially filled with mercury. He removed his finger and the mercury came out of the tube into the bowl – but not all the mercury came out. The top edge of the mercury stood just about 30 inches above the level of mercury in the bowl. The space above the mercury in the tube was filled with – nothing. Torricelli slanted the tube. The mercury filled more of the tube but the height was still 30 inches. Slanting it still more, the top of the tube was less than 30 inches above the mercury in the bowl and the mercury filled the tube completely. Again he straighted out the tube and the space reappeared. The space, we know now, was filled with a few molecules of mercury vapor, but it was practically a vacuum.

There was still a question to be settled: why did the

column of mercury remain? Why did it not all fall into the bowl? Torricelli had the answer. "We live," he wrote, "submerged at the bottom of an ocean of air, which by experiment, is known to have weight. On the surface of the liquid in the bowl," Torricelli added, "a fifty-mile column of air presses down. It is therefore not to be wondered, that in the tube, with nothing to oppose its entry, it rises until it balances the weight of the air on the outside, which supports it." The pressure of the air keeps the mercury up: this was the meaning of the experiment.

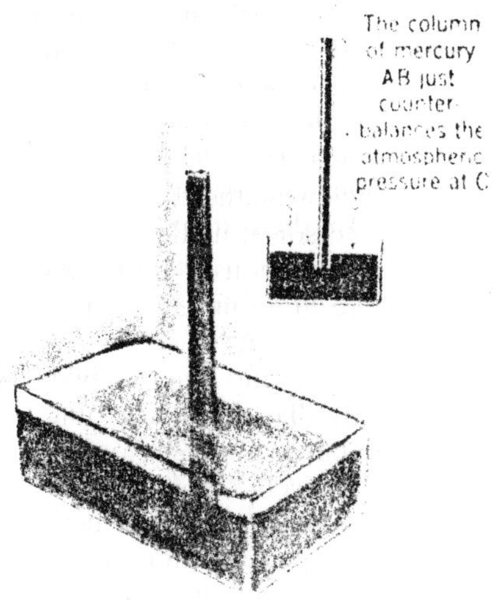


*Torricelli's experiment on air pressure.*

Torricelli was able, now, to explain why the water could not be lifted higher than 32 feet by means of a suction pump. That is all the weight of water that the pressure of the atmosphere can support. It is higher than the column of mercury because mercury is about 13.6 times as dense as water. Torricelli realized too that he had an instrument for measuring the density of the air, although it was Blaise Pascal who called the device a barometer. If the "ocean of air" is not so deep, as on a mountain, the column of mercury the air is able to support will be less. At the top of Mt. Everest, the weight of the air would support a column of mercury only about 11 inches high.

The barometer is one of the instruments used in predicting weather. Surprisingly perhaps, the weight of "damp" air is less than that of dry air. Thus the barometer "falls" when the air is moist, and moist air means that rain is to be expected. The barometer will rise again when the air is dry. There is more to weather prediction than watching a barometer, but in general a drop in air pressure means bad weather ahead, while a rising barometer presages fine weather.

Torricelli used his newly discovered vacuum to make other experiments. He noted that light was transmitted as readily through a vacuum as through the air and gave Huygens a clue to the wave theory of light. He worked with sound and magnetism as well. Torricelli also made notable contributions to mathematics and to hydraulics.

Torricelli accomplished much in a relatively short life; he died in 1647 at the age of thirty-nine. We are in his debt whenever we read a barometer or listen to a weather forecast. By the way, it is the "ocean of air" that keeps the water from coming out of that tumbler, and pushes the handkerchief up into the glass.

## ROBERT BOYLE

Robert Boyle was born on January 26, 1627, in Munster, Ireland. He was the fourteenth child and the tenth son of the very wealthy Earl of Çork. There was never any question that he was extraordinarily bright. In addition he enjoyed the tremendous advantages that an enlightened parent with great wealth can supply. He learned Latin and French along with English, and later on added Hebrew, Greek, and Syriac to his language arsenal. These enabled him to make extensive studies of the Bible in its original languages.

When he was eight he entered Eton College, the largest and most famous of English preparatory schools. He was taken out of the school after three years to tour the European continent. This kind of a tour was considered the final polish for an English gentleman, but rarely was this taken by an eleven-year-old. In 1641 the fourteen-year-old Robert visited Italy and came under the influence of the famed Galileo. Boyle decided that he would spend his life in science.

Back in England, he entered Oxford, then the leading

center of scientific study in England. At Oxford, Robert Boyle found himself among an informal group of brilliant scholars who called themselves the "Invisible College." In 1660 the king granted these scientists a charter, The Invisible Society became the Royal Society. These men were devoted to the scientific experimental method. Truths could be gained only from experience and experiments.

Boyle, an experimental scientist, is celebrated as the author of Boyle's Law, a mathematical formula that tells how gases behave under pressure. Boyle's Law was discovered experimentally and only later was it translated into its mathematical form.

This is how Boyle conducted his famous experiment. First he had prepared a glass tube in the form of a letter J with the shorter end of the J closed. This was a long tube. The long side was more than ten feet tall. The experimenters couldn't fit it into the room so they had to use a stairwell. He carefully poured some mercury into the tube so that the level was the same on each side of the bend of the tube. The pressure of the gas in the closed section was now the same as the pressure of the atmosphere in the open section. You can see that if one side had a greater pressure than the other the mercury would not stand even.

These scientists knew well the materials they were working with; the bottom of the J tube rested in a large box. If the glass broke (and it did several times) the box would catch the quicksilver. Now that the mercury stood even, he pasted scales, strips of paper marked in inches and in eighths of an inch, on each side of the tube. Mercury was poured slowly and carefully into the open end. The level of the mercury increased on both sides of the tube, but unevenly. The air in the closed section was compressed by the mercury and therefore resisted the mercury; thus the level on the open side was higher than the level on the closed side of the tube. But in spite of the difference in levels there was a balance. The pressure of the air on the inside depends on the height of the column of mercury in addition to the normal atmospheric pressure. The volume of compressed air can readily be figured out from the measurements of the cylinder. Boyle found an interesting thing: when the long side had 29 inches of mercury more than the short side the volume of the gas was exactly half of its original value! Boyle knew that the atmosphere itself had pressure and he knew that the pressure was enough to support a column of mercury 29 inches high. The additional 29 inches had doubled the pressure on the air in the closed section and this doubled pressure had cut the volume in half. Of course he didn't stop; he made hundreds of measurements. A column of mercury almost eight feet high compressed the air into a quarter of its volume.

What Boyle found to be true about pressure and volume is now used by every chemist and physicist and is known as Boyle's Law: "The volume of a gas is inversely proportional to the pressure." Later scientists, notably Jacques Charles, added the phrases "providing the temperature does not change."

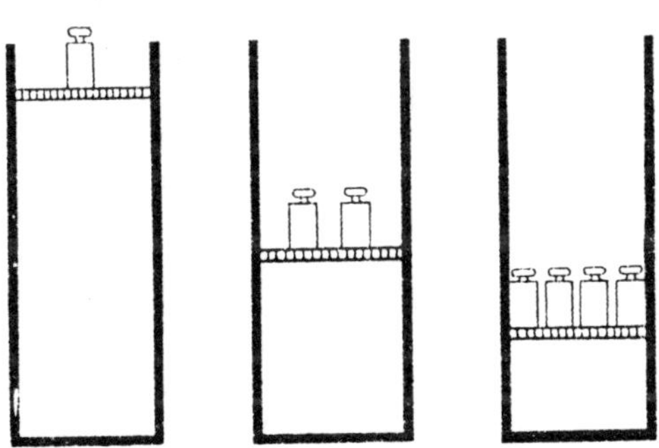

*Boyle's Law: The volume of a gas varies inversely with the pressure.*

Many of Boyle's experiments and discoveries are described in letters to his nephew, who became the Earl of Cork. These letters sometimes ran to more than a hundred pages.

Like other great scientists, Boyle was interested in many branches of science. He investigated the speed of sound, the reasons for color, crystal structure, static electricity. He came close to discovering oxygen. He had developed a vacuum pump (man driven) and used to show that an animal could not live in an air-free space. He showed that sulphur would not burn if heated in a vacuum. Boyle is credited with a definition of a chemical element which comes close to present-day theory. He defined an element as a substance "incapable of decomposition," and like a true scientist, added the prophetic "by any means with which we are now acquainted." Elements have been changed in the atomic laboratories of today.

Robert Boyle was a generous man, and if he had not discovered Boyle's Law might well live in history as the benefactor who paid the publication costs for Newton's "Principia."

He died in London on December 30, 1691. He was 64 years old. Born into an age of superstition and belief in witchcraft, he made notable advances in science and scientific method. He provided his contemporaries with inspiration and support. Their tribute was, "Robert Boyle smells the truth."

## CHRISTIAN HUYGENS

The pendulum clock that Christian Huygens invented lost time when it was taken to French Guiana. When he found out how much time it lost, Huygens calculated that the earth bulges at the equator.

This outstanding scientist, a student of pendulum clocks and of the theory of light, was born on April 14, 1629, in the Netherlands at the capital city of The Hague. Constantyn Huygens, his father, was an influential member of the community, a statesman, a poet, a musician, and a gymnast of note. Christian showed great interest in mathematics and in science very early in life. He attended the universities at Leiden and at Breda. When only twenty-two, Huygens published some astronomical and mathematical theses which attracted the attention of the mathematician-philosopher René Descartes.

The scientific world of the day revolved about the study of astronomy, and Huygens, too, worked in this field. The telescope was just coming into use. Huygens, dissatisfied with the poor equipment available, learned to make his own lenses. He was assisted in this by his friend Benedict

Spinoza, the great Dutch-Jewish philosopher who supported himself by grinding lenses.

The improvements he made in the telescope enabled Huygens to identify the "halo" that Galileo had noticed around the planet Saturn. Huygens explained this "halo" as a large flat ring. As a result of the much more effective telescopes of the present day, it is known that the ring is really three rings, and that the three rings are really large pieces of "dust" moving about the planet at high speeds. Huygens' work in optical instruments is still with us: the Huygens' eyepiece is part of many modern microscopes.

At thirty-four, Huygens was elected a Fellow of the Royal Society of London. When he visited England to accept this honor, he met with Isaac Newton who was greatly impressed with Huygens' abilities. Newton attempted to obtain a position in England for Huygens but was unsuccessful. The Hollander was not yet well known outside of a small scientific group and Newton was unable to locate a wealthy patron who would be willing to sponsor the foreign scientist.

Several years later King Louis XIV, determined to maintain French ascendancy in scientific studies, offered Huygens a position in charge of scientific research. He retained this post from 1666 to 1681.

While in France he composed his great work, *Treatise on Light,* which was not published until 1690. Huygens explained the delay as due to his own human failings. He had written the original in French and had intended to translate it into Latin. But the "pleasure of Novelty" having worn off, he became absorbed in other projects, and the translation was "put off from time to time." Finally he gave up and published the treatise in French because he was afraid that delay might deprive him of credit for the originality of the ideas.

In his own day, Christian Huygens was famous for his invention of the pendulum clock and for his masterful analysis of its action. The fact that a pendulum could be used to keep time was discovered by Galileo, who suggested that a clock could be made on this basis. But no successful application of the pendulum was made at that time.

Many scientists had worked on the problem, but no satisfactory result had been obtained. In 1657 Huygens succeeded where others had failed. He had found out the laws governing the compound pendulum: he had managed to build an "escapement," which allowed the hands of the clock to move an exact amount for each swing of the pendulum, and he had worked out the principle of the cycloidal suspension shown in the illustration. His clock was accurate, for the first time a mechanical device kept time with the stars and with the sun. The pendulum clock was sent out to sea to aid in navigation. Success was not complete. The matter of gravity entered into the pendulum clock.

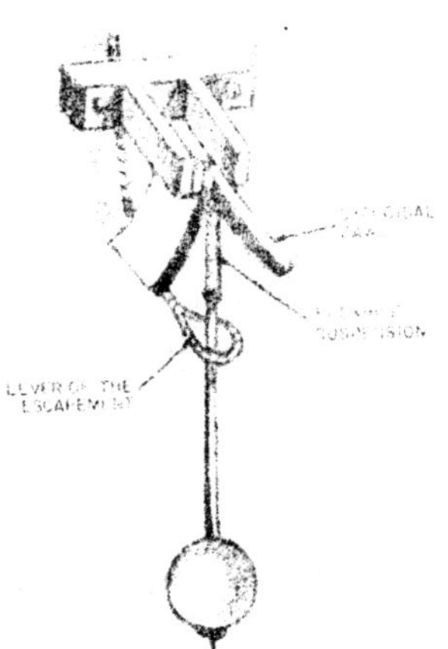


Each swing of the pendulum takes the same time — provided the pull of gravity remains the same. The reason the pendulum "falls" from its high position to the low point is because it is attracted by the earth's gravity. Take the clock to a mountain top, farther away from the center of the earth, and the pendulum does not fall as fast; it will take longer to swing to and fro. The clock will lose time. This is true and to be expected on a mountain top. When the pendulum clock was taken to Cayenne in French

Guiana it lost time, but Cayenne is at sea level, not on top of a mountain. What had happened?

Huygens analyzed the problem. He knew that a stone tied to a string and whirled round and round, hugs the outside of the circle in defiance of gravity. In fact if the speed were great enough the string would break. He called this "centrifugal" force or center-fleeing force. The earth spins and it moves fast. It turns about its axis once every 24 hours. At the equator the surface of the earth moves with the jet-age speed of over 1,000 miles per hour. A body on the equator is turning like the stone on the end of the string; it is forced away from the earth. As we travel North and South from the equator the earth still turns once in 24 hours but the surface speed is less because the circle about the earth's sphere is less. If you turn your bicycle wheel the spokes will be blurred near the rim, but you can still see them near the hub because they do not travel so fast. At the exact center of rotation there is no motion at all.

At every place on the earth the pull of gravity will cause objects to fall toward the center of the earth. At the North Pole that is all gravity has to do, but at every other place gravity has, in addition, to keep people and things from flying off the earth because of centrifugal action. At the equator the centrifugal action is greatest, because at the equator the earth moves fastest.

The amount of gravitational attraction that remains will therefore be less at the equator. Since the amount of available gravitational attraction is less at the equator, the pendulum clock *should* lose time; the pendulum won't "fall" as fast. Huygens calculated how much slower the clock should go at the equator basing his calculations on the speed of the earth at the equator and at Paris, but the clock was even slower than he figured. There could be only one explanation: the earth, he predicted, was bulged at the equator, reducing the effect of gravity still more! The total effect of centrifugal force and of the equatorial bulge was to cause the clock to lose two and a half minutes a day.

The failure of the pendulum clock as a navigational aid

set Huygens to thinking of other methods of keeping time. He came up with the idea of the spiral watchspring, which he patented, not knowing that Robert Hooke had thought of the idea before. However, Hooke did not bring his idea forth until Huygens' discovery had been acclaimed. Huygens' work in clocks was important in his day, and his cycloidal suspension is still used wherever pendulum clocks are made.

He is important, too, because of his work on the theory of light. In this work he discussed possible explanations for the behavior of light rays. He likened the behavior of light to that of sound and of water waves. "It is inconceivable to doubt," said Huygens, "that light consists in the motion of some kind of matter." He felt that light spreads in waves, like sound, but realized that light, unlike sound, could travel through a vacuum.

He set up a model of the method of travel of waves. "When one takes a number of spheres of equal size, made of some very hard substance, and arranges them in a straight line so that they are in contact with one another, one finds, on striking the first sphere with a similar sphere, the motion passes as in an instant to the last of them, without being able to perceive that the others have been stirred."

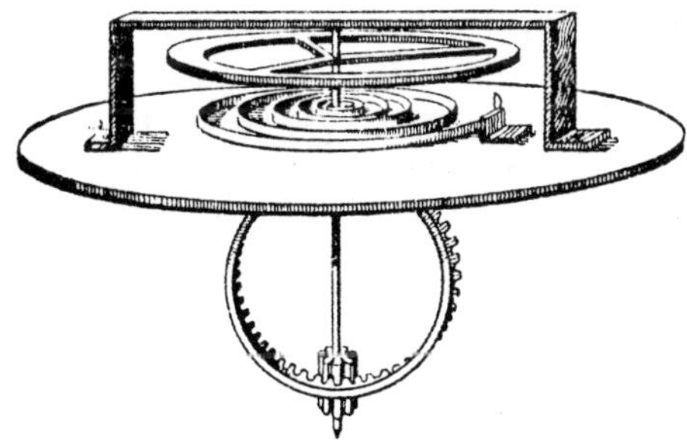

*A seventeenth-century balance spring. From a drawing of the time.*

He used the same model with two sets of spheres at right angles and saw that both motions were transmitted simultaneously. In this way he explained why light waves can pass each other without getting mixed.

Huygens thus proposed the wave theory of light, and used it to explain refraction, reflection, and polarization. But Newton had advanced the corpuscular theory and Newton was the leader of the day. The corpuscular theory held that small particles traveled from the source of light. The corpuscular theory was accepted for almost two hundred years until Maxwell showed that the wave theory could be applied more simply. Einstein and Planck revived the corpuscular theory in the study of photoelectricity. Modern views combine with the Huygens wave theory and Newton's corpuscular theory of light.

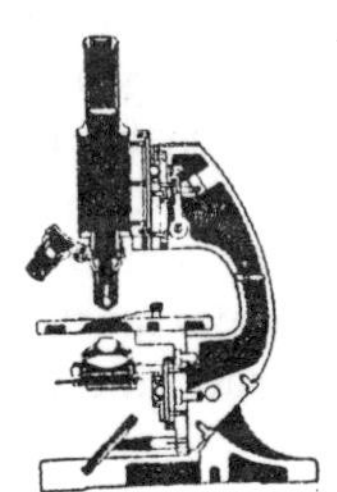

## ANTON VAN LEEUWENHOEK

In 1673 the Royal Society of London received a long and curious letter, which sent its erudite members into bursts of laughter. The letter was from a Dutch storekeeper and part-time janitor. Laughter soon changed to astonishment and to respect. For this simple, artless man who wrote at great length about his own health, about his neighbors and their superstitions, had titled his letter, "A Specimen of Some Observations made by a Microscope Contrived by Mr. Leeuwenhoek Concerning Mould upon the Skin, Flesh, etc.; the Sting of a Bee, etc."

In an age where the magnifying glass was, as yet, a simple hand-lens of meager magnifying power, an uneducated storekeeper with a passion for grinding glass had produced a device which enlarged objects many hundreds of times. The Royal Society invited Mr. Van Leeuwenhock to continue his contributions and received 375 letters from him during the next fifty years.

Anton van Leeuwenhoek was born in Delft, Holland, on October 24, 1632, into a respected family of basketmakers and brewers. When Anton's father died, the boy left the pretty town of blue windmills and canals to go to Amsterdam, where he was apprenticed as a clerk in a dry-goods store. At the age of twenty-one, he left Amsterdam and returned to Delft where he married and opened his own dry-goods store. He also got the job of janitor of the City Hall.

Anton had a great and consuming passion: the grinding of lenses. He made lens after lens. He was determined to make as perfect a lens as possible; in all he made over 400 magnifying glasses. These lenses were small, scarcely one-eighth inch in diameter, about as large as this letter O, but they have not yet been surpassed in quality. Van Leeuwenhock made "simple microscopes" with his lenses, but they were remarkably effective. He was a superb craftsman and made the delicate, strong stands that supported the lenses.

Galileo had turned his telescope on the vastness of the heavens, but Leeuwenhoek turned his lenses on the vastness of the microscopic world. He looked at everything he could find, skin fibres, ox eyes, animal hairs, the legs and head of a fly.

He was, the neighbors felt, slightly mad – hour after hour of peering through his microscope. But he paid no attention to the good folk of Delft. Van Leeuwenhoek kept looking through his microscope and discovered new wonders all the time. One day he looked at some rain water which he scooped up from a puddle and discovered "little animals, swimming, playing, a thousand times smaller than you can see with the eye alone." "Wretched beasties," he called them.

He had a feeling that they didn't come from the sky. To prove it he collected rain water as it fell into a perfectly clean bowl. The microscope showed there were no "beasties." He kept the water in the dish for several days and gradually the "animalcules" appeared. He decided that they came from particles of dust blown by the wind.

He stuck his finger and examined the blood, and discovered the red blood corpuscles. Faithfully, in 1674 he related his findings to the Royal Society. Three years later he described the sperm cells produced by dogs and other animals.

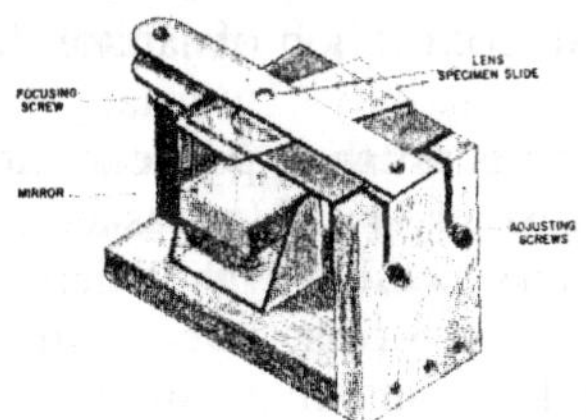


*Leeuwenhoek's microscope. From a model.*

The Royal Society was intrigued – was this fellow in Holland a scientist or a science-fiction writer? The Society asked to borrow a microscope. They got a nice long newsy letter describing more miracles of the very small world, but they could get no microscope from the suspicious Leeuwenhoek. Robert Hooke and Nehemiah Grew were commissioned to build the best microscope they could. Science had to verify Leeuwenhoek's findings. So they did, and they too looked at blood and grew bacteria in pepper water and scraped their own teeth and killed germs with hot water and they saw the same microscopic world that had been reported to them. The Royal Society honored the untutored Dutchman. Van Leeuwenhoek was elected a Fellow of the Society in 1680.

Van Leeuwenhoek first made drawings of bacteria in 1683. In an age of superstition, where the common belief was that certain forms of life, such as fleas, were produced spontaneously or bred from decaying matter, he was able to prove that even the lowest forms of animal life reproduce. He studied grain-destroying weevils and reported that the grubs were hatched from eggs deposited by the insects. In the tail of a fish, examined with his microscope, he discovered the capillary blood vessels.

His fame spread, thanks to the publicity the Royal

Society and the Paris Academy of Sciences (which also had received letters) gave to this grinder of lenses and to the discoveries he had made. The Russian ruler, Peter the Great, came to visit him, as did the Queen of England. They wanted to look through his microscope. There was little change in his daily activity. Unusually healthy, he continued working until his death at 91 years of age. Just before he died on August 26, 1723, he asked a friend to send off his last two letters to the Royal Society.

Van Leeuwenhoek's microscope was a simple instrument. It had only one lens, and that one was very, very small. The compound microscope, with two systems of lenses, had been invented in 1590, but the technical problems were so great that Van Leeuwenhoek's simple magnifying glass was superior. Since then, lens making has been improved and a modern optical microscope can be made to magnify about 2,500 times in diameter. Scientists have need for greater magnification. The virus, for example, is much, much smaller than the bacteria "beasties" Van Leeuwenhoek saw. The electron microscope which uses streams of electrons instead of light is the present tool of

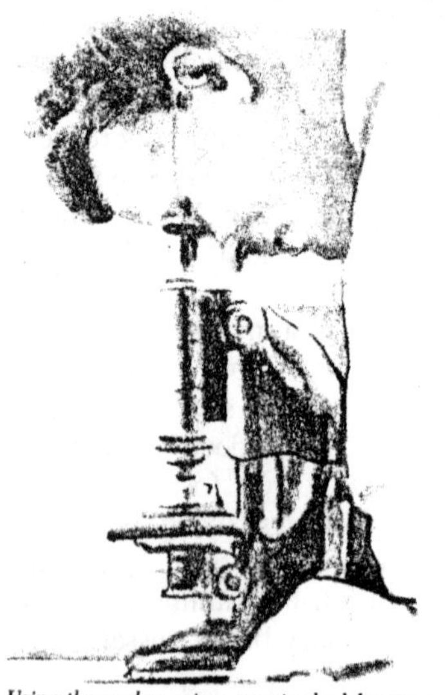

*Using the modern microscope in the laboratory.*

science. The magnification possible is upwards of 100,000 diameters.

Anton Van Leeuwenhoek did not have the instruments of present day science, but there were scientific tools he had that have never been surpassed; dedication to an idea, infinite patience, extraordinary powers of observation.

## ROBERT HOOKE

Do you play anagrams? See what you can do with C E I I I N O S S T T U V?

Robert Hooke was born on September 18, 1635, on the Isle of Wight off the south coast of England. His father, the local curate, was fairly well off financially, considering his position. However, he died when Robert was thirteen. As a consequence the boy went to London where he was apprenticed to Sir Peter Lely, a leading portrait painter. Although he showed talent, Robert was a sickly child and the oils and paints associated with the job were more than his allergies could stand. He was forced to quit an otherwise promising apprenticeship; but his art training was useful to him in later life.

Fortunately his father had left him 100 pounds, a fairly large sum in those days, and he was able to attend Westminster School. When he was eighteen he entered Oxford. He worked his way through college; he sang in the choir of Christ Church, acted as a valet, and did all manner of odd jobs. He possessed many skills, was a good draftsman and illustrator, and could work with wood and metal, and above all he was a brilliant student.

While at Oxford, Robert Hooke met Christopher Wren and Robert Boyle. Robert Boyle, brilliant, wealthy scientist, eight years Hooke's senior, employed the unprepossessing student as a research and laboratory assistant. Christopher Wren distinguished himself for his work in geometry and in 1660 was made Professor of Astronomy at Oxford. In 1663 Wren began a career as an architect and is still famous as the designer of St. Paul's Cathedral in London. The home of Christopher Wren was the meeting place for the scientists of England. This was the gathering point for the "Invisible College" which later became the famous and important scientific Royal Society.

Many believe that much of Robert Boyle's work, including Boyle's law for gases, was the result of Hooke's intellectual abilities and mechanical skills. In fact Hooke lays claim to this achievement. However, Boyle seems to have been a most fair-minded man and when the vacuum pump was developed in his laboratories, he publicly gave Hooke the credit although the pump was known at the time as Boyle's engine.

Hooke had a very interesting job – unpaid – with the Royal Society. Before each meeting he prepared the experiments which the Fellows of the Society wished to have performed. This experience brought him into association with all the branches of science then in existence and enabled him to enhance his experimental abilities.

The Royal Society had been the recipient of long letters from Anton van Leeuwenhoek, describing his marvelous findings in the world of microscopy. Leeuwenhoek worked with a single lens of remarkable magnifying powers, and although he had made many lenses, he refused to part with any of them. Robert Hooke, commissioned by the Royal Society to investigate the matter, designed and built a practical compound microscope. Using his artistic skill he then made remarkable drawings of some sixty microscopic items. The eye of a fly, the metamorphosis of a gnat larva, the structure of feathers, a louse, a flea, all were drawn many times life size with meticulous accuracy. These remarkable drawings were published in his *Micrographia* in 1664. Hooke showed how to make and use the microscope, but it is Leeuwenhoek who is thought of as the father of microscopy.

In 1666 the Great Fire of London broke out. Before the flames were conquered, eighty per cent of the city had been destroyed. Christopher Wren enlisted Hooke's aid in his architect office. The plan for rebuilding London, attributed to Wren, was drawn up by Hooke. The recommendation was for rebuilding on a rectangular plan, with streets at right angles to each other. This was rejected, not because it was inadequate, but because of opposition from the owners of buildings still standing. As a result, London is still beset with many narrow crooked streets.

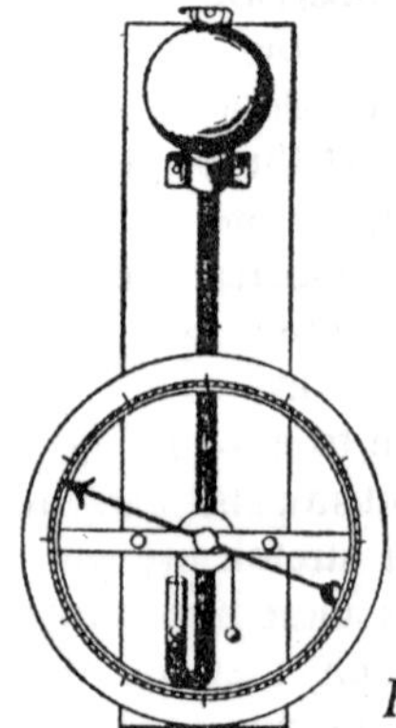

*Hooke's dial barometer.*

Hooke was an ingenious instrument maker. He brought his knowledge of optics to astronomical measurements and devised a quadrant with telescopic sights and a screw adjustment. He invented various mechanical devices for survey work in navigation including sounding instruments and devices for collecting water at different depths. Weather investigations were advanced by his ingenious wind gauge, dial-type barometer, rain gauge and humidity measuring devices. He instituted a weather publication under the auspices of the Royal Society. Hooke may be thought of as the father of weather prognostication. He appreciated the role played by the sun's radiation and the rotation of the earth in determining the weather.

Five years before Newton published his "Principia," outlining the gravitational attractions among various planets, Hooke delivered a lecture before the Royal Society that disclosed his grasp of the law of universal gravitation. He said, in part, "All the celestial bodies are of a globular figure, and several of them do turn round on their axes. Were there not in them such a gravitating power, all the loose parts must be thrown away from them like a stone out of a sling."

Newton had formulated his gravitational theory ten years before but had not published it. When he finally did write the "Principia," Hooke was upset since he felt that Newton had used some of his work without acknowledgment. This incident led to a good deal of bitterness and wrangling between these scientific prima donnas.

Have you solved the anagram at the head of this story? The correct answer is *Ut tensio, sic vis.* This is the Latin expression of Hooke's law of elasticity. In 1676 Hooke tucked this anagram into a scientific publication of an entirely different matter. In this way, although not quite sure of all the facts, he was able to establish the date that he began to develop the idea and so establish priority. The translation of the Latin is "The stretch is proportional to the force." Hooke's Law seems incredibly simple: if one pound stretches a spring one inch, then two pounds will stretch it two inches, and ten pounds will stretch it ten inches and so on within the limit of the strength of the spring.

This principle Hooke applied immediately to the invention of the spring balance. Hooke took the balance and a known mass to the top of St. Paul's Cathedral and attempted to show that the pull of gravity was less as he went higher. The theory behind his experiment is that the earth will have a greater gravitational pull on a mass that is closer to the center of the earth than on one that is farther away.

His analysis of the spring led to the invention of the watch. The pendulum clock was in general use but it had to be kept in one place. Its use aboard ships was very undependable and a pendulum clock lost time as it approached the equator, due to the reduction in gravity at the equator. Hooke replaced the pendulum with a balance wheel and a hairspring. The idea is that the hairspring will vibrate at a constant rate back and forth about its center position. Here again Hooke was frustrated. Christian Huygens, in France, had worked out a similar system and had patented it in 1675. Hooke was able to establish priority of discovery, but Huygens' patent stood. Hooke had neglected to follow up on his invention.

Hooke acted as secretary of the Royal Society, and although he gave up this job in 1682 he continued to contribute scientific papers. He had never married but had a niece who lived with him and acted as housekeeper. She died in 1687 and the shock was so great that Hooke broke down completely. Two years after his death in 1703, his notes were published – 400,000 words which revealed the full extent and variety of his interests.

Worldly fame and success had eluded him, but his original mind had anticipated many inventions and theories. When he held the blade of a screwdriver to his watch and the wooden handle to his ear, and heard the works of his watch, he predicted the invention of the stethoscope. This was achieved 150 years later. He invented the word "cell" to describe the structure of cork which he saw in his microscope and which he compared to a honeycomb.

Like many scientists of his time, he was interested in

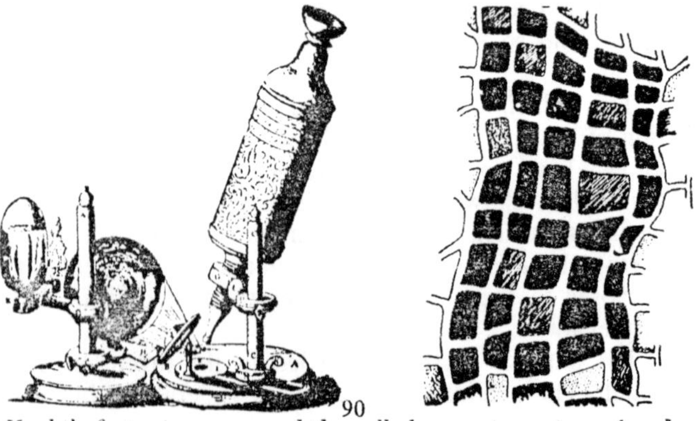



*Hooke's first microscope and the cells he saw in a piece of cork. From a drawing of the time.*

social welfare and concentrated on studies which would improve the conditions of man. He tackled the problems of the miner and the farmer from a practical point of view.

Robert Hooke was an amazing scientific genius – he made discoveries as great as Newton and Huygens and Leeuwenhoek, but he is remembered now mainly for his law concerning the spring, *Ut tensio, sic vis.*

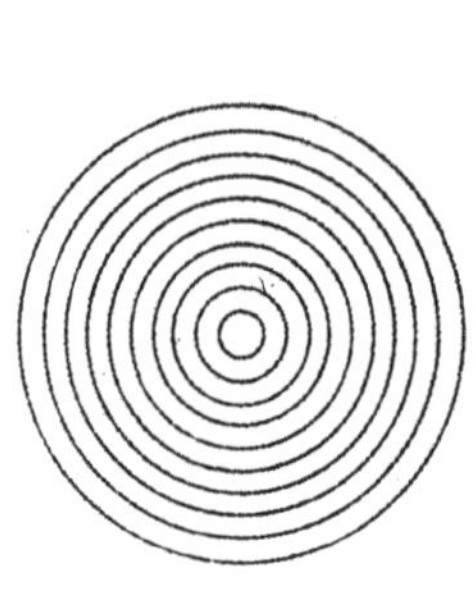

## SIR ISAAC NEWTON

Isaac Newton was born in a farmhouse in a tiny village in England on Christmas day in 1642, a Christmas gift to the world. He must have seemed a small present indeed. His mother had said that he was so tiny at birth that he might well have been placed in a quart-size pitcher. This undersized child, born prematurely to an already widowed mother and not expected to live, grew up to be one of the world's greatest scientists.

Newton's achievements in mathematics, in mechanics, in gravitation, in optics, were so vast and fundamental that each would have brought renown to the scientist even if he had accomplished nothing else.

When his mother remarried – he was about two at the time – Isaac was sent to live with his grandmother. There is very little in his early record that suggests an exceptional genius. He showed a great deal of interest in doing things with his hands: he made a model of a windmill (it actually worked), he made water clocks, and he made a stone sundial (which is now in the possession of the Royal

Society of London). He was fond of reading and of copying drawings, and he collected flowers and herbs.

When Isaac was fourteen he was taken back to live with his mother, whose second husband had just died, to help her run the farm. The young Newton proved to be totally inadequate at farming. Instead of paying attention to his duties, he would read or daydream or make wooden models. His mother at last agreed that Isaac be prepared to enter college. At the age of eighteen, then, the youthful Newton went off to Cambridge University where he had been accepted at the famous Trinity College.

Newton spent four years at Cambridge and received his B.A. degree in 1665. While at Cambridge, he was befriended by Isaac Barrow, his mathematics professor. Professor Barrow recognized that Newton was out of the ordinary and encouraged him to develop his mathematical abilities.

England was suffering from an epidemic of the bubonic plague, which had wiped out about one-tenth of the population. Cambridge was shut down and the students dispersed to their homes. Newton went back to his mother to the small farmhouse of his birth and spent most of his time there until the University reopened about a year and a half later.

The eighteen months he spent at his mother's farm were probably the most fruitful in science history. Newton devised the basic laws of mechanics and applied them to heavenly bodies, he discovered the fundamental law of gravitation, he invented the methods of differential and integral calculas, and he laid the foundation for his great optical discoveries. He was to spend the rest of his scientific life explaining, expanding, and applying these discoveries, but the creation took place in those eighteen months during his twenty-third and twenty-fourth years.

Newton did not make his wonderful discoveries known to the world. This secretiveness was to involve Newton in controversy and argument throughout his career.

Newton returned to a minor teaching position at Cambridge when it reopened in 1667. He advanced rapidly and, when he was twenty-six, became a professor of mathematics, succeeding his own teacher and sponsor Isaac Barrow.

Newton had been doing a considerable amount of experimental work in the study of light. He was annoyed by the fact that his telescopes, like all others of the time, gave images that were fringed with color and were therefore indistinct. In an attempt to solve this problem he made a detailed study of light, using a triangular glass prism for the purpose. The basic experiment consisted of shining a beam of sunlight on the prism. He worked in a darkened room and obtained the beam through a hole in the shutter. He noted that the white light was spread out in a rainbow strip, which he called a spectrum. The colors were in the following order: red, orange, yellow, green, blue, indigo, violet.

He then blocked off all the colors but one, for instance violet. The violet beam was allowed to pass through another prism. Newton observed that the violet was bent but did not change color, that violet remained violet. He repeated this experiment with each color. The colors did

not further split as white light had done. He noticed, however, that each color was bent a different amount as it passed through the second prism. Newton came to a simple but startling conclusion: the white light of the sun was in fact a mixture of all the colors of the spectrum! The glass of the prism bent each color a different amount and so separated them.

From these experiments Newton concluded that it was not possible to construct a lens without color fringes. Turning away from the use of lenses, Newton devised the reflecting telescope which makes use of a bowl-shaped metal mirror to focus the light from the stars. Since the light does not pass through glass in this type of telescope, there is no uneven bending of the light and no color fringes. It is interesting to note that lenses without color fringes were produced about 100 years later. These acromatic lenses were made by combining different types of optical glasses.

Newton did the mechanical work on his telescope by himself. The mirror was about one inch in diameter. The observatory of the California Institute of Technology at Mount Palomar has a reflecting mirror almost seventeen feet in diameter.

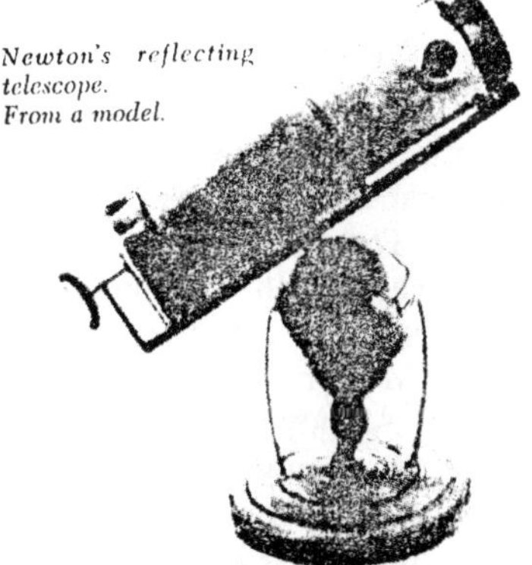

*Newton's reflecting telescope. From a model.*

His work on optics, the subject of his first published scientific paper, was greeted with a good deal of criticism as well as applause. Newton was forced to defend his theories against the ablest scientists of the day, Christian

Huygens, Robert Hooke, and others. During this controversy he had occasion to state a cornerstone of scientific method: "The best and safest way of doing scientific work seems to be, first to enquire diligently into the properties of things, and of establishing these properties by experiment, and then to proceed slowly to theories for the explanation of them."

Newton, now in his early thirties, was known to the scientific world as a brilliant experimenter and theoretician. He had grown tired of the necessity of answering critics, and he determined not to publicize any more of his discoveries. He continued, nevertheless, to work at his theories and somehow found time to serve in Parliament as a representative of the University.

In 1684 the famous astronomer Edmund Halley visited Newton in order to discuss Kepler's theories of the motions of the planets. From these discussions it became evident to Halley that Newton had worked out in detail one of the most fundamental of all laws, the law of universal gravitation. Halley somehow convinced Newton that he must publish his findings. In order to save Newton every difficulty possible, Halley agreed to take care of all details and, although he was not a wealthy man, to defray the printing costs.

The result, titled *Philosophiae Naturalis Principia Mathematica* consisted of three sections called "books" and was written entirely in Latin, the scientific language of the day. A rough translation of the title is *Mathematical Principles of Science*. The "Principia," a landmark in the history of the world, showed that all motions, whether on earth or in the heavens, were expressed by the same laws.

Newton's Laws of Motion were outlined in the "Principia." The first law is: A body that is at rest remains at rest unless forced to change; a body that is in motion will continue to move with the same speed and in the same direction unless forced to change. Newton realized that in order to get an object to move, whether it was an apple that fell out of a tree or the tides that rose in the oceans, there had to be a force present. Consider what happens when the automobile in which we are riding is suddenly stopped.

We continue to move forward; thus we remain in motion until forced to stop, perhaps by banging against the seat in front of us. These ideas were observed before Newton, but he explained them mathematically.

The second law of motion showed that the amount of force may be measured by a rate of change of motion. Rate of change of motion is called acceleration and refers to the rapidity of increase or decrease in speed. For example, it takes a greater force to bring an automobile from standstill to twenty-five miles an hour in five seconds, than it does to bring that automobile from standstill to fifteen miles an hour in the same time.

From the second law we also learn that it takes the same force to stop a car going sixty miles an hour in ten seconds, as it does to stop the car going thirty miles an hour in five seconds.

The third law of motion is that action causes a reaction and that these are equal and opposite. This has many applications; the most spectacular is that of rocket flight. As the hot gases move back the rocket moves forward. Or examine your lawn sprinkler: as the water leaves the nozzle, the nozzle spins backwards.

The universal law of gravitation was the most astounding. In it Newton contended and proved that every particle of matter attracted every other particle of matter. Not only does the earth pull on the apple in the tree but the apple pulls on the earth. This law applies to all of the planets. The sun pulls on – attracts – the earth, the earth attracts the moon, and the moon attracts the earth. He showed that the force between bodies depended on the mass of the bodies and how close they were to each other, and showed how to calculate these forces.

The second book of the "Principia" developed the ideas of the first book but included some idea of resistance offered to motion. He discusses, for example, the shape of a ship that will meet with least resistance. In this book he also gives a mathematical treatment of wave motion, which has proved essential in modern physics.

The third book is recognized as an outstanding triumph of human intelligence. Newton took the principles of motion and of gravitation as deduced from observations of earthbound objects and extended them to the motions of the earth and of the planets around the sun. He calculated the mass of the sun and of the earth. He showed how to account, mathematically, for the fact that the earth is flattened at the poles and bulges at the equator. He worked out the main wobbles in the orbit of the moon about the earth, showing exactly how they are caused by the attraction of the mass of the sun. Newton explained the attraction of the moon and of the sun on the waters of the earth and worked out the mathematical theory of tides.

Newton, although he calculated the attraction between masses, refused to entertain any discussion of the cause of the power of gravity, saying, "It is enough that gravity does really exist, and act according to the laws which we have explained, and abundantly serves to account for all the motions of the celestial bodies, and of the sea."

Newton had gained renown as a scientist through his "Principia." He wrote further treatises – more on optics – and published his invention of the calculus.

In 1699 he was made Master of the Mint and supervised a reform in the manufacture of coins, making them tamp-erproof. In 1703 Newton was elected President of the Royal Society and remained in that office until his death. He was knighted by Queen Anne in 1705.

Sir Isaac Newton died in 1727, at the age of eighty-five. He was buried in Westminster Abbey. An outstanding scientist of the ages, he recognized his debt to those who went before. He said: *"If I have seen further it is by standing on the shoulders of giants."*

*When white sunlight is broken down by a glass prism, the spectrum of colors is revealed.*

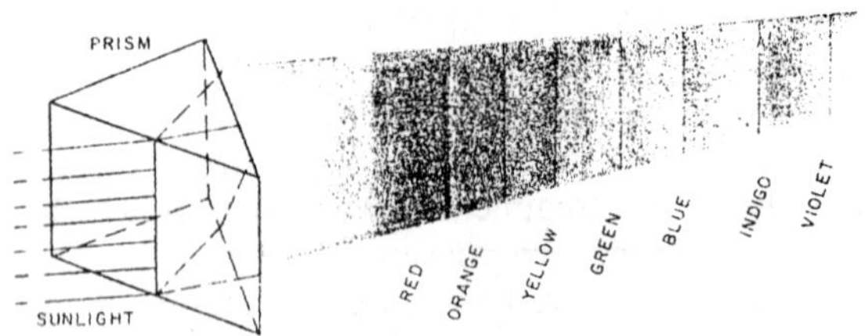

## BENJAMIN FRANKLIN

"Debby, I wish the good Lord had seen fit to make each day just twice as long as it is," said Benjamin Franklin to his wife. "Perhaps then I could really accomplish something."

Really accomplish something? Benjamin Franklin made outstanding contributions to national and international life in many fields – in science, invention, education, literature, publishing, social service, and international diplomacy. It is hard to think of what else he might have done, if the days were twice or even three times as long.

Ben Franklin was born in Boston, Massachusetts Colony, on January 17, 1706. He had fourteen older brothers and sisters; altogether there were seventeen children in the family. His father worked at candlemaking which was an important, but scarcely a well-paying vocation.

Ben taught himself to read and when he was eight years old he was sent to school. His schooling was stopped two years later; schools were not free in those days and Ben's father, unable to pay, reluctantly put Ben to work in his candlemaking shop. But Ben was restless. He looked out on Boston Harbor and talked of going to sea. Alarmed, the elder Franklin prevailed on his son James to teach Ben to a be a printer. Brother James published a weekly newspaper, *The New England Courant.* Here the twelve-year-old was happy for a while. He learned to set type and to run the presses.

Franklin, eager to educate himself, read all the books he could lay hands on, frequently doing without food to buy books. This remarkable boy taught himself arithmetic, algebra, geometry, navigation, grammar, and logic. He learned to write well. When his *Autobiography* was published after his death, it was judged one of the classics of American literature.

Franklin was determined to write for the *New England Courant,* but when his brother would not take the youngster seriously, Ben submitted articles under the assumed name of Mrs. Silence Dogwood. When James discovered the author, his short temper gave way, and he made life miserable for Ben. Franklin decided to strike out on his own; at eighteen he went to Philadelphia.

In Philadelphia, his abilities as a printer quickly became known, and his services were eagerly sought. He wished, however, to establish his own printing plant. There was, at the time no printing machinery manufactured in the Colonies; it had to be imported from England. Ben Franklin, with the promise of financial support from Sir William Keith, govenor of the colony of Pennsylvania, sailed for England to select printing presses.

Somehow the promised finances did not arrive. Franklin spent a year and a half working in England to raise funds for his business venture. Meanwhile, home in Philadelphia, with no word from her missing sweetheart, Deborah Reed married another man. Some years later, after the disappearance of her first husband, Benjamin and Deborah became man and wife. They had three children.

Upon his return to Philadelphia he established the *Pennsylvania Gazette.* In addition he began publication of the annual *Poor Richard's Almanac. Poor Richard's Almanac* was a calendar that provided information about the sunrise and the phases of the moon, a long-range weather forecast, and church holy days. In addition it contained many pithy sayings on various subjects: honesty, industry, thrift, and patriotism. Some that have come down to us today are:

> God helps them that help themselves.
>
> Early to bed and early to rise makes a man healthy, wealthy and wise.
>
> Never leave that till tomorrow which you can do today.

By the time he was forty-two, Benjamin Franklin had made enough money to enable him to retire from business and to devote himself completely to public service and to a scientific career. He had started these activities even while he was engaged in the printing business.

At age twenty-one he had organized a discussion group among young mechanics and tradespeople of Philadelphia. This group expanded beyond Philadelphia and grew into the American Philosophical Society. This Society included the best minds of the colonies. They set up Committees of Secret Correspondence which laid the foundation for the stirring Declaration of Independence and the American Revolution. The American Philosophical Society building still stands in Philadelphia.

Benjamin Franklin obtained an appointment as Postmaster General of the Colonies in 1753. He brought his usual energy and abilities to his new job, vastly improved service between the various colonies, and placed the post office on a paying basis. In 1847, when the United States printed its first postage stamps, the likeness of Benjamin Franklin appeared on the stamp, a tribute to his contributions to our postal system.

At age twenty-five Franklin has founded the first circulating library in America, remembering his own early days when he went without food to obtain books. He set up a fire department in Philadelphia, and to cut down on the distress among burned-out unfortunates, helped to establish the first American fire-insurance company. He helped establish the Academy of Pennsylvania, which grew into the University of Pennsylvania. Philadelphia owed much of its reputation as the leading city of the colonies to the influence of this great man. And he is a great man in science.

Franklin began his scientific work when he was about thirty-eight; he already had had a successful career in business and in public service. His most important work was done in electrostatics, the study of electricity at rest.

Everyone has heard how he flew a kite in an electrical storm and proved that lightning is electricity. This story is one of the most popular in the American legend, and, unlike many stories that have come down to us, this one is true. He published it in the *Scientific Journal* of the day, and many scientists all over the world repeated the experiment.

Franklin's electrostatic theory is fundamentally simple and has remained with us to the present. He said that all bodies are composed of "common matter" and of "electrical matter" or "electric-fluid." In its normal condition, every material contains a certain amount of the electric fluid. Franklin stated that a body may gain or may lose some of the electric fluid. If it has gained or lost "fluid" the body will be charged, or "electrified." If it has gained

*Franklin's experiment with lightning.*

"electric fluid" it will be charged positive, if it has lost "electric fluid" it will be charged negative.

Today we would say that all bodies are composed of protons and electrons; and that in an uncharged body the number of electrons equals the number of protons, but the idea is the same as Franklin's theory.

Franklin developed experiments to support his theory. When a piece of glass is rubbed with a silk cloth, the glass has a positive charge and the silk has a negative charge. Many scientists thought that the friction created the electric charge. Franklin correctly insisted that the electricity was not created but that the electric fluid was moved from the silk to the glass.

Franklin made his demonstrations of this electric fluid theory dramatic. He placed two men on stools, insulated from ground by means of glass. One man was charged positive, an excess of "electric fluid." The other was charged negative, a deficiency of "electric fluid." When the two men touched each other both men lost their charge and got a shock. The excess "electric fluid" of one supplied the lack in the other. If an uncharged person touched either the positively or the negatively charged person, he, too, got a spark or a shock, because he had more electric fluid than the man charged negative and less than the man charged positive.

Franklin's studies of electricity led him to the invention of the lightning rod. He discovered that a sharp point held near a charged body would draw off the charge of the body. He knew that clouds were electrically charged and suggested that a sharply pointed iron rod be placed on the highest point of a building and that a wire be run from the rod to the ground. This scheme would protect the building from lightning by discharging the cloud slowly instead of violently. Franklin's experiments led him to speculate that clouds may be charged either positive or negative and that, therefore, the lightning discharge rises from the ground to a cloud as often as it goes from the cloud to the ground. This fits in with up-to-date lightning research.

Franklin studied the Leyden jar, which was universally

used as a collector of electrical charge. This is simply a glass jar, the outside coated with metal, and the inside filled with water. Franklin startled the scientific world by analyzing the action of the Leyden jar. He poured out the water of a charged Leyden jar and then poured in fresh water. The Leyden jar was still charged! He proved thus that the charge was in the glass and not, as had been supposed, in the water. As a result of these experiments he invented the parallel plate capacitor used in your TV and radio today.

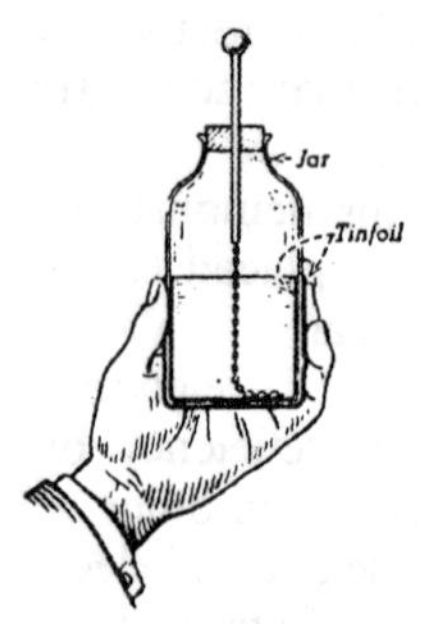


*The Leyden jar. This early form of condenser was used by Franklin in his experiments on electricity.*

Franklin's scholarly book *Experiments and Observations on Electricity made at Philadelphia in America* contained the principles of electricity he discovered and deduced. This great book was published throughout the world, and was translated into German, French and Italian.

Leading scientists of the world compared his book with the "Principia" of Sir Isaac Newton. "The experiments and observations of Dr. Franklin constitute the "Principia" of electricity, and form the basis of a system equally simple and profound," one journal said. Franklin was awarded every scientific honor possible. He was elected to the Royal Society in London and to the Royal Academy of Science in Paris. His contribution was the "one-fluid" theory of electricity. Now we say that electric current is a flow of electrons – still a theory of one "fluid."

Despite all his scientific research and publications

Franklin found time to remain active in public affairs. The American Revolution was in progress and the Continental Congress appointed Thomas Jefferson, John Adams and Benjamin Franklin to serve as a committee to draft the Declaration of Independence.

Franklin – an acknowledged giant of American social and political history – is, in the development of electrical theory, one of the giants of science.

## HENRY CAVENDISH

Henry Cavendish was the richest man of his time in England. When he died he left an estate of more than a million pounds, but while he lived he wore clothes so old and shabby that they literally fell apart. He was an eccentric – but he was one of the world's very great scientists.

Cavendish was born at Nice, France, in October of 1731. He was the first of two sons of Lord Charles and Lady Anne Cavendish of England. He counted among his forebears, if he ever bothered to notice such things, ancestors who had become British nobility in the fourteenth century. One of his ancestors was a Lord Chief Justice, and another, Thomas Cavendish, was the second Englishman to sail around the world. Henry's father, Lord Charles, was a scientist of note. He had received the important Copley medal of the Royal Society of London for the invention of the maximum-minimum thermometer.

Unfortunately his mother died when his brother was born, but Henry Cavendish's education was conventional for the son of a nobleman. At the age of eleven he was sent to a boarding school at Hackney, England, and at the age of eighteen entered Cambridge, where he studied for four years. He was unwilling, however, to spend any time studying religion. Since this was a required subject for all candidates for graduation, he left the university without a degree.

He and his brother Frederick went to London and then to Paris to study mathematics and physics. As a student he had received only a moderate allowance from his father, but he inherited an enormous fortune at the age of forty. He had no concern about funds at any time in his life.

Henry Cavendish, although well educated and wealthy, could never have been considered an eligible bachelor. If he was uncomfortable in the company of men, he was panic-stricken in the presence of ladies. Even the women who did his housekeeping were required to keep out of his sight. He communicated with them by means of notes, and dismissed the maid if she came into the same room with him.

He had absolutely no fund of small talk and was unable to engage in any kind of social conversation that was not related to science. He would not even discuss business matters with his bankers. When they asked for guidance in investing his very considerable fortune, Cavendish asked them not to bother him, to invest the funds as they saw fit. Cavendish never wasted words, in fact, he hardly used them.

Almost his only point of contact with the world was through the Royal Society of London. He was elected a Fellow in 1760, at the age of twenty-nine and ate regularly at the club formed by the Fellows.

The big science problem of the day was fire. What was fire? Johann Becher and his student George Ernst Stahl, German scientists and inventors, had proposed a theory of burning that seemed to work, and which was, in spite of its defects, generally accepted by the scientific community. Even Priestley, the discoverer of oxygen, accepted Becher's erroneous theory of burning, the "phlogiston" explanation. The theory ran like this: All substances that will burn contain ash (called calx) and a combustible substance called phlogiston. When the substance burned, the phlogiston was released, when no more burning took place there was no more phlogiston present.

Nobody had ever isolated phlogiston, and Cavendish determined to try. He spent some time in library research and found out that Theophrastus Paracelsus and Jan van Helmont had found a "flammable air." They had placed some iron into sulphuric acid, caught the bubbles of "air" that were released and noted that the "air" had burned, but they had done no further work with the remarkable "flammable air." Perhaps, thought Cavendish, this "air" was the phlogiston that science was looking for.

Cavendish went to his own laboratory, which he had built in the family residence. He experimented with and enlarged upon the findings of Paracelsus and Van Helmont. He took bits of iron and of zinc and of tin, and sulphuric acid and hydrochloric acid and made "air." Into a container of sulphuric acid, Cavendish dropped pieces of iron. Bubbles formed on the iron and floated to the surface of the acid. These bubbles were caught in an animal bladder like a toy balloon. Six bladders in all were filled with "air," each separately obtained. One was from the iron and sulphuric acid, the second from zinc and sulphuric acid, the third from tin and sulphuric acid. The fourth, fifth and sixth were filled with "air" from iron, zinc, and tin respectively in hydrochloric acid.

Was this really phlogiston? Cavendish ignited a sample of each of these "airs." Each burned with the same pale beautiful blue flame. Now to make sure. Cavendish weighed each of these "airs" and found they weighed the same. They were very light, but they weighed the same. Another experiment showed that the amount of inflammable "air" obtained depended on the amount of metal used, and he reached an erroneous conclusion. He decided that the "air" did not come from the acid, but from the metal. He thought he had isolated "phlogiston" and published his findings before the learned men of the Royal Society in 1766.

We may wonder now how the scientists of the day accepted this material as "phlogiston," or accepted the phlogiston idea altogether. Henry Cavendish was so extraordinarily skillful in the laboratory that he was able to weigh the very light inflammable air. He knew that after a material burns the ashes weigh more than the material itself, and yet he was willing to accept the idea that phlogiston escapes from a substance when it is burned. Cavendish was not alone; other leading scientists were also enthusiastic in accepting this inflammable air as phlogiston.

Sometime later, Lavoisier helped to destroy the phlogiston theory and identified the "air" Cavendish discovered. He called it hydrogen.

Call it phlogiston or hydrogen, its discovery created quite a stir. Scientists and non-scientists alike made their own. Many must have been injured and killed their experimenting for hydrogen mixed with a certain amount of oxygen is violently explosive. It is reported that an enterprising Frenchman filled his lungs with hydrogen and set fire to the gas as he exhaled it through his mouth.

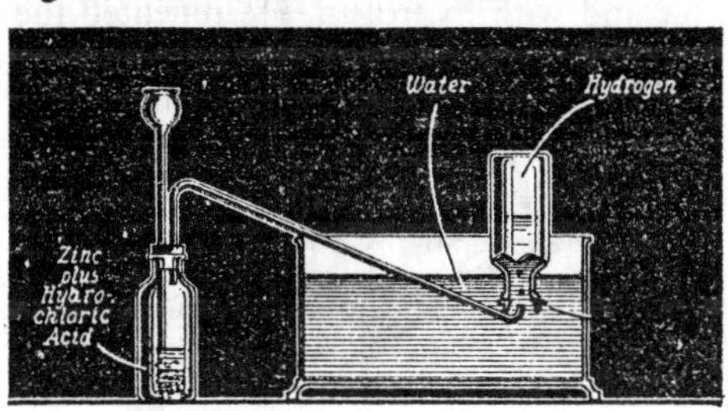


*Making hydrogen in the laboratory.*

The first hydrogen-filled balloon was flown in 1783. Hydrogen is the lightest element, and in 1781 an Italian living in England showed that a hydrogen-filled soap bubble would float upwards. Balloons had already been constructed of paper-lined cloth bags and had ascended when filled with hot air. Jacques Charles, a famous French physicist, constructed a hydrogen-filled balloon. This made a successful flight without passengers but was destroyed by frightened peasants when it landed some fifteen miles outside of Paris. In 1785 a hydrogen-filled balloon exploded, killing its occupants. Some 150 years later in 1937 the enormous and palatial dirigible *Hindenburg* exploded in Lakehurst, New Jersey, killing thirty-six persons. It contained 7,000,000 cubic feet of hydrogen. It had crossed the Atlantic many times.

Along with the explosions of the hydrogen-filled balloons, there were controlled explosions in the laboratories. Scientific reports reached the Royal Society that told of experiments in which hydrogen was burned with the formation of dew, a British experimenter had exploded hydrogen in a closed container by means of an electric spark, and had noted the formation of moisture. A French experimenter had held a porcelain saucer over a hydrogen flame and the saucer became wet. Priestley described the explosion of air and hydrogen in a thick glass container and, too busy with other things, decided that it would not take the place of gunpowder. He had a clue but did not follow it.

The explosions in the glass containers and the reports of moisture triggered an idea in the mind of Henry Cavendish. He went back to his laboratory and filled his glass tubes with air and with hydrogen. He repeated the experiment with oxygen and with hydrogen. He passed an electric

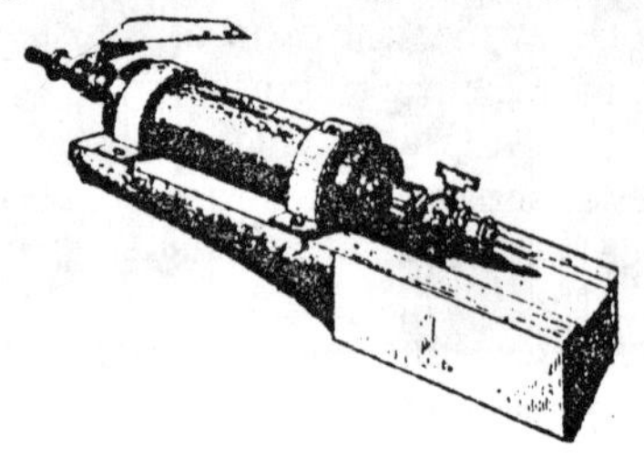

*Cavendish's eudiometer, an instrument for measuring and analyzing gases. From an old drawing.*

spark through the mixture. Sure enough, there was a fog on the inside of the cylinder. Experiment followed experiment – *ten years* of careful measurement of gases going into the tube, and of gases and water coming out. Pure oxygen, ordinary air, hydrogen, were measured and exploded. The results were carefully recorded.

In 1784 Cavendish published his *Experiments on Air* before the Royal Society of London. The conclusions of his work were startling. Water, Cavendish found, resulted when phlogiston (as he called hydrogen) united with dephlogisticated air (as he called oxygen). And further, he had proof that two volumes of hydrogen combined with one volume of oxygen and produced water. He had combined enormous volumes of hydrogen and of oxygen to produce a weight of water equal to the original weight of the gases. Cavendish had proved conclusively that water was not an element but, unbelievable as it might seem, water was made up of two colorless gases.

In the course of his work, Cavendish discovered that twenty per cent of the air we breathe is oxygen. His careful analysis of the explosion of hydrogen and air led him to this result. When the air was expanded with hydrogen by means of an electric spark, Cavendish also noted a small amount of acid. He tracked this down to the nitrogen in the air; he realized that oxygen combines with nitrogen when there is an electric spark. This method is the basis of nature's production of fertilizer. Nitrogen is combined with oxygen during lightning discharges and the compound is rained down on the earth, fertilizer from the sky. Cavendish squeezed almost the last drop of information out of the air. He kept up his electrical discharges, adding oxygen until no nitrogen was left. A small bubble of "air" still remained. This was mostly argon, a rare gas that makes up less than one per cent of the atmosphere.

Cavendish died as he had lived, alone and unattended, at the age of seventy-nine in the year 1810. He was buried at Derby, England, where the cathedral set up a monument for this eccentric scientist, who during his lifetime had paid no heed to organized religion.

Henry Cavendish was not content with the study of chemistry alone. He made some remarkable discoveries in electricity. He had established, using Newton's Laws of Attraction, the surprisingly accurate figure of 5.48 for the specific gravity of the earth. He literally weighed the earth.

A good part of his fortune was used by his heirs to establish the Cavendish Laboratories in England, where the great J. J. Thompson discovered the electron in 1897, and from whose halls have come at least six Nobel Prize winners in physics or chemistry.

For his discovery of hydrogen and nitrogen and his

determination of the composition of air, and of the composition of water, and for his magnificent experimental and analysis techniques, Henry Cavendish is foremost among the giants of science.

*This simple apparatus was used by Cavendish for a very important experiment. With a mixture of oxygen and air in the bent tube, he passed electric sparks through it until all the oxygen and nitrogen had combined, and showed that air is composed almost entirely of these gases.*

# JOSEPH PRIESTLEY

When was the last time you had an ice cream soda or a bottle of soda pop? Americans spend an astonishing $1,000,000,000 a year on ice cream sodas, soda pop, cola drinks, ginger ale, and just plain charged water. When Joseph Priestley received a gold medal for his invention of carbon dioxide gas dissolved in water, he never dreamed that he was starting a billion-dollar soda water industry. But it was not the invention of soda water that made Priestley a giant of science. It was the discovery of the gas of life.

Joseph Priestley was born on March 13, 1733, in a small town near the city of Leeds in England. His father was a weaver, a poor man, who died leaving Joseph an orphan at the age of seven. The child was taken by an aunt who brought up her nephew in an atmosphere of free discussion. She belonged to a small religious group called "Dissenters" and sent Joseph to the non-conformist academy to study for the ministry. Joseph was an able scholar and showed a remarkable ability to learn languages. He had mastered French, Italian, German, Arabic, and Aramaic. He had a speech impediment however, and upon his graduation he was able only to obtain the pastorate of a very small church where his salary was less than a pound a week. In order to make ends meet, or perhaps because he was indefatigable, Priestley taught at a local school all day, and then gave private lessons. At the same time he managed to find time to write an English grammar. Soon he obtained a position as a language teacher at the Academy of Dissenters. At this institution he attended some lectures in chemistry and began to experiment on his own. He became well known among the local scientists.

Benjamin Franklin, the roving ambassador of the American colonies, visited England to stir up sympathies for the cause of Independence. Franklin came in the guise of a scientist, which, in truth, he was. Priestley hurried to London to meet the great electrical scientist of the age and was inspired to write a book, the *History and Present State of Electricity*. This book resulted in Priestley's election to membership in the Royal Society in 1766. Incidentally Priestley was convinced of the justice of the American revolutionary cause, and was to maintain a lifelong friendship with Benjamin Franklin. As we may well realize, the history of electricity that Priestley wrote was not merely a collection of the facts already known, but contained original experiments.

Still a minister and only a part-time scientist, Priestley took charge of a chapel in Leeds. Underpaid, and by this time with a family to support, he made his home in a building next door to a large brewery. It was this fascinatingly odorous neighbor that started him on his chemical career in earnest. He obtained permission of the brewers to capture the "air" which came off the mixture in the vats. He studied the gas, noted that a burning splint of wood was extinguished in this "air." Priestley searched through the writings of scientists; he found other ways to prepare this fixed air, which we now know as carbon dioxide. Happily, he succeeding in dissolving some of the gas in water, and received the medal we spoke about earlier.

His success was acknowledged in France; he was honored by election to the French Academy. Most important for science, he was to be freed from his time-consuming church position. And just in time; the bewildered congregation could not quite get used to the idea of a minister who was continually surrounded by flasks and bottles and smells, and who spent so much time in a brewery. Lord Shelburne, a scholar and statesman, offered Priestley a position as his librarian. Along with the job went a laboratory. Lord Shelburne provided Priestley with winter quarters in London, a summer lodging at his castle in Calne, laboratories in which to work, and an annual salary of 250 pounds.

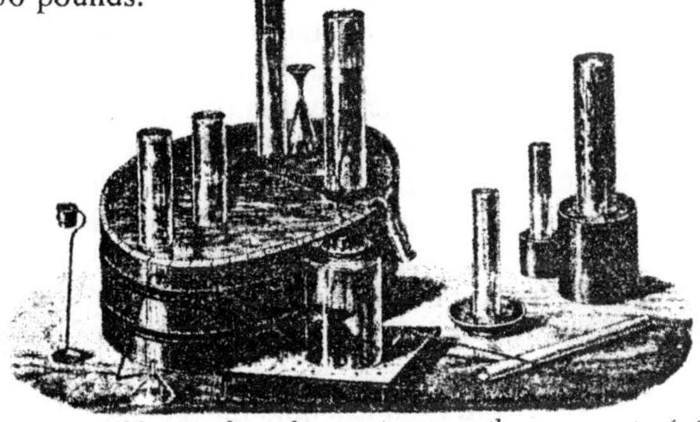

*Apparatus used by Priestley in his experiments on the components of air. From a print of Priestley's time.*

It was during his association with Lord Shelburne that Priestley made some of his most important scientific experiments. With Shelburne, he visited France and Antoine Lavoisier. To Lavoisier, belongs credit for the insight that Priestley's "dephlogistinated air" was in reality a new substance which Lavoisier named "oxygen."

In 1780 Priestley became a member, by invitation, of the Lunar Society. This famous organization included the leading scientists and industrialists of the day. Josiah Wedgwood, the pottery magnate, James Watt, the steam engine pioneer, and scientist Erasmus Darwin, grandfather of Charles Darwin, the naturalist, were members of the group. The "Lunatics" met once a month on the Monday nearest the full moon. This date was chosen so that there would be moonlight for the trip home after their six-hour dinner meeting. In addition to supplying him with good food and stimulating conversation, some wealthier members of the Lunar Society undertook to subsidize Priestley's experiments. Priestley was an idealist who "never did intend or think of making any pecuniary advantage from any of his experiments, but gave them to the public." Nor would he take large sums from the Lunatics, but only enough to maintain his experiments.

But Joseph Priestley was not to continue his peaceful scientific life. The idealistic minister was caught up in the enthusiasm of the French Revolution. He wrote and preached of the doctrines of "liberty, equality and fraternity" and applauded the separation of church and state. Edmund Burke, who had tried, in 1775, to persuade the British government to conciliate the colonies, opposed the violence of the French Revolution and attacked Priestley in a speech in the House of Commons. On July 14, 1791, the second anniversary of the French Revolution, a mob, inflamed by the controversy, attacked Priestley's home. An eye witness described the action as follows:

"They broke in at once, emptied the cellars, smashed the furniture, tore up the books in the library, destroyed the philosophical and chemical apparatus in the laboratory, and ended by setting fire to the house. The roads for miles around were afterwards found strewn with shreds of the valuable manuscripts in which were recorded twenty years' labour and study" – a loss which Priestley continued to bitterly lament until the close of his life.

Fortunately Dr. Priestley and his family had escaped. They left Birmingham and fled to London. As the French Revolution gave way to the reign of terror, the clamor against Priestley increased. He was branded a traitor and called an anti-Christ. His former colleagues in the Royal Society no longer associated with him. In 1794 Priestley set sail for America.

Dr. Priestley arrived in New York City, greeted joyously by the cheers of the people. He was hailed by religious, scientific, and political leaders. Once in the United States he joined his sons, who two years before, had settled in Northumberland, Pennsylvania. He was offered all manner of positions: minister of the Unitarian Church, professor of chemistry at the University of Pennsylvania, lecture tours. Benjamin Franklin opened the gates of Philadelphia; Priestley met with Thomas Jefferson and took tea with George Washington.

He preferred, however, to stay in Northumberland, and he established a laboratory in that quiet place. His home is now a national museum and visitors may see the flasks and crucibles, the vials and troughs that Dr. Priestley used in his chemical quest.

What discoveries did Priestley make that place him so high in the rank of chemists and scientists? He discovered that wonderful element – oxygen. His method was simple and beautifully effective. He placed a sample of mercuric oxide in a glass flask partly filled with mercury. He inverted the flask over a trough of mercury. The next step was to heat the mercuric oxide from the outside by focussing the rays of the sun on the sample with a magnifying glass. If the chemical reaction produced a gas, the level of mercury went down; if, on the other hand, it used a gas the level of mercury went up. Priestley found that the mercuric oxide gave off a large amount of gas. He noticed, quite by chance, that a candle burned more brightly when placed in this gas. He tried the gas on some mice and discovered that a mouse could live much longer in a container of this material than in a container of air.

Priestley discovered that vegetation, plants, "reverse the effects of breathing and tend to keep the atmosphere sweet." He had placed a plant in a container from which the oxygen had been removed and discovered that after ten days, a candle would again burn in the container. Nature's method of the production of oxygen was thus discovered.

An important discovery was made by Priestley after he had established his laboratory in Pennsylvania. Here he uncovered the useful, but deadly, gas – carbon monoxide. Carbon monoxide is produced when coal, gasoline, fuel oil, or any fuel that contains carbon, is combined with less oxygen than is necessary for complete burning. This happens accidentally when an automobile is run in a closed garage. Soon the oxygen is used, and instead of producing carbon dioxide (the nice gas in sodas), the burning fuel can't get enough oxygen and so produces carbon monoxide, the deadly gas. Carbon monoxide can be produced on purpose and is the chief material of much of the gas that cooks our coffee and heats our homes today.

Sir Humphry Davy got quite a kick out of another gas discovery made by Joseph Priestley. He inhaled some of it and described the effects as follows: "The gas raised my pulse upwards of twenty strokes and made me dance about the laboratory as a madman." The gas he wrote about is often called "laughing gas" and has been used as an anesthetic before pulling teeth. Chemically, it is known as nitrous oxide.

Americans can well be proud that they have offered refuge to so many people, oppressed in the lands of their birth. Joseph Priestley was among them.

Joseph Priestley died in 1854, three score and ten years of age.

## ANTOINE LAURENT LAVOISIER

In 1796 the government of France arranged for a funeral in honor of Antoine Laurent Lavoisier. This was an impressive ceremony with many orations in praise of the great scientist. It was the best they could do; they could not bring him back to life. Two years before, in 1794, the terrorists of the French Revolution had sent Lavoisier to the guillotine and had thrown his body into an unmarked grave.

Antoine Laurent Lavoisier was born in Paris on August 26, 1743. His father was a wealthy merchant and owned a considerable amount of land. His mother died when he was very young. Antoine was cared for by a selfless and devoted unmarried aunt, and by his loving father.

His father wished him to follow the law. Dutifully, Antoine completed his legal education and was admitted to practice. However, he was more interested in the study of science than in the law. At college he attended the chemistry lectures of Professor Bourdelian, a theoretical chemist. But he was most fascinated with the demonstrations that accompanied and explained the lectures. A meeting with the great Swedish naturalist Linnaeus also influenced his choice of a scientific career.

At the age of twenty-two, he was awarded a gold medal by the French Academy of Sciences for his competition-winning plan for lighting the streets of Paris. Two years later he became a member of this academy in recognition of his work in preparing a geological study of France and for chemical research on gypsum and plaster of Paris.

Lavoisier's path to the guillotine was established when he became *Fermier General,* the chief tax collector for the monarchy of France, but at that time he was happy to have the position which gave him time for scientific work.

Through a colleague in this tax-collecting organization he met Marie Anne Paulze. Antoine, a tall, handsome, charming man of twenty-eight, fell in love with the beautiful precocious Marie, who was just half his age.

This was a happy, fortunate and intellectually productive marriage. Marie became her husband's secretary and assistant. Antoine had no bent for foreign languages, so Marie learned English and Latin. She translated the scientific papers of Priestley, of Cavendish and the other English scientists of the day. Clever and beautiful, she made the Lavoisier home a popular meeting place for visiting scientists of France and of all nations. She had artistic abilities and made the drawings for his books.

Antoine completed the manuscript for his great work, *Memoires de Chimie* while in prison awaiting execution, and it was Marie who afterward edited it and had it printed.

For many years scientists had concerned themselves with the problem: "What is fire?" The ancients considered fire an element, the most perfect of the earthly elements. Some early civilizations worshiped fire as a god. One explanation of burning that was popularly accepted during Lavoisier's time was called the "phlogiston" theory of combustion.

According to this theory, a material that could burn was rich in a substance called phlogiston. No one had ever seen this material or had any idea of what it was, nevertheless the idea of it was widely accepted. Even the great scientist,

Priestley, who discovered oxygen, was a firm believer in the phlogiston theory until the day of his death. The apparent proof of one theory was that when things burned they seemed to lose something in the rising flames. What they lost, said the scientists, was phlogiston.

Lavoisier had been devoting himself to the experimental study of the rusting of metals and of combustion. His experiments with sulfur and phosphorus convinced him that instead of losing something when they were burned, the materials actually weighed more after burning than before. This shook his belief in the thoery that phlogiston was released upon burning.

Lavoisier now devised what is thought of as one of the classic chemistry experiments of all time. He placed a very carefully weighed quantity of mercury in a retort (see the picture). This was connected to a bell jar that contained a measured volume of air. The bell jar was sealed off from the atmosphere in a trough of mercury. Lavoisier gently heated the mercury in the retort, some of it turned to a red powder. The level of the liquid rose in the bell jar, showing that the volume of air had been reduced. Lavoisier continued his experiment. After twelve days there was no further change. The mercury did not acquire a further red coating, nor did the volume of air reduce further. When he started, the retort, tube and bell jar had fifty cubic inches of air, when he finished heating the mercury he found that there were forty cubic inches of "air" left.

*Lavoisier's apparatus for decomposing water. From a drawing of the time.*

After the first part of the experiment was completed he carefully collected the red powder and heated that, strongly this time. He collected the gas that was driven off and found the missing ten cubic inches of "air"! He correctly interpreted his results. One fifth of the air is a gas that can unite with mercury to form the red powder. This gas – Priestley had called it perfect air – Lavoisier named oxygen. This name comes from the Greek *oxus* (acid) and *glunan* (to produce). He erroneously thought that all acids had to contain this material.

Lavoisier was a very careful experimenter. He devised very delicate balances to enable him to do his work. He said:

"As the usefulness and accuracy of Chemistry depend entirely upon the determination of the weights of the ingredients and products, too much precision cannot be employed in this part of the subject, and for this purpose we must be provided with good instruments."

He is one of the acknowledged fathers of modern chemistry as a result of these experiments which demonstrated the important law of the conservation of matter, which can be stated: "Nothing can be lost, nothing can be created." The law is the cornerstone of present day chemical formulas; everything has to come out even.

Lavoisier did another interesting experiment. He burned a diamond in pure oxygen and obtained carbon dioxide as a result. This pròved, of course, that diamonds and coal are chemically the same: both are carbon.

The building up and breaking down processes that go on in our body – the chemical and energy changes that take place when we eat food and give off waste materials – are known as metabolism. Of course, when we are at rest we need less energy. Physicians are interested in what is called the basal metabolism or basic needs of the body, the food we need just to stay alive. Lavoisier made studies in physiology and biochemistry that established the methods of basal metabolism tests. He performed experiments on guinea pigs, accurately measuring their intake of oxygen and output of carbon dioxide.

He was the first to show that body heat is produced by the process of "burning" that continually takes place in the body, and is a result of the combination of food and oxygen. It was while at work on an experiment to measure the waste products of the body that he was arrested during the reign of terror following the French Revolution.

Henry Cavendish, working in England, was experimenting with a combustible gas – inflammable air, he called it. In 1781 he had shown that when this gas burned, water was produced. Lavoisier repeated Cavendish's experiments and publicized its meaning. Water is a compound of two gases, oxygen and hydrogen. This was too much to accept for some of the scientists of the day, one of whom said, "This arch magician so imposed on our credulity as to persuade us that water, the most powerful natural antiphlogistic we possess, is a compound of two gases one of which surpasses all other substances in inflammability!"

Perhaps it is still a wonder that water is made up of hydrogen, which burns so readily, and oxygen, without which nothing else will burn, and yet water stops most fires. Lavoisier gave the present name to the "inflammable air" – he called it hydrogen, from the Greek *hydro* (water) and *gennan* (to produce).

Throughout his lifetime Lavoisier interrupted his research to devote himself to public services. He was a versatile man, as versatile as our own Benjamin Franklin. He pioneered in chemistry, physiology, scientific agriculture, finance, economics, government and public education.

At the time of the American Revolution, Lavoisier performed a service to France that also resulted in an advantage to the American Revolutionary Army. A private organization in France had a monopoly on the supply of gunpowder. This group fell down on the job and was able to manufacture only a small amount of gunpowder, which was, at the same time, of inferior and uncertain quality.

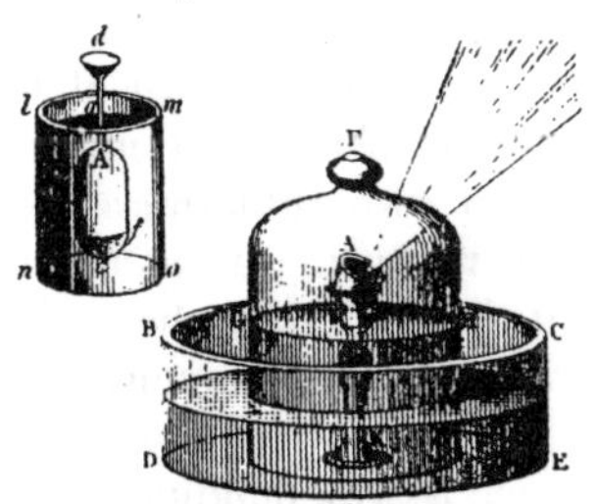

*Hydrometer developed by Lavoisier. From a drawing of the time.*

Lavoisier formed a government-owned agency and within three years had improved on the quality and in addition more than doubled production. This added supply enabled France to provide the fighting colonists with munitions. While experimenting with gunpowder Antoine and Marie Lavoisier were almost killed in an explosion which cost the lives of two colleagues.

Irenee du Pont was an apprentice at the arsenal, and it was Lavoisier who later helped du Pont start a gunpowder factory in Delaware. Irenee wanted to call his enterprise the Lavoisier Mills, but his family prevailed upon him to name it du Pont. That gunpowder factory has grown into a vast industrial-chemical company, still known as E. I. du Pont de Nemours.

Lavoisier had a keen and personal interest in agriculture. He owned a very large farm at Le Bourget, where he demonstrated the importance of fertilizers and the proper apportionment of acreage for pasture and for cultivation. In a relatively short time, by the application of scientific principles to agriculture, he doubled the yield of wheat and produced a five-fold increase in the size of his herd.

He was a political figure, representing the Third Estate (the people) in the provincial Parliament of Orléans. Democratic in his philosophy, he expressed his ideas in this statement: *"Happiness should not be limited to a small number of men; it belongs to all."* He believed that all men have the right to individual liberty.

In 1789 Lavoisier was made President of the Bank of France. He presented a report to the National Assembly which is an acknowledged masterpiece in the study of financial inflation. In 1791 the Republic of France reprinted his treatise "On the Land Wealth of France." He had also suggested a system of national education for France, which is similar to our own modern educational system.

Lavoisier had the misfortune to incur the wrath of Jean Paul Marat, one of the leaders of the Terror following the French Revolution, because Lavoisier had rejected a chemical treatise submitted by Marat to the French Academy of Science. Marat denounced the scientist and succeeded in requesting the arrest of all the members of the tax collecting *Fermier Generaux* as robbers who despoiled the people. Lavoisier and his father-in-law were thrown into the overcrowded prison. All petitions to free Lavoisier as a great scientist who had rendered invaluable services to the state failed. On May 8, 1794, the guillotine ended his life.

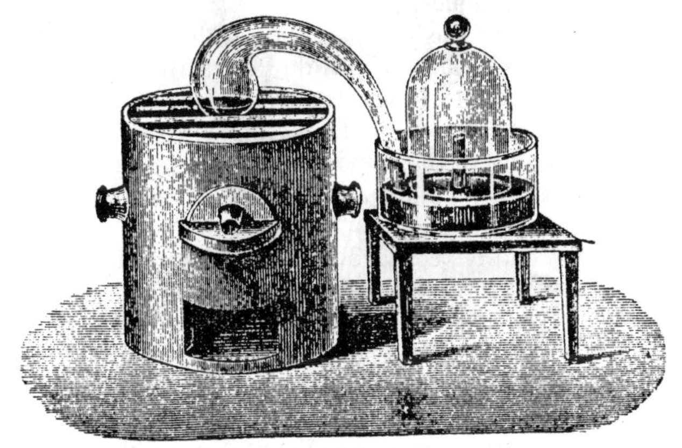

*Lavoisier's mercury oxide apparatus.*
*From a drawing of the time.*

## ALESSANDRO VOLTA

Have you ever "tasted" electricity? "I covered the point of my tongue with a strip of tin. With the bowl of a silver spoon, I touched the tongue further back; then I touched the handle of the spoon to the tin." This is how Alessandro Volta, Professor of Physics at the University of Pavia, in Italy, described an experiment. He expected his tongue to twitch, but instead there was a sour taste.

Volta was born on February 18, 1745, at Como, Italy. Como is the largest town on beautiful and famous Lake Como, at the foot of the Italian Alps. Lake Como has attracted the wealthy as residents and has always been popular as a tourist attraction.

Alessandro Volta's family were not among the wealthy, but through the intercession of some relatives who were influential in the Church, the brilliant boy was able to get an education. Upon completion of the university course in which he earned a degree at the age of seventeen, he obtained a teaching position at the high school at Como. He remained there until 1779 when, at the age of thirty-four, he was appointed to the University of Pavia to establish a Department of Physics. There was time also for research.

While still a teacher at Como, Volta invented the electrophorus which he described in a letter to Joseph Priestley in England. The electrophorus has no practical value but is still used in science classrooms to explain and demonstrate static electricity.

Volta used the electrophorus to discover many of the laws which govern the operation of that important electrical component now called the capacitor or condenser. Volta called it the condensator, but the name was shortened to condenser by the translator for the *Transactions* of the Royal Society of London. Volta used the device, ingeniously, to magnify the effect of an electric charge so as to operate the not very sensitive electroscopes or electrometers with which electricity was measured in those days. He charged an electrophorus and separated the plates. This has the effect of increasing the potential or voltage between the plates. He suggested the name of microelectroscope for the device.

In 1791, Luigi Galvani, professor of biology and physiology at the University of Bologna, had been studying some dissected frogs in the university laboratory. A sharp brass hook had been forced into the spinal cord of the frog. An assistant touched a leg muscle with an iron

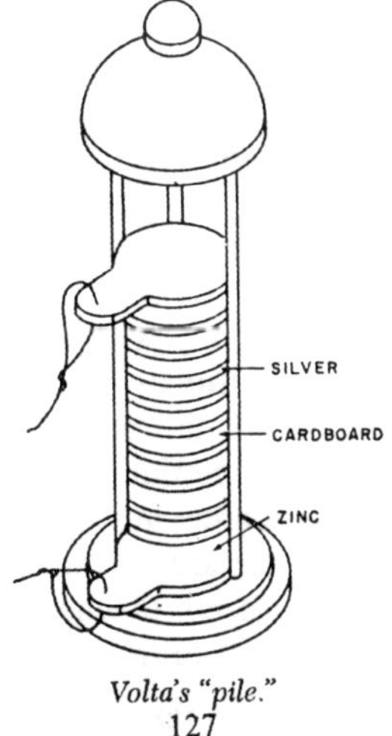


*Volta's "pile."*

scalpel. As the upper end of the iron scalpel touched the brass hook the frog's muscle twitched violently! Galvani tried again – again the same result, the muscle jerked.

Galvani published his observations. He felt that the action was the result of electricity which had originated in the animal itself. Volta read of the experiment and doubted. But when he tried it himself, he said, "Indeed I have performed the miracles myself and have swung over from incredulity to enthusiastic belief."

Volta was not convinced that it was "animal electricity," however, and continued his studies. On March 20, 1800, he wrote a famous letter to the Royal Society of London. In it he described what is known as the Voltaic pile. You can make one yourself. Volta took dry clean disks of silver, dry clean disks of zinc, and disks of cardboard soaked, but not dripping, with salt water (very salty) and arranged them in a pile – silver, cardboard, zinc, silver, cardboard, zinc, and so on.

From the ends of the pile a continuous flow of electricity was possible. Volta had made the first electric cell, forerunner of the dry-cell "battery" used in your portable radio. He had produced a continuous source of electricity for the first time in the history of science. When he put the tin and silver spoon in his mouth, these, too, produced an electric cell. Here, too, he had used two different metals and a liquid conductor of electricity.

His discovery opened up whole new fields of electrical and chemical research. In a short time, using Voltaic piles, scientists decomposed water into hydrogen and oxygen; Davy discovered sodium and potassium, and the study of electricity and magnetism was able to proceed at a rapid pace.

Many honors came to Volta. Napoleon invited him to Paris to address the Institut de Paris. A gold medal was struck in his honor. When he tried to resign his position at the university because of his age, he was persuaded to stay, if only to deliver one lecture a year – and at full salary! He was elected a senator from Lombardy. The Emperor of Austria gave Volta the job of director of the Philosophical Faculty of Padua. In 1819, at the age of seventy-four,

Volta retired to his native town of Como, where he died in 1827.

There is an impressive statue at Como, commemorating Volta's achievements; but a more universal monument is the use of his name whenever electricity is mentioned. In 1893 the Congress of Electricians called the unit of electromotive force the volt. It was Volta's pile which placed man on the threshold of the electrical age.

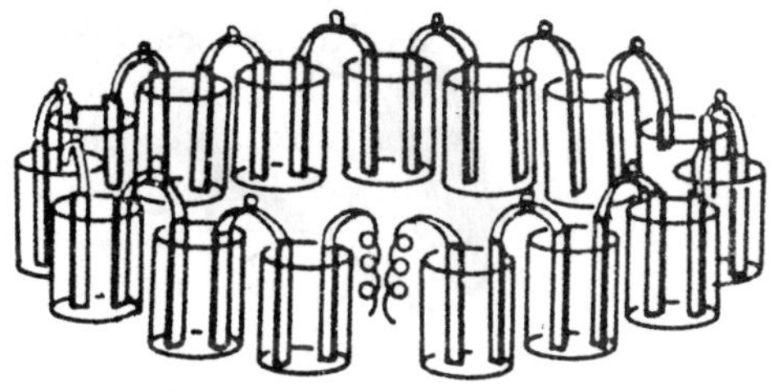

*An early battery. After the voltaic pile, the next step was to connect a number of chemical "cells" together. The principle is the same as in the modern automobile battery where a chemical reaction occurs between two metals in a solution called an electrolyte.*

## EDWARD JENNER

Sixty million persons is about twice the combined population of London, New York City, Tokyo, Shanghai, and Moscow! It has been estimated that about 60,000,000 Europeans died of smallpox between 1700 and 1800.

In the epidemic of 1721 more than half the population of Boston had smallpox and one out of every ten victims died. This frightful disease is now so rare that the vast majority of doctors have never seen an actual case. This once dread disease has been wiped out by the principle of vaccination, a principle advanced by Dr. Edward Jenner in 1796.

Edward Jenner was born on May 17, 1749, in Gloucestershire, England. His father, a clergyman, sent the boy to the local schools for his elementary education. Jenner showed an early interest in biology and took up the study of medicine. One way to become a doctor in those days was to study with another doctor, and Jenner was "apprenticed" to the surgeon Daniel Ludlow. At the age of twenty-one, Jenner went to St. George's Hospital in London to work and study under John Hunter, the leading surgeon of the day.

Dr. Hunter had boundless curiosity and enthusiasm; he was a physician who believed in trying things out. Unfortunately he used himself as the subject of his experiments and contracted an incurable disease which destroyed his health and shortened his life. However, though he infected himself with disease, he infected his student with his philosophy: "Why wonder, why not try an experiment."

John Hunter corresponded with Jenner and remained his life-long friend and adviser. After Jenner's graduation from St. George's Hospital, Hunter sent him back to Gloucestershire to set up a practice. He apparently was of the opinion that the country-bred Jenner would not be happy in the confines of the city. The world owes much to this decision to return to the country.

Before the advent of scientific medicine and of the modern wonder drugs, the usefulness of homegrown remedies was generally recognized. Certain plants were known to have valuable medical effects. Digitalis had been used as a medicine for heart disease long before medical men knew why it was effective. Many people used molds to cure infections long before Fleming found penicillin. Many people insist that raw onion will cure them of a sore throat; and indeed raw onions have been found to have germicidal effects.

Among other things that were known long before analytical science took a hand was that certain diseases could be caught only once in a lifetime. Modern parents are especially content when their little girls have German measles. German measles can be a very serious matter in a grown woman, but in a child it is of no great consequence. If the little girl has German measles she is immune for the rest of her life.

Knowledge had grown that if a person had smallpox and recovered, that person would never have smallpox again. The peoples of the East took advantage of this idea and deliberately injected smallpox germs into the body. They had devised a method to weaken the germs so that the injected person suffered only a mild case of smallpox, recovered, and was, thereafter, safe from the disease. Unfortunately, the method worked only fairly well; many people did not recover from the injection.

The country folk of Gloucestershire knew that anybody who suffered from a disease called cowpox would never get smallpox. Cowpox, as its name implied, was a disease affecting cows and was caught by humans from cows. Curiously enough, the cows became infected as a result of a malady which attacked the hooves of horses.

Dr. Jenner interested himself in the strange matter of cowpox-smallpox cases. He was encouraged by his old teacher, Dr. Hunter, who said, "try: be patient, be accurate"—good advice for any scientific investigator. In all, Jenner investigated twenty-seven cases. He published his findings in 1796.

Jenner carefully documented his cases. In the early stages of his investigations, the doctor noted that people who had had cowpox did not contract smallpox, even though they came in contact with smallpox sufferers. He took some small pox fluids and inserted it into the arms of these people and still they did not contract the disease.

*Dr. Jenner inoculating his son. From a famous engraving.*

Finally—and we must pay tribute to the courage of the child's parents—Jenner inoculated a healthy eight-year-old boy, Jimmy Phipps, with cowpox virus and produced that illness in the youth. He then injected some smallpox material into the boy and into another person who had not had cowpox. Smallpox resulted, but only in the person who had not been protected by cowpox, not in lucky Jimmy Phipps.

When Jenner published his findings a storm arose. There were those who objected to tampering with nature. There were others who rushed to claim the credit for the discovery, and there were some who used the idea, but mixed in some smallpox matter and so killed rather than cured the patients.

When the excitement died down, and Jenner was able to prove his method and his claims, honors and recognition poured in from all the civilized world. Parliament knighted him and rewarded him with 20,000 pounds sterling. Oxford gave him an honorary degree. The Czar of Russia gave him a gold ring. Napoleon of France praised his discovery. And from the United States came a delegation of Indians bearing gifts and thanks to Edward Jenner.

*Dr. Jonas Salk, discoverer of the vaccine for polio.*

This man had taken an old country superstition and proved that it had scientific accuracy. He had the considered courage to infect humans with a mild disease to protect them from a terrible scourge. He was a country doctor at heart and having won great honors, turned from London to return to Gloucestershire to spend his last years on the farm. Edward Jenner died in January, 1823.

When you look at your own small vaccination scar think of the courage of the many unknown people who allowed themselves to be used for experimentation. And think of that genius, Edward Jenner, who devised the vaccination and so protected all of us from smallpox.

And think also of all the types of vaccinations that protect our health, including the one discovered by Dr. Jonas Salk to protect us from polio.

## Benjamin Thompson, COUNT RUMFORD

You probably know many people who will say, more than half-believing it, that one of the most important things in life is a good cup of coffee. To these people, Count Rumford would be a Giant because it was he who invented the drip coffeepot. To more serious students of science Count Rumford is celebrated for his contribution to the study of heat.

Count Rumford was born Benjamin Thompson in 1753, in the town of Woburn, in the British colony of Massachusetts. His father, a farmer, died when Benjamin was but a few months old. His education was in the hands of a private tutor, a local Harvard graduate, and finally in the local schools. Although he showed unusual abilities as a student, as an experimenter, and as a mathematician, he was forced to go to work as a store clerk at the age of thirteen. His ambition to be a doctor was unfulfilled because of lack of funds.

When eighteen years old, he obtained a job as a schoolteacher in Concord, New Hampshire. Concord was the capital of the colony and had previously been called Rumford. Benjamin Thompson was an extremely handsome, six-foot-tall youth. Auburn-haired, blue-eyed, he sat a horse with magnificent grace. He caught the eye and heart of the thirty-three-year-old wealthy widow Rolfe. Benjamin and the influential widow were married in 1772; he was nineteen years old. Mrs. Thompson introduced her husband to the society of the colony. The British-appointed governor of New Hampshire made Benjamin a major in the local militia.

The former farmer boy had developed a superior, snobbish manner which irritated the local revolutionary patriots, and they suspected him of informing to the British. After the "Sons of Liberty" had arrested him as a spy on several occasions, Thompson decided to leave the colonies. In October of 1775 he sailed for England leaving behind his wife and his baby daughter. He never again saw his wife who died seventeen years later.

In England, Thompson became an expert on American affairs for the British Colonial office. At the same time he experimented with gunpowder and made improvements in the explosive power of firearms. For this achievement he was elected a Fellow of the Royal Society and was knighted by the king in 1784.

Impressed by his record of service to the British Government, the ruler of Bavaria invited Sir Benjamin Thompson to serve as his advisor. In Bavaria, the charming man of many talents was made Minister of War, Minister of Police, and Grand Chamberlain. Next to the king himself, this onetime American farm boy was the most influential man in the kingdom. He spent eleven successful years in Bavaria. Thompson applied himself to all manner of social reforms – in education, sanitation, housing, land reclamation and utilization, hospitals, and relief of the poor. He improved the rations of the soldiers, making studies in nutrition for the purpose. For his services to Bavaria he was made a Count of the Holy Roman Empire. He chose the name of Rumford, the name by which Concord, New Hampshire, had been known. His daughter Sarah, who had joined him after her mother's death, was made a countess and provided with a large pension.

Count Rumford is memorialized with a large statue in Munich. He expressed a forward-looking philosophy in these words, "To make vicious and abandoned people happy it has generally been supposed necessary first to make them virtuous. But why not reverse the order? Why not make them happy and then virtuous?" But Count Rumford couldn't make his own daughter happy; she returned to America. Later she was to upbraid him for interfering with her opportunities for marriage.

Benjamin Thompson, or Count Rumford as he was now known, returned to England to pursue his scientific investigations. In January of 1798 Rumford read to the Royal Society the paper *"An Inquiry Concerning the Source of Heat Which is Excited by Friction."* This scientific paper resulted from observations he made of cannon manufacture in Munich. He had observed, as had countless others before him, that the brass guns got very hot while being machined. The current theory of heat was called "caloric." According to the caloric theory, heat was a material thing. "Caloric" was supposed to pass out of bodies when they were cooled. The caloric theory of heat by friction was that the friction squeezed out the "caloric" from the bodies much as water is squeezed from a sponge. It is difficult for us to believe now that men of science held this wrong theory.

Count Rumford had a watertight box constructed around the cannon cylinder. A team of horses operated the cannon boring machine; the boring tool was pressed against the cannon. After several hours of this action the water boiled.

Count Rumford reasoned as follows: the water cut off the air from the cylinder; hence, the heat or "caloric" could not have come from the water, which started out cold and was now boiling hot. It could not have originated in the brass, because if the brass gave up "caloric" it should get colder, but the cannon also got hotter. The only place that heat could come from was the action of the tool against the cannon.

This demonstration was associated with another experiment designed to destroy the erroneous idea of caloric.

Rumford took two containers, exactly alike. He filled one with water and the other with an exactly equal weight of mercury. The containers were sealed so that no liquid could escape and both were placed in a cold room where the temperature was just above freezing. There they remained for 24 hours. They were weighed, and they weighed exactly the same cold as hot. They had lost heat but they had not lost or gained weight. "Caloric" did not exist. The destruction of the theory of caloric is an important milestone in the history of science, as important as the destruction of the "phlogiston" theory, explained in the article on Lavoisier.

Count Rumford performed experiments and published findings on the methods of heat transfer. In working out a chemical experiment he had heated a flask of colored liquid in which there were dust particles. This was placed on the window sill to cool and the streaming sunlight made the particles quite visible. Rumford noted that the dust flowed rapidly up the center and then down the sides of the flask. As the flask cooled, the rate of flow decreased; when room temperature was reached the motion stopped.

Of course, he tried the experiment many times and checked the results, but, by chance, he had discovered the way in which liquids and gases transfer heat from one place to another. The warmer fluid rises to the top and the cooler drops to the bottom. Although the experiment was a chance, the conclusions Rumford drew were the mark of the great scientist. Many people had noted the same action, as many people had known about the cannon getting hot, but Rumford drew correct scientific conclusions.

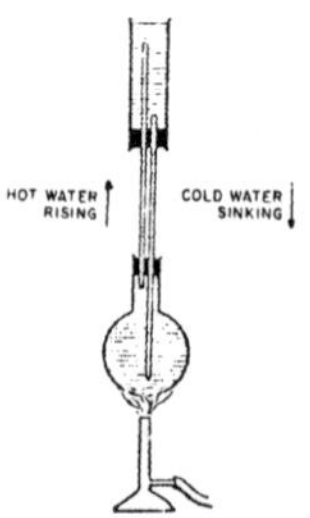


*A laboratory model of convection heating, the basic principle of a central heating system.*

If you place a thin sheet of tissue paper on top of a radiator you should be able to see the movement of the air due to the heat. This movement is called convection. As a result of Rumford's studies, the heating systems of England and the world were redesigned, with considerable saving of fuel and increase in comfort.

Count Rumford's scientific achievements and international fame were so great that the newly established American government offered him the position of Inspector General of Artillery of the United States. Considering his past behavior as a British sympathizer during the American Revolution this was a considerable honor. He preferred, however, to remain in Great Britain.

By now a man of great wealth, he created the famous and fruitful Royal Institution in London. This scientific laboratory was intended as a kind of popular rather than theoretical scientific institution for "diffusing knowledge and facilitating the introduction of useful mechanical inventions and improvements, and for teaching the application of science to the common purpose of life." Two important scientists who worked at the institution were Humphry Davy and his assistant and successor Michael Faraday. Humphry Davy worked with Rumford to help establish the theories of heat and, although the Institute was intended as a practical rather than a theoretical institution, the results achieved there showed that the most practical results always came from theoretical studies.

The final years of Rumford's life were unhappy and relatively unproductive. He married Marie Lavoisier, the widow of the brilliant French chemist Antoine Lavoisier. This should have been a fine marriage. Both were wealthy, brilliant, charming and interested in science. However, they could not agree on anything, and after four years of unhappiness they parted.

Benjamin Thompson Count Rumford died in 1814. This honored Count of the Holy Roman Empire, Knight of Great Britain, wealthy and successful, must have been lonely for the land of his birth. In his will he left money to Harvard University.

Count Rumford was a practical scientist who laid the

foundation for the science of heat, a science which has made our homes more comfortable and has given us the engines that pull our trains, propel our cars, and run our factories.

## JOHN DALTON

Before he became one of the world's outstanding scientists, John Dalton was the headmaster of a school. There is, of course, nothing unusual in a scientist-teacher, but John Dalton was the school headmaster at the ripe old age of twelve.

The idea of a basic particle of matter had been in the minds of men for many centuries. The ancient Greeks spoke of the elements: earth, air, fire and water. Aristotle attempted to explain the makeup of all materials on the basis of these four, plus the heavenly element. Democritus, the Greek scientist and mathematician, formulated the idea that there was a limit to the smallness of particles. The particles, he said, would become so small that they could no longer be split. Democritus called this final particle an atom, a word derived from Greek words meaning not cuttable.

Why then, if the idea of the atom is so ancient, do we honor John Dalton? The progress of chemistry from Dalton to the present day is largely associated with elements, compounds, atoms, molecules – all of which stem from the work of John Dalton. This hardy scientist proposed an atomic theory that went far beyond the thoughts of the ancients.

John Dalton was born on September 6, 1766, the son of a poor hand-loom weaver, in the English village of Eaglesfield.. There were five children in the family. He attended a school run by the Quakers where he learned, in addition to religion, some mathematics, science, and English grammar. He had gained a local reputation as being a mathematical genius. When he was twelve years old the authorities of the village granted him permission to open his own school. Many of his students were older than the youthful schoolmaster.

At about this time Dalton took up what was to be a lifelong interest in meteorology. He made his own weather instruments and began a series of written observations that he was to continue, unfailingly, every day of his life. The last entry was made on the same day he died. Altogether he recorded more than two hundred thousand observations on the weather.

He did not, however, neglect his other studies. Somehow while teaching, helping his father on the small farm, and studying the weather, John Dalton mastered Latin and Greek, studied mathematics, and added to his knowledge of natural philosophy, as science was then called.

At the age of fifteen, Dalton, lacking students, closed his school and joined his brother Jonathan at the village of Kendal. There he taught for twelve years, adding to his stock of mathematics and science and continuing his hobby, weather study. While at Kendal he attempted to start a Science Discussion Forum, but his unattractive platform personality and inadequate speaking voice ruled against the success of this venture.

In 1793 Dalton became an instructor at a college in Manchester, England. There he taught mathematics and science but was unhappy because of the amount of time required by his duties. While at Kendal, Dalton had come under the influence of John Gough, a well-known and distinguished scholar. Gough, blind from birth, knew several languages and was familiar with every type of plant within twenty miles by touch, taste and smell. In addition, he was a meteorologist and this formed a common bond with the awkward-looking John Dalton.

John Gough encouraged Dalton to publish his meteorological observations, with the result that Dalton was invited to membership in the Manchester Literary and Philosophical Society. He maintained his association with this society for the rest of his life and read over a hundred scientific papers to the membership during his fifty years of activity.

Dalton modestly credited hard work for his success, saying to the Manchester Society, "If I have succeeded better than many who surround me, it has been chiefly – may I say almost solely – from universal assiduity." Thomas Edison was to say a similar thing a hundred years later – but he phrased it, "Genius is one percent inspiration and ninety-nine percent perspiration."

Dalton left the University at Manchester to devote his time to scientific study and conjecture. Not wealthy, he was content to give only private lessons so that he could retain his leisure to study the air about him.

It was Dalton's extensive study of the atmosphere that led him eventually to the atomic theory of matter. Robert Boyle, the Irish chemist and physicist who preceded Dalton by a century and a half, had done a considerable amount of work on air and air pressure. He had concluded that air was made up of several gases. More lately Cavendish, Lavoisier, and Priestley had established that the atmosphere was composed of oxygen, nitrogen, carbon dioxide, and water vapor.

Dalton had collected hundreds of samples of air from various places in England, from mountain tops and valleys, from city and rural countryside. He had analyzed them, and in every case the air had about the same composition. This bothered Dalton. Why didn't the heavy carbon dioxide settle to the bottom? Why should the gases be so thoroughly mixed? Did the winds and thermal currents mix the gases? Dalton, not a great experimenter, tried to check the matter in the laboratory. He placed a flask of heavy gas on the table and upended a flask of light gas so that the mouths of the flasks met. The flasks did not stay with the heavy gas at the bottom and the light gas at the top; pretty soon the gases were thoroughly mixed.

Dalton explained this by a statement that has come to be known as the theory of partial pressures: "The particles of one gas are not repulsive to the particles of another gas, but only to the particles of their own kind." This led Dalton to the belief that a gas consists of tiny particles separated from each other by great distances. This idea is still accepted.

Dalton defined chemistry and chemical analysis. All chemistry could do, he said, is separate particles from each other or join particles to each other. These particles he spoke of are the indestructible bits of matter which make up all materials – and they were indestructible until the discovery of radioactivity and atom-smashing.

It is of very great importance to any chemical manufacturer to know how much of each material must go into a process in order to produce the amount of compound required. By trial and error this information had been collected for many things, but it was Dalton who used this collected data to obtain the relative weight of the ultimate particles; we call it atomic weight now. Dalton realized that he could use the atomic weights to predict how much of each material would be needed to make up a compound.

Dalton proceeded to make up a table of atomic weights. His results were inaccurate but his thinking was precise. The errors that he made were the result of faulty laboratory work. He established his atomic weights by assigning a weight of *one* to the hydrogen particle. Now, he said, one "simple" of hydrogen combines with one "simple" of oxygen to give us one compound of water. The weight of the oxygen is seven times the weight of the hydrogen, so the relative weight of the oxygen particle is seven times that of the hydrogen particle. He didn't know that it takes two hydrogen atoms to combine with oxygen, and he made an error in weighing the materials. Nowadays we say that the atomic weight of oxygen is sixteen. That is, the weight of the oxygen atom is sixteen times that of the hydrogen atom.

Dalton's atomic theory, which has, for the most part,

stood the test of time, contains the following ideas: All materials are made up of small, uncuttable particles called atoms. Atoms of different elements have different properties, but all atoms of the same element are exactly the same. The whole atom takes part in chemical changes. Atoms are not changed as they enter into chemical compounds. Atoms cannot be created or destroyed.

In order to explain the combination of his "simples" he drew little circles with different center symbols for the atom of each element. These, along with some compounds, are shown in the illustrations.

Dalton's atomic theory was accepted by his fellow scientists with unusual speed and appreciation. The French elected him to their Academy of Sciences and he was hospitably received in Paris. He was awarded the Medal of the Royal Society of England in 1826. He had this to say of his visit to London. "It is a surprising place and well worth one's while to see once, but the most disagreeable place on earth for one of a contemplative turn of mind to reside in constantly." A good place to visit but he wouldn't want to live there.

A problem arose; Dalton was to be presented to the King. Court etiquette required knee breeches, buckled shoes, a sword. These things were forbidden to the Quakers. Fortunately Dalton had just received an honorary degree from the University of Oxford and he could wear the university robes. But how could a Quaker wear scarlet. Dalton inspected the collar of the robe and decided that it was green. He had always been color blind. He had experimented with this defect; color blindness is still called Daltonism.

Dalton never married. He was not, however, unaware of the opposite sex. His report to brother Jonathan of the visit to London in 1809 contained the following: "I see the belles of New Bond Street every day. I am more taken up with their faces than their dress. Some of the ladies seem to have their dresses so tight around them as a drum. Others throw them round like a blanket. I do not know how it happens, but I fancy pretty women look well anyhow."

Dalton's atomic theory brought mathematical exactitude to chemistry; it brought together the sciences of physics and chemistry. It resulted in the discovery that all matter is electrical. It led to the atomic bomb. It is in the background of the peaceful application of atomic energy.

Forty thousand people filed past his bier when he died in 1844. Even then they knew that John Dalton was a giant in the world of science.

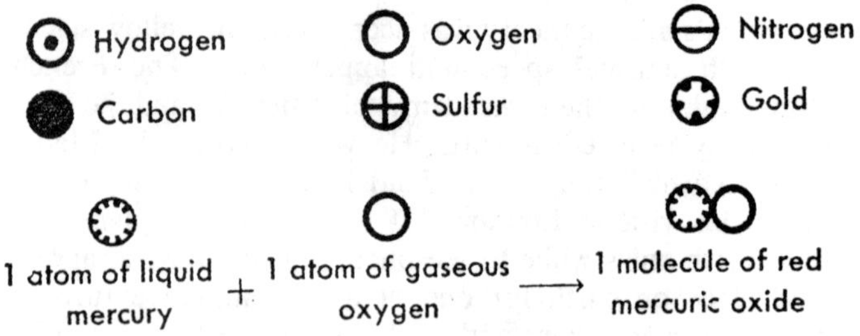

Hydrogen  Oxygen  Nitrogen

Carbon  Sulfur  Gold

1 atom of liquid mercury + 1 atom of gaseous oxygen ⟶ 1 molecule of red mercuric oxide

*Dalton's symbols for chemical elements.*

## ANDRE MARIE AMPERE

At various stages in history the cruelty of man to his fellow man has been unbelievable. The "Reign of Terror" following the French Revolution was such a period in France. The "Committee of Public Safety" made a mockery of the glorious revolutionary slogan "Liberty, Equality, Fraternity." Thousands of people were beheaded by the guillotine on mere suspicion and with scarcely the formality of a trial.

An unwilling witness to one of these monstrous executions was the eighteen-year-old André Marie Ampere. He was forced to watch the death of his beloved father. André was thrown into the blackest despair; the boy was emotionally and mentally ill. For a full year he could do nothing but wander about, forlorn and disconsolate. The world almost lost this great scientist even before he started his career.

Ampere was born on January 22, 1775, the son of a hemp merchant, in a suburb of Lyons, France. His father was an intellectual as well as a merchant and soon introduced his son to the Latin and Greek classics, but it was obvious that the boy was to become a mathematician. As a very young child, before he could read or write, André had worked out arithmetic problems using pebbles to assist in obtaining the solution. By the time he was eleven, he had mastered Latin and had a working knowledge of calculus.

Recovery from the shock of his father's death brought him to the necessity of earning a living. The family resources had been destroyed by the revolution and Ampere sustained himself by giving private lessons in mathematics, languages, and science, meanwhile continuing his studies. He was not, however, too busy to fall in love with the attractive Julie Carron and get married.

A year later, in 1800, the happy couple had a son, Jean Jacques Ampere. The son was to become a first rank writer and historian and member of the French Academy. Ampere's happiness in his personal life was not to endure. In 1804 his beloved wife died. His escape from this blow was to plunge indefatigably into scientific work.

Ampere had come to the attention of the scientific-mathematical world as a result of an article he had written on the mathematical theory of games of chance. In this paper he had solved a problem that had baffled mathematicians for a long time.

Two noted French mathematician-astronomers, Jean Delambre and Joseph Lalande, were impressed with the young man's ability and recommended Ampere as teacher of mathematics and astronomy at the secondary school at Lyons. He stayed there for two years, moving to Paris in 1805 to accept an appointment at the Polytechnic School, an engineering college. In 1809 Ampere was elected to the chair of mathematics and mechanics at this institution. He published scientific papers on a wide range of subjects: calculus and chemistry, optics and zoology. These resulted in his election to the exclusive Institute of Arts and Sciences.

In 1819 Johann C. Oersted, a Danish scientist, published an account of an experiment. He described the deflection of a magnetized needle in the vicinity of a wire carrying electricity. This was a great discovery because it somehow linked electricity and magnetism.

It seems to us today that it should have taken very little more to perform Ampere's famous experiment. It even occurred to Ampere that Oersted might have done the job himself. He said, "When Oersted discovered the action which a current exercises on a magnetized needle, one might certainly have suspected the existence of a mutual action between two circuits carrying currents." But Ampere went on to explain why Oersted may have missed the idea. "A bar of soft iron also acts on a magnetized needle, although there is no mutual action between two bars of soft iron."

Ampere set up an experiment in which he arranged two conductors (metal rods), placed parallel to each other. One conductor was suspended from knife edges and counterbalanced so that it would move very easily. The other conductor was held rigidly in place. When he connected both conductors to voltaic batteries, the movable conductor swung toward, or away from, the fixed conductor, depending upon the direction of current flow in each. When the currents were in the same direction the conductors attracted each other. When the currents were in the opposite direction the conductors repelled each other.

Ampere had established the amazing fact that magnetism could be produced without iron, without magnets, but with electricity alone! The space surrounding an electric current was the same kind of field of force that surrounds a magnet!

Ampere published his famous treatise on magnetism and electricity in 1823. In this masterwork he included, in addition to the expcrimment detailed above, an explanation of magnetism in a permanent magnet as being due to molecular electricity. Modern theory holds that an atom consists of a nucleus about which electrons rotate, and, of course, a moving electron constitutes an electric current. So Ampere may not have been far off. Perhaps modern science will solve the riddle as to why some materials can be magnetized, while others ignore the magnetic field, and still others weaken the field set up by a current in a conductor..

André Marie Ampere is one of the band of immortals. The greatness of his work might some day fade into the background as a result of the press of newer and newer discoveries, but the world cannot forget him. Scientists have given his name to the unit of electric current – the ampere.

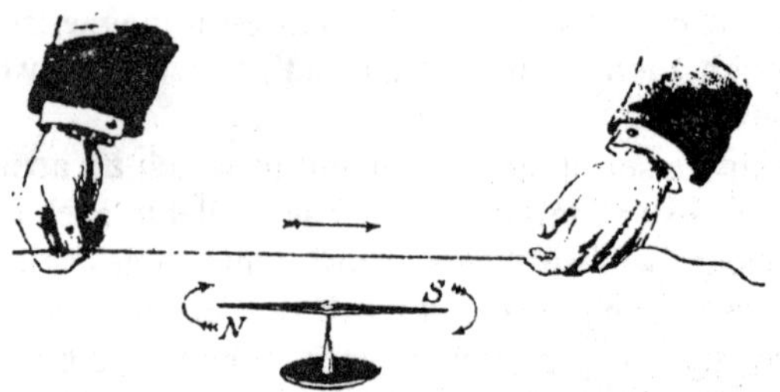


*Oersted's experiment. A wire carrying an electric current will cause the magnetic needle to turn.*

# AMEDEO AVOGADRO

One of the greatest problems faced by scientists at all times has been to know what other scientists are doing. Scientists, as a rule, do not keep their work secret. They are happy to have others know what they have discovered and what they have thought. It is the free exchange of ideas among scientific workers that enables progress to be made most rapidly. The scientific workers of another age published their findings in Latin, the universal learned language of the time.

Nowadays the science student is required to learn a foreign language as part of his education. Electronic machines have been built to translate foreign languages, especially Russian, into English so that scientific treatises can be made available. Other electronic devices have succeeded in summarizing the vast number of scientific reports that are printed in every nation every year. Scientists spend a good part of their time reading the reports of other scientists. Very few published discoveries are overlooked by the scientist working on a problem.

Sometimes, however, there is a slip; an article goes

unnoticed or is misunderstood. Such an article was published in France, but it was unnoticed by the scientific community for over fifty years. The ideas in the paper were vital to the advance of chemistry and physics. In 1811, Amedeo Avogadro made a clean-cut distinction between the atom and the molecule, an important idea that was ignored at the time but is now known to be of central importance.

Amedeo Avogadro was born on June 9, 1776, in Turin, Italy. His father was a lawyer and it was decided that he was to follow in his father's footsteps. He was a brilliant student, and by the time he was sixteen he had earned a bachelor's degree. By the time he was twenty he had earned his doctor's degree in church law.

Three years of practice convinced him that the legal profession was not for him, and he plunged into the study of mathematics, chemistry, and physics. He attracted local attention for some original work on electricity. At the age of thirty-three Avogadro was appointed Professor of Physics at the Royal College at Vercelli, in the North of Italy. Two years later, in 1811, he published the now famous, but then unnoticed, article on molecules in the French *Journal de Physique*.

Avogadro spent the rest of his life in scientific studies and in scientific teaching. His university life was interrupted from time to time because of wars and revolutions. As the leaders of Italy changed, they opened and closed the universities. From 1820 to 1850, with time out for university closings, Avogadro was professor of physics at the University of Turin. He died at the age of eighty, the world at that time still unaware of his scientific genius.

It is common knowledge now that the chemical formula for water is $H_2O$ and we are all aware that this means that two hydrogen *atoms* combine with one oxygen *atom* to produce one *molecule* of water. Atoms and molecules are very small. Scientists have now worked out methods of counting molecules and have learned that a quart bottle filled with any gas contains about 25,000,000,000,000,000,000,000 molecules. Long before scientists had worked out methods of measuring molecules, Avogadro had proposed the idea that equal volumes of gases – of any kind of gas – contained the same number of molecules. Of course the gases had to be measured under the same conditions of temperature and pressure. This idea is known to modern chemists as Avogadro's Law.

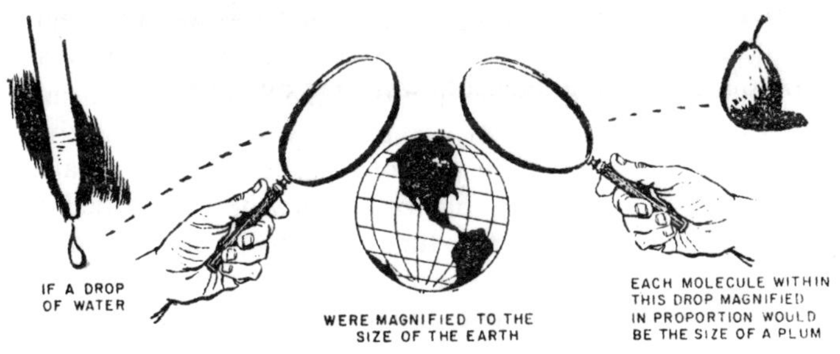


*The size of a molecule of water.*

Dalton, the father of the atomic idea was satisfied to think of water as HO; and in general chemists were able to accept the idea that the formula showed the elements that went into compounds. But this is not enough to explain all the things that happen. Scientists need to know exact quantities.

In 1808, Joseph Gay-Lussac, a famous French chemist performed some demonstrations that seemed to dispute parts of Dalton's theory. Dalton and Gay-Lussac were both right and Amedeo Avogadro said as much in his now famous paper of 1811. But no one read the paper; it was entombed in the scientific archives, and chemists were at an impasse. In 1860 a meeting of scientists was held in Karlsruhe, Germany, to try to settle the problem. The view-points of many learned men were considered. Stanislao Cannizarro, an Italian chemist, advanced the theory of Amedeo Avogadro. "See how easy it all is," he pleaded, "all we have to do is accept the fact that *molecules* need not be formed only of separate kinds of atoms, but that a molecule could also be made up of two atoms. Thus a *molecule* of oxygen consists of *two atoms of oxygen.*" This time a few scientists listened, but the meeting ad-journed without really deciding anything.

Cannizarro did not give up. He taught and wrote and explained and finally the world heard. Water was now accepted as $H_2O$. In 1891 Cannizarro was awarded the Copley medal of the Royal Society.

In 1911, hundreds of scientists from every country in the world gathered in Turin, Italy. They met to unveil a monument commemorating the 100th anniversary of the publication of Avogadro's Law. Recognition of the genius who discovered the molecule was long overdue.

## GEORGE SIMON OHM

George Simon Ohm resigned from his position as professor of mathematics at the Jesuit College of Cologne. This was in 1827 and Professor Ohm was forty years old. He had just published a treatise entitled "Mathematical Measurements of Electrical Currents." Instead of the acclaim which he felt was due, his paper was virtually ignored. Those who did read it felt that Ohm had contributed nothing new to mathematics or to science. This impulsive mathematics teacher, who expected a promotion as a result of his publication, was drawn into an argument with the Ministry of Culture and found himself with no job at all.

George Ohm was born in Bavaria in southeast Germany on March 16, 1787. His father had been a locksmith and gunsmith, as had *his* father before him. For generations the trade had been handed down from father to son. But Johann Ohm broke the succession. Until his fortieth year he wandered over Germany and France, plying his skilled trade. He then settled in his home town of Erlangen where he married, and fathered two sons, George and Martin.

At the same time he turned to the study of science and mathematics. And it was the love of learning, rather than the mechanical skills of his forebears, that he fostered in his sons. Both sons became mathematics teachers after attending the local university.

At eighteen George became a teacher in the town of Gottstadt in the Swiss canton of Bern. His supervisor, who had hired him sight unseen, was dismayed by the appearance of the smallish, skinny, young mathematician. But he soon recognized and appreciated the young man's ability. Ohm continued his studies and received a doctorate in mathematics in 1811. He wanted to join the army opposing Napoleon but the pleadings of his father prevailed and he remained a teacher. When he was thirty he joined the faculty of the Jesuit College at Cologne as professor of mathematics.

Ohm's most famous contribution to electrical science was published in 1827. This paper, unrecognized at the time, might well be considered the cornerstone of electrical circuit calculations. It is so simple in appearance that it was received as a truism and not an original concept. By this time his mathematical formulation is known to every high school student of physics; it is called Ohm's Law. It is usually written in mathematical symbols as $I = \frac{E}{R}$. This means that the electrical current (I) in a circuit will increase as the electromotive force (E) gets larger and will decrease as the resistance (R) gets larger. This is almost an expression of a universal law – the more difficult a job is to do, the greater effort we have to exert in order to get it done.

After he had resigned his job, Ohm found it rather difficult to make a living, tutoring and such. In about six years he managed to return to teaching. While he still did not receive very great acclaim in Germany, his achievement was recognized in Great Britain. In 1841 he received the Copley Medal of the Royal Society of London.

George Ohm died in Munich, Germany, in 1854, at the age of sixty-seven. In 1881, at the meeting of the International Congress of Electrical Engineers at Paris, it was decided that the unit of electrical resistance was to be known as the ohm. This posthumous honor tried to make up for the years of neglect that he had suffered. It is a happy circumstance that the three great units of electricity, the ampere, the volt and ohm, are named after an international trio – a Frenchman, an Italian, and a German. It was Ohm, the German, who showed the relation between the three units. His law could be written:

$$\text{amperes} = \frac{\text{volts}}{\text{ohms}}$$

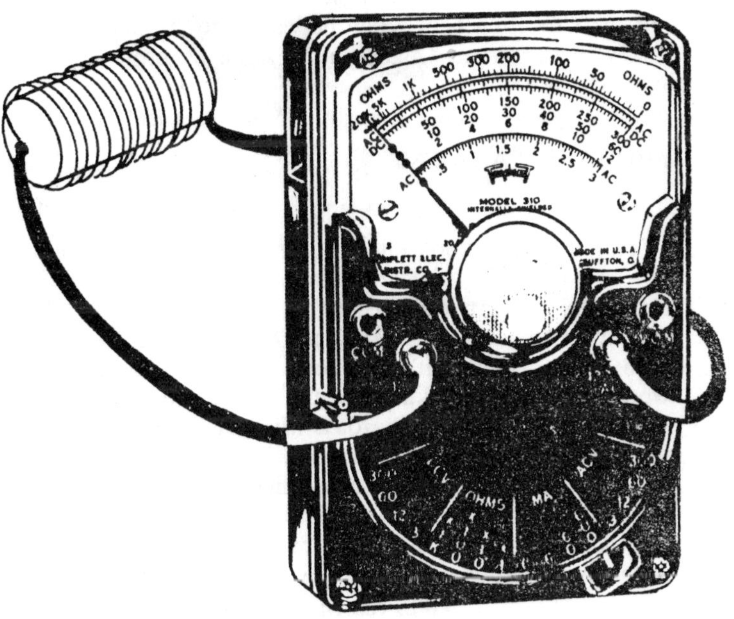


*The ohmmeter, a modern device for measuring resistance, is named for Ohm.*

## MICHAEL FARADAY

"Convert Magnetism into Electricity."

This terse notebook entry was made by Michael Faraday in 1822. The staccato command to himself was the outline of a scientific problem that needed an answer. But it had to be laid aside. Michael Faraday was too busy with some "practical" problems. Other scientists the world over were looking for the answer to this purely theoretical problem of the day. Michael Faraday holds a foremost place among experimental scientists for many reasons, but his crowning achievement came when he was able to show the world how to "convert magnetism into electricity." In 1831 when he finally got around to the problem he had the historic answer in just ten working days.

Michael Faraday was born in a suburb of London on September 22, 1791. His father was a blacksmith and poor. Michael received very little schooling, was barely taught reading, writing and arithmetic. At the age of thirteen the boy was forced out of school and into a job delivering newspapers for a bookseller. About a year of this and the bookseller was happy to have Michael as an apprentice in bookbinding.

Here was a real break for the lad. As was usual with the apprenticeship system in force at the time, Michael went to live with his employer. In his spare time he was able to read many of the books that were available. His kindly and understanding master encouraged him in this self-education.

Later on Faraday was to write, "There were two [books] that especially helped me, the *Encyclopedia Britannica,* from which I gained my first notions of electricity, and Mrs. Jane Marcet's *Conversations on Chemistry,* which gave me my foundation in that science." These must have formed firm foundations indeed, for Faraday was to spend his life in chemical and electrical research. In 1810 he attended a short course of lectures in natural philosophy. He took full notes of these lectures and, using his skill as a bookbinder, bound them into volumes. His ability to record what he heard and saw was especially important to him as we shall see.

His apprenticeship as a bookbinder was completed when he reached the age of twenty-one and he left his master to obtain employment as a journeyman. Faraday was unhappy. His new employer was bothersome, and the work was monotonous and irksome – and the world of science had begun to catch his imagination.

Faraday wrote a letter of application to the brilliant Sir Humphry Davy at the Royal Institution. The bookbinder desired to leave his trade and wished to obtain employment at the scientific laboratory. Faraday enclosed a neatly written notebook, notes he had taken at Sir Humphry Davy's lectures. The notebook turned the tide, he was granted an interview. Faraday was able to show that he himself had performed chemical and electro-chemical experiments. He had kept notes of his own work too. Faraday had made a voltaic pile and had electrically decomposed several compounds. Davy was greatly impressed and recommended Faraday for an appointment to the Royal Institution as a laboratory assistant. Years later Sir

Humphry Davy was to say, "The greatest of my discoveries is Faraday."

Faraday started to work in March 1813; in October, seven months later, Sir Humphry and the newly acquired Lady Davy left on a two-and-a-half-year combination honeymoon and scientific tour of the continent. Faraday was taken along as secretary and scientific assistant. In less than a year the blacksmith's son had had his whole outlook changed. The erstwhile bookbinder now met the leading scientists of the age, as he assisted Davy in his demonstrations and lectures. In April of 1815 the tour was over and Michael Faraday went back to work at the Royal Institution. Here he remained for the rest of his prolific life, becoming successor to Davy as Director of the Laboratories.

For many years, Faraday devoted himself to the same researches that interested Sir Humphry Davy. He experimented in chemistry, electro-chemistry and in metallurgy. He assisted in the development of the famed Davy safety lamps.

From his interest in electro-chemistry came the Laws of Electrolysis also known as Faraday's Laws of Electrolysis. Electrolysis is the name given to the action of electricity in

*Faraday experimenting with electricity.*

passing through a liquid. Scientists had found out that electricity could break down (decompose) water into oxygen and hydrogen. Sir Humphry Davy had passed electricity through a block of caustic potash. The electricity decomposed the potassium hydroxide (the chemical name for caustic potash) and potassium was discovered. Faraday made many careful experiments and was able to prove that a given amount of electricity passing through a substance always decomposes a definite amount of its component parts.

This law enabled the manufacture of the first commercial electric meters. The electricity used in the home passed through a small jar which held silver electrodes. At the end of each month the electrodes were weighed and the change in weight told how much electricity had been used. Incidentally the technical terms used in electrolysis – electrode, anode, cathode, electrolyte, ions – were all coined by Faraday. Another important point was to be able to define *exactly* the value of an ampere, the unit of current. An ampere is the amount of electricity needed to obtain 0.001118 grams of silver per second by decomposing nitrate of silver. It is interesting to note that the ampere was thus defined by an act of the United States Congress in 1894.

On a cold morning in 1821, Michael Faraday brought his wife from their apartment at the Royal Institution to his laboratory. It was Christmas and the young bride must have wondered what surprise gift was in store. Filled with excitement and delight, she reached the laboratory to find – not a gift for her alone, but a magnificent present for the whole world. For the first time a continuous mechanical motion was produced by the action of an electric current. Every electric motor, from the tiny one in a toy train to the great engines in electric locomotives, operates on the same basic principle uncovered by Michael Faraday on that historic Christmas.

What did the fortunate Mrs. Faraday see on her visit to the laboratory? Upon the table stood a small vessel, filled almost to the brim with mercury. One end of a bar magnet had been carefully fastened to the bottom of the vessel;

the other end protruded slightly above the mercury. A copper rod was supported above the magnet and the bottom end was stuck in a cork which floated on the mercury. The copper rod was free to rotate about the magnet. A battery was connected to the upper end of the rod and to the mercury, which went to the lower end of the rod. When the circuit was completed, the copper rod revolved about the magnet.

The explanation, and we know it now, is that the electricity through the wire produced a magnetic field. This reacted with the magnetic field of the permanent magnet and the force between them sent the copper wire rotating madly about the magnet. All the variations of the principle were investigated and demonstrated. The system was arranged to reverse direction–either by reversing the battery connection or by reversing the pole of the magnet. Faraday changed the setup and held the rod stationary while the magnet rotated.

He realized that a magnet might not be needed. The earth itself is a magnet, and he set up a demonstration to use the earth's magnetic field as a part of his "motor." He made the arrangement shown in the illustration. The conductor, hooked at its upper end, was floated in mercury at an angle of about 40 degrees. The earth's magnetic field had a magnetic dip of about 72 degrees in London at that time. When the current was turned on the conductor rotated about the earth's lines of force.

Thus the electric motor was born. But, curiously enough, inventors did not rush to make it practical. Perhaps their lack of interest – although a few inventors did work on the

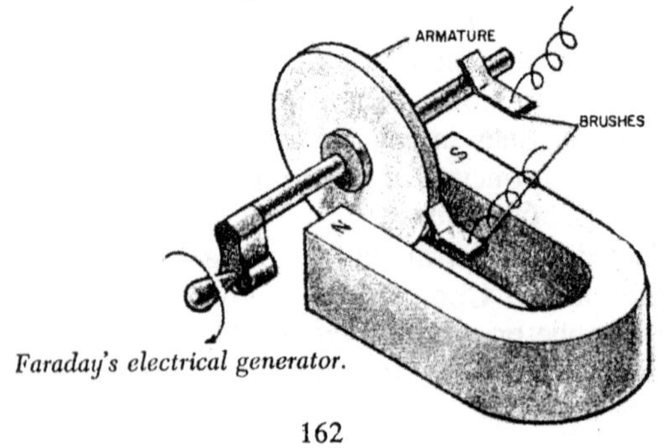


*Faraday's electrical generator.*

idea – stemmed from the very high cost of electricity and the nuisance of maintaining electric batteries, voltaic piles as they called them.

Faraday was beginning to be appreciated by the scientific world. Up to now he had been known only as the assistant to Sir Humphry Davy, but his researches and successes with the electric motor principle brought him into prominence as a scientist in his own right. He was nominated and elected to the Royal Society. Curiously, Sir Humphry Davy opposed his selection. It is not known whether Davy was jealous of the rapid rise of his assistant or whether he felt this "late bookbinder's apprentice, now turned philosopher" was not yet ready for the honor.

For ten years after his Christmas Day demonstration, Faraday was busy with chemical investigations, but he had not forgotten the important memo to himself.

*"Convert Magnetism into Electricity"!*

In October of 1820 the Danish physicist, Hans Christian Oersted discovered that a current of electricity flowing in a conductor had the power of deflecting a magnetized needle away from its North-South position. He realized that the current produced a magnetic field about the conductor. As soon as the scientific world recognized the importance of this discovery, the hunt was on to reverse the effect.

Electricity could produce magnetism. Could magnetism produce electricity? How?

When Faraday found the answer it was so simple that it is difficult for us to believe that the scientific world took so many years to find the method. After many dead-end trials the answer was found on October 17, 1831.

This is how he found the principle of electric induction. Copper wire, 220 feet long, was wound on a cardboard cylinder. Between the turns he had wound twine and between the layers he placed calico cloth. The ends of the wire were connected to an instrument that could detect electricity, a galvanometer. Faraday thrust a bar magnet into the cylinder; the galvanometer showed the presence of an electric current. He pulled the magnet out; again the meter moved, this time in the opposite direction. When the magnet was at rest no electricity was produced. He tried it the other way: move the coil, keep the magnet still – again success. The solution was here: *relative motion between the conductor and the magnet would convert magnetism into electricity.*

Quickly Faraday devised a method of making the motion continuous in order to obtain a continuous rather than a momentary induced voltage. He mounted a copper disk a foot in diameter and almost a quarter of an inch thick on a brass axle. The disk was mounted between the poles of the most powerful magnet in the Royal Society. A piece of copper was arranged so that it would make contact with the rotating copper disk; a second copper "brush" made contact with the axle. The copper brushes were connected to an electric meter. When the disk was rotated the meter deflected and showed that electricity was being produced. This first electric generator, the granddaddy of the giant dynamos of today, is shown on Page 165.

In November of 1831, Faraday described his discovery before the Royal Society. When he explained the laws of electric induction he used the idea of magnetic lines of force and of tubes of force. His law – the induced electric force depends on the number of magnetic lines of force cut by the wire each second – is a cornerstone of electrical theory and practice to this day.

Faraday made no attempt to develop his idea for any commercial purpose; he was only interested in scientific research. Once he had cracked the fundamental problem, he lost interest and turned to other investigations.

From 1831 to his death on August 26, 1867, he continued his scientific studies except for a period between 1841 and 1845 when he suffered from an illness that may have been mercury poisoning, contracted from his work in the laboratories. Of the additional studies he made any one of them would have marked him as a scientific genius. He established, for example, the fact that light is electromagnetic in nature by deflecting polarized light with a magnet.

Michael Faraday was the father of the electric motor and of the electric generator. He was a dedicated, an unselfish genius. The entire electrical industry rests on the shoulders of this giant. His name has been immortalized by being applied as an important unit of measurement in electrical science, the farad.

## JOSEPH HENRY

Joseph Henry neglected to publish his experiments as he performed them, and thus lost for himself and for the United States a deserved place of honor in the history of electrical science. This professor of science at the Albany Academy in New York State had made discoveries in magnetic-electric induction several years before Michael Faraday, but through modesty and neglect had failed to publish his findings. There were many superpatriots of the day who called him a traitor to his country because of the scientific reports he did not write.

Joseph Henry was born on a small farm near Albany, New York, on December 17, 1797. His family was extremely poor and his schooling was badly neglected. He spent most of his time helping on the farm. However, he had taught himself to read well and had absorbed all the books – mainly romantic novels – he could find. When he was fourteen he was sent to Albany to earn his own living as a store clerk and found, as well, the make-believe world of the theatre. After two years as an amateur actor – and he showed great promise – he discovered a new, real world, the world of science.

Joseph Henry applied for entrance at the Albany Academy, which, fortunately, had evening classes, and in seven months, including private tutoring from the sympathetic headmaster, had earned the qualifications to become a country schoolteacher. He turned to school-teaching to make a living and continued his evening studies at the Albany Academy. There wasn't time left to do very much more; teaching and attending classes, traveling between school and the academy took up most of the day. Fortunately an opening in the Chemistry department at the Albany Academy, as laboratory assistant, developed, and Henry was able to get this post. Here indeed was a wonderful job. Henry had an opportunity to work with the equipment all day, to set up demonstrations for the lectures, and to perform the demonstrations himself. Meanwhile he continued with his education, specializing in mathematics and in science.

Henry completed all the courses available at the Albany Academy and reluctantly left the laboratories to accept a job on the Erie Canal. He was hired as a surveying engineer. The success of the canal was immediate; it brought great financial gains to New York City and to New York State and opened an era of public works in various states that wished to emulate New York. There were many highly paid engineering jobs available for the talent and training of Joseph Henry. However, in 1826, at the age of twenty-nine, he turned his back on the engineering job offers and accepted the position as professor of science and of mathematics at the Albany Academy.

His teaching schedule was arduous, for Professor Henry was a popular teacher. He was a well-proportioned, blond-haired, blue-eyed young man, well bronzed from the outdoor life he had led. His years as a lab assistant had made him a master demonstrator and his apprenticeship as an actor stood him in good stead as he brought a dramatic flavor to his classroom. His winter was filled with school work, but the departure of the students for the summer was the signal for Joseph Henry to begin his own scientific investigations.

In England, William Sturgeon had invented the electromagnet. He had taken a soft iron rod and bent it into horseshoe form. The rod was coated with varnish and a single layer of bare copper wire was wrapped around the iron. An electric current passed through the wire made the rod magnetic. Sturgeon's electromagnetic rod was reportedly able to hold, by magnetic attraction, nine pounds of soft iron. Joseph Henry reconstructed and improved Sturgeon's electromagnet. He insulated the wire with silk and was able to wrap many turns of wire about an iron core without danger of short circuits between the turns. His magnet was capable of sustaining 2,300 pounds.

The construction of the electromagnet led Henry to the famous quest to convert magnetism into electricity. He coiled a length of insulated wire about a soft iron bar and connected the ends of the coil to a galvanometer. The iron bar was placed across the poles of the electromagnet. At a signal, an assistant connected the coil of the electromagnet to a battery. Henry watched the galvanometer; it indicated a voltage and then it returned to rest at zero. At another signal the assistant disconnected the coil and the galvanometer again showed that a voltage had been produced in the second coil, but this time in the opposite direction. Henry had found the principle of electromagnetic induction, but he did not publish his discovery and Faraday deservedly got the credit.

There was one facet that did not occur to Faraday, however, and that is the idea of self-induction. Happily the credit for this discovery, made in 1829, rests with Joseph Henry. If a coil of wire has an electric current through it, a magnetic field will be produced. When the circuit is broken the magnetic field disappears. While this is happening, a voltage will be produced in the coil. The change in the magnetic field due to the change in its own current produces a voltage. The coil, in effect, induces a voltage in itself, hence it is called self-induction.

While Henry was experimenting in Albany, confident that he was years ahead of the scientific world, Faraday was experimenting in London. In 1832, Faraday published his results and the race was lost. A scientific race that Joseph Henry felt confident wasn't even close.

Nevertheless, at the urging of his scientific friends, Joseph Henry prepared a series of articles for publication in the American Journal of Science. These articles, and of course, the scientific investigations upon which the articles were based, helped earn an appointment to the faculty of Princeton University. Professor Henry spent fourteen years at Princeton, from 1832 to 1846, in teaching and in research.

Ask anyone who invented the telegraph and the answer is almost certain to be Samuel F. B. Morse. However Joseph Henry, long before Morse, had a workable model of a telegraph system operating over a mile of wire. Further, he invented the electric relay and showed how he could use this device to repeat the signal indefinitely. The electric relay is still in use in the present day and although billions of relays have been built, the basic method that Henry discovered has not been improved upon. The method then and the method now (although refined in details) is to use an electromagnet to attract a piece of magnetic material (called an armature) which in its new position closes an electrical circuit. Henry demonstrated his telegraph system to Morse and to Charles Wheatstone, the father of the British Telegraph System.

In fairness, the telegraph system in the United States was largely a result of Morse's untiring efforts. The system that Joseph Henry demonstrated consisted basically of a switch and a bell. Morse assumed that an automatic mech-

*One of Henry's experimental devices. From a drawing of the time.*

anism must be employed to assure accuracy of transmission and that the messages must be permanently recorded. He built complicated mechanisms to perform these functions and succeeded in recording dots and dashes on paper tape; the tape then was translated into language. Within a short time, however, the operators learned to read the sounds as they came in, and little by little the complicated mechanisms were discarded, so that the telegraph system was in essence a switch and a bell.

In 1842, fifty years before the experiments of Heinrich Hertz, Professor Henry demonstrated the transmission and reception of radio waves. He set up a spark gap in the laboratory and noted that a second coil thirty feet away, responded as a receiver by magnetizing a needle, although not connected to an electric source. Henry published this experiment later, but he was too far ahead in the race, this time, for the world to understand what he had accomplished.

James Smithson, a British chemist and mineralogist, who had never even visited the United States, left the government more than half a million dollars for the establishment of a scientific establishment. The money was accepted by an act of Congress in 1846 which established the Smithsonian Institution. This building located in Washington, D. C. is a museum as well as a scientific research organization. Joseph Henry accepted the position of executive head of the institution, a position which he held until his death in 1878. The Smithsonian Building, still a magnet for Washington visitors, was completed under his guidance in 1852. Henry established the weather service and collected telegraphed meteorological data from over five hundred observers throughout the country. The department published weather maps and made weather predictions. The astrophysical observatory made studies of the sun, and Henry is given credit for measuring the relative temperature of the sun spots, finding they were cooler than the surrounding areas of the sun.

Joseph Henry will be remembered for all time, because scientists took the capital away from his name. There is an important electrical measurement having to do with the size of the magnetic field and the amount of current needed to produce this field. The measurement is called inductance and the unit is the henry.

FRIEDRICH WOHLER

"I can make urea in the laboratory without the help of a man or a dog or a kidney." This was the startling announcement by Friedrich Wöhler of a major breakthrough in chemical theory. For the first time man was able to produce in the laboratory a compound which had been manufactured heretofore only by living animals. When Friedrich Wöhler synthesized urea in 1828, he established the branch of science now called organic chemistry.

The word organic is derived from the word organism which means a living thing. It was thought that some "vital force" entered into the making of the fats, sugar, vitamins, hormones and the many other complex compounds that are present in plants and in animals. The great English chemist William Henry wrote, "It is not probable that we shall ever attain the power of imitating nature in these operations." He made this statement only one year before Wöhler's achievement.

Organic chemistry is now thought of as carbon chemistry. Thousands upon thousands of organic compounds, based on the element carbon, have been produced in chemical laboratories and factories for the betterment of the world standard of living. For example, the historic urea has been combined with formaldehyde to make a light, almost unbreakable type of tableware, dishes, cups and saucers.

Friedrich Wöhler was born in a village near Frankfort-am-Main, Germany, in July 1800. His father, an educated man with a strong streak of independence, took care of the early education of Friedrich. Under his father's influence the boy became interested in minerals and in chemistry. He was fortunate in having a fine library and a private chemical laboratory available for his use. Young Wöhler built voltaic piles and performed all manner of chemical experiments, some dangerous enough to have killed a less fortunate young man.

When Wöhler entered Marburg University at the age of twenty his purpose was to study medicine. Prophetically, perhaps, he made a study of urine and the methods by which waste materials are converted into this body fluid. Meanwhile he continued, on his own, the study of chemistry, converting his room into a laboratory. This displeased the authorities and brought an admonishment from his professor. Friedrich decided to go elsewhere.

The University at Heidelberg gave a medical course and had Leopold Gmelin as professor of chemistry. Wöhler obtained his medical degree, but Professor Gmelin convinced him that chemistry, not medicine, held greater promise.

So instead of rounding off his medical education with an interneship at the hospital, Friedrich Wöhler set off to work under the famous Swedish chemist Berzelius in Stockholm. While there, he succeeded in preparing a compound of nitrogen, carbon, oxygen and silver, called silver cyanate. This discovery was published and was picked up by another German chemist, Justus Liebig, who was working on explosives in a Paris laboratory. He too had prepared a compound, apparently the same as Wöhler's. It had the same number of parts of nitrogen, carbon, oxygen and silver, but something was wrong. The two materials, both with the same chemical makeup, just didn't act the same way.

This was a remarkable discovery. Up to this point chemists could use a simple formula to describe a compound, but now it was plain that the formula was not enough. Wöhler took the matter up with Berzelius who recognized the importance of this new idea and invented a name: *isomer.* Compounds which have the same chemical elements in exactly the same proportions, but have different arrangements of atoms in their molecules are called isomers.

As a result of this chance meeting over a chemical formula, the two young chemists – Liebig was twenty-one and Wöhler was twenty-three – became lifelong friends and scientific associates. Liebig was already a professor of chemistry at the University of Gniessen. Wöhler, upon his return from Sweden, obtained a teaching position in a trade school in Berlin.

Still working in the laboratory on the cyanates, Wöhler made potassium cyanate. Then, when he treated the potassium cyanate with ammonium sulfate, the great discovery was made. Out of the solution came white needle-like crystals of ammonium cyanate, or urea, a substance that had never been made in a laboratory before. These crystals opened up a whole new world to mankind.

If Wöhler had not been the father of organic or carbon chemistry, he would still be a noted chemist. In 1827 he succeeded in preparing the metal aluminum for the first time. And it was his student, Professor Frank Jewett of Oberlin who inspired *his* student Charles Martin Hall to discover the modern, inexpensive method of aluminum manufacture. Wöhler also discovered the elements beryllium and yttrium and just missed isolating vanadium.

How shall we measure Wöhler's contribution? Urea, the material he taught the world could be made in the chemical laboratory, is in use today in adhesives and agriculture, in construction and cosmetics, in medicine and pharmaceuticals, in plastics and in textiles.

But urea is only one item; there are thousands upon thousands of compounds in use that depend on the synthesis of "organic" materials, materials that man thought could come only from the living, until Wöhler showed the way.

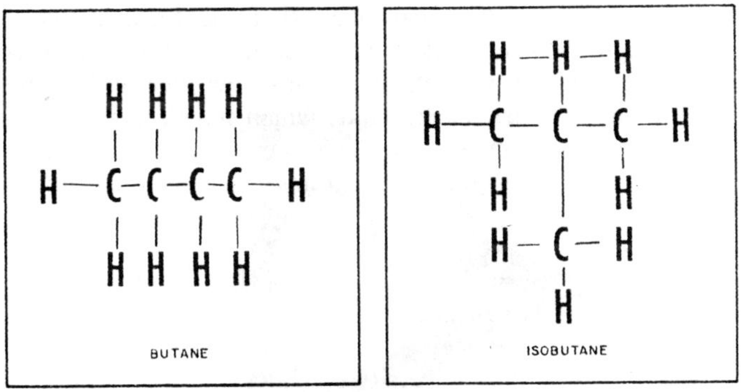

BUTANE

ISOBUTANE

*The same number of carbon and hydrogen atoms make different compounds, called isomers.*

# CHARLES DARWIN

"You care for nothing but dogs, shooting, and rat-catching. You will be a disgrace to yourself and all your family." So said an angry and distraught father to his son, Charles Darwin, the boy who was to become one of the foremost naturalists of all times and the author of the monumental book *The Origin of Species by Means of Natural Selection.* The book presents a once controversial but now generally accepted explanation of the method by which new forms of plant or animal life come into being.

Charles Darwin was born in 1809 in Shrewsbury, England, on the same day as Abraham Lincoln, but into a very different kind of household. His father Robert, a successful and wealthy physician, provided the children with everything that money could buy. They lacked for nothing material, but they were motherless from the time that Charles was eight.

His grandfather Dr. Erasmus Darwin was well-known as a doctor, a naturalist, and an author.

In this well-educated family, Charles was considered to be rather dull. At one time his school headmaster called him a dullard. But Charles was not stupid. The trouble was his lively imagination did not fit into a school pattern. He showed great interest in all animals and in insects. He was, in spite of what his father thought, preparing himself for his life work, sharpening and developing the primary tool of science, the art of observation. He was later to say, not boastfully, "I think that I am superior to the common run of men in noticing things which easily escape attention and in observing them carefully."

His powers of observation were, in fact, appreciated by his father. Dr. Robert Darwin was a big hulk of a man – some three hundred pounds – who frequently had difficulty in visiting some of his less prosperous patients. Their stairs and floors were adjudged too weak for the stress. In his early youth Charles accompanied the doctor on his rounds, visited patients and reported to his father, who then prescribed on the basis of Charles' observations. The medical laws were quite lax in those days.

Charles was sent to the University at Edinburgh, with his brother Erasmus, to study medicine. At Edinburgh, as expected, he was a poor scholar, but he took great interest in the student discussion sessions – especially those about the origins of life, a favorite topic of the day. After two unsuccessful years as a student it was agreed that Charles was unfitted for medicine.

As a last resort, in order for this scion of an educated family to enter one of the learned professions, Charles agreed to study for the ministry. And so to Cambridge, where he spent less time on theology than on "bug-hunting"; his insect collection was outstanding.

At twenty-two, Darwin had a theological degree but was not at all eager to begin work as a minister. A letter from John Henslow, a young botany lecturer he had met at Cambridge, gave him a chance to avoid settling down. Henslow introduced Darwin to Captain Fitzroy, master of the 235-ton barque-rigged *H.M.S. Beagle*.

The *Beagle* was to survey the South American coastline. Would Charles like to go along as a naturalist? He would have to pay his own way. The trip was scheduled to take two years. Would Charles like to go along!

Back to his father for funds – and father said "No, the whole idea is nonsensical." More pleadings and family conferences and finally consent. As the *Beagle* slipped out of Devonport harbor in the winter of 1831, Charles Darwin looked over the rail. He didn't know it then, but he was not to see home for five years; he was to have the greatest naturalist adventure on record.

Darwin was a keen observer, an accurate reporter, and an indefatigable collector. Patiently and persistently he collected plants, rocks, insects, animals, and fossils by the trunk load. He filled all available deck space. At every port of call his collections were sent home.

The voyage was full of adventure and danger. Inland there were savages and outlaws to avoid. There was fever, the danger of being marooned, and the hardships of storms and cold. In contrast there were elegant receptions in some of the large South American cities where Darwin met beautiful ladies, "nice round mermaids" as he described them, and very civilized men. These contrasted strangely with the savages he met on some of the coastal islands.

On this trip Captain Fitzroy returned three savages to their barren island. They were natives of Tierra del Fuego whom he had taken as hostages on a previous trip. Darwin

*Darwin's theories were based on intensive field work.*

noticed that these savages, whom nature had fitted to their harsh climate, were already changed by their contact with civilization.

After surveying many uncharted coasts, and observing many strange forms of plant and animal life, the *Beagle* dropped anchor at the Galapagos Islands, some five hundred miles west of South America. Here nature provided the laboratory that started Charles Darwin on the path that led to the "Origin of Species." The unusual, primitive quality of the various creatures gave him a clue to the theory that changes take place in living forms. "One might almost fancy that from an original paucity of birds in this archipelago, one species had been taken and modified for different ends," he wrote. Reptile, bird, and animal life differed from island to island and yet there were similarities. If all creation had taken place at the same time, why were there so many organisms with slight differences? By examining fossils that resembled organisms still living, he decided that some species were replaced by closely related ones.

A vice-governor of one of the islands told Darwin that he could tell from which one of the various islands each tortoise came. Darwin felt that the resemblances and differences could be understood if the inhabitants of the several islands had descended from common ancestors, but had undergone a series of small changes in the course of their development. Thus the germ of his own evolution theory was planted in Darwin's mind. There were changes in species: that was evident, but what was the mechanism of this change? How did it happen?

It was not till 1838, on reading Thomas Malthus' *Essay on Population* that Darwin got the answer to the problem of how and why living things change from generation to generation. Malthus held that the human population tended to increase faster than its food supply. This set up a struggle for the food and hence a struggle for existence.

Darwin knew that domestic animals were bred to bring out selected qualities. In domestic animals, man controlled the qualities desired by preventing reproduction of the animals without the desired qualities, and by encouraging reproduction of the animals with the selected qualities. Darwin had observed that variations existed in wild animals, but how did the selection take place without human assistance?

Malthus gave the clue: man had to struggle for his food supply and to cope with his environment. The wild animals had the same problem. If there wasn't enough food to go around, then only the animals most fitted by nature to obtain the food would survive. The "survival of the fittest" was the key to the constant change in species.

In the struggle for existence, Darwin said, "Favorable variations would tend to be preserved and unfavorable ones to be destroyed. The result of this would be the formation of a new species."

For 20 years, Darwin gathered evidence to support his theories while he continued the studies he had begun during his trip on the *Beagle*. In 1855 Alfred Wallace, a biologist, wrote an article "On the Law Which Has Regulated the Introduction of New Species." This article contained many ideas which were similar to Darwin's unpublished studies. Darwin was advised to release a summary of his theory, but he kept putting it off. In 1858 Wallace sent Darwin the manuscript of an article, "On the Tendency of Varieties to Depart Indefinitely from the Original Type." Darwin felt this could well be a short abstract of his own theory if he had written it out, and he decided, therefore, to announce his findings to the world. On July 1, 1858, Wallace's essay and Darwin's sketch of his own theory, arrived at independently, were read to the Linnean Society of London.

"The Origin of Species" was published the next year. In it Darwin set forth his theory; he dealt with geology and with the geographic distribution of plants and animals. The whole volume is "one long argument for evolution," according to Darwin. Controversy has raged about Darwin's theory since it was first published.

In 1860 two papers attacking Darwin were presented at a meeting of the British Association for the Advancement of Science. The Bishop of Oxford took the platform, savagely ridiculing Darwin and his supporter, Thomas H.

Huxley. The Bishop asked his famous question, "Was it through his grandfather or his grandmother that Huxley claimed descent from an ape?" When Huxley answered that he would prefer an ape to the Bishop as an ancestor, the meeting dissolved in an uproar.

In 1925, John T. Scopes, a schoolteacher, was prosecuted for teaching the theory of evolution in the state of Tennessee. He was defended by the famed lawyer Clarence Darrow. The prosecution was conducted by the equally famous William Jennings Bryan. Scopes was convicted, but the decision was later set aside. Thus, more than 40 years after his death, in these modern times, Darwin's theory was still the subject of controversy.

Darwin, whose carefully written book stirred up a great controversy, was a mild, gentle man. He came home from his voyage on the *Beagle* a sick man, suffering from constant headaches and nausea. He lived until he was past 70 but never traveled again.

He married his cousin Emma Wedgewood and lived happily with his family in a small village in Kent. He had sufficient income so that he did not have to worry about earning a living. He spent his time in going over the tremendous body of evidence that led to his theory of evolution. A lovable and sweet-tempered invalid, he wandered about his garden, caring for his flowers. He made botanical experiments which he used to test his theory.

Darwin wrote other books besides "Origin of Species." His book *Formation of Vegetable Mould through the Action of Worms* showed that worms were of great impor-

tance in the history of the world. No book, however, created the excitement of "Origin of Species."

Like Aristotle, Darwin was greatly impressed with the efficiency and effectiveness of nature in designing its creatures to do special jobs. He wrote, "The more I study Nature, the more I become impressed that the contrivances and beautiful adaptations, slowly acquired through each part occasionally varying in a slight degree . . . transcend in an incomparable manner the contrivances and adaptations which the most fertile imagination of man could invent."

Charles Darwin died in 1882. If he were to make his voyage today, the Galapagos Islands would no longer be of help to him in the study of natural selection. The giant tortoises and the lemurs are gone; the rare plants and the curious birds are vanishing. The islands are now used as air bases and the roar of jet planes drowns out the animal noises that Darwin once heard.

His was "the prepared mind" that was on the job at the right time in history to bring us the Theory of Evolution. He must have known that even scientific theories undergo evolutionary changes. He said, "I look at it as absolutely certain that very much in the 'Origin' will be proved rubbish; but I expect and hope that the framework will stand."

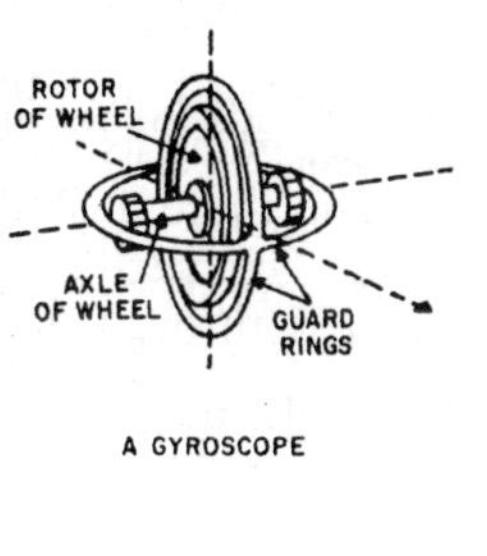

A GYROSCOPE

## JEAN BERNARD LEON FOUCAULT

In the United Nations building in New York a small sphere, suspended on a long steel rod, moves in pendulum fashion but seemingly changes direction as the hours pass. This golden sphere, slowly swinging, simple in appearance, is ingenious proof that the earth rotates on its axis. Named after its inventor, it is called a Foucault pendulum.

Jean Bernard Leon Foucault was born in 1819, in Paris. His early education took place at home; his well-to-do parents hired tutors for him. As a youth, Jean demonstrated great interest and ability in mechanical devices of all types. He built a boat, a mechanical telegraph system, and a working steam engine, among other things.

Entering the University in Paris, Foucault turned to the study of medicine, but unable to stand the sight of blood, soon abandoned the idea of becoming a doctor. He got a job in the medical school as a technician in the preparation of microscope slides.

The development of a photographic process by Louis Jacques Daguerre, described in 1839, ignited Foucault's interest in the physics of light and optics. He soon realized that mechanical skill, by itself, was insufficient to pursue his new interest. He restudied mathematics and enlarged his knowledge of science.

Foucault developed some ingenious methods to measure the speed of light, but due to the short distances chosen, and the imperfect mechanical techniques of his time, was unable to obtain the accurate results necessary. His experiments were not without positive results, however. Foucault established the important principle that light travels more slowly through water than it does through air. This helped establish the theory that light is made up of waves rather than a stream of "corpuscles" as scientists then believed. Later, Albert A. Michelson, an American physicist, using Foucault's rotating mirror method, measured the speed of light with astounding accuracy.

Foucault, a remarkably prolific scientist, did not confine himself to the study of light; his talent and curiosity led him into the fields of electricity and mechanics. The electric arc lamp, really a huge electric spark jumping between two sticks of carbon, was beginning to come into use. The space between the carbons increases as the carbons burn, until soon the space is too large and the light goes out. Foucault invented an automatic regulator to feed the carbons toward each other, as they tended to burn out.

Additional work in electricity included studies of the relations between mechanical energy and heat, and mechanical energy and magnetism. He discovered the existence of eddy currents, or, as they are called, Foucault's currents. These currents are induced in a copper disc moving in a strong magnetic field. This idea is still used as part of the electric meter in our homes.

The Foucault pendulum is a dramatic demonstration of Newton's law that "a body in motion continues in motion along the same path, unless acted upon by some outside force." At the same time it offers proof that the earth rotates on its axis. The pendulum is suspended by means of an almost frictionless ball and socket bearing. As the sphere swings back and forth the earth rotates under it. To the observer it seems as though the pendulum is changing direction. This is the same kind of illusion that causes

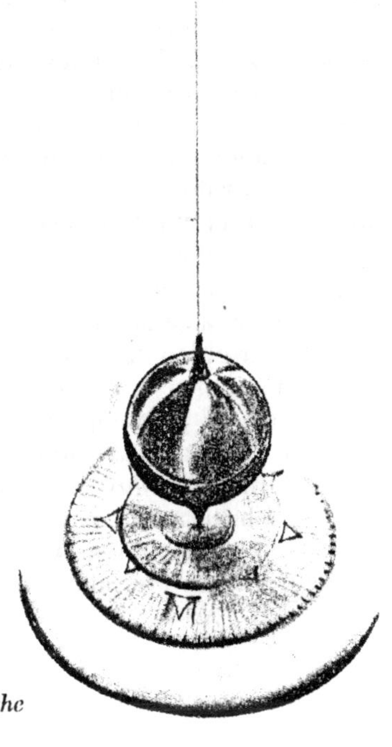

*The Foucault pendulum in the Smithsonian Institution.*

the sun to seem to rotate from east to west, when in reality it is the earth that rotates from west to east.

All of Foucault's inventions and discoveries have contributed importantly to the fund of human knowledge, but perhaps the most important thing he did was to invent a toy. This toy is a small metal wheel with a heavy rim. When set spinning, the wheel amazingly maintains its axis in the same direction.

For many centuries mariners had depended upon the magnetic compass to point the way North. The compass is a small magnet and falls in line with the earth's magnetic field. The use of steel ships made the compass difficult to use; the needle no longer pointed north but was attracted erratically to the steel of the ship. The problem was to find something that pointed North, but would not be influenced by the steel of the ship.

Elmer Ambrose Sperry, an American inventive genius, found the answer in Foucault's gyroscope, which he developed into the gyrocompass. If the gyrocompass is set rotating with its axis pointing true North, it will continue to hold its position no matter how the ship turns. The first gyrocompass was installed on the battleship Delaware, in the Brooklyn Navy Yard, in 1911 and proved an immediate and outstanding success.

The principle of the gyroscope has been extended in many ways. It became an automatic pilot, holding ship or airplane on course despite wind and weather. A gyroscope control maintains the accurate course of a torpedo. A complex system of gyroscopes and electronic computers makes up the "inertial" navigation system that enabled the atomic submarine *Nautilus* to sail under the North Pole.

Sperry's sophisticated gyroscopes are in the forefront of space travel, guiding missiles and setting space satellites on course. But it was Foucault's toy that set Sperry on the course in the first place.

## LOUIS PASTEUR

The village blacksmith was the doctor in case of a dogbite. If the dog were mad – had rabies – the standard treatment was to cauterize the wound. The blacksmith heated an iron until it was red hot. He then plunged the red-hot iron into the patient's wound. A "lucky" patient survived both the disease and the cure. Louis Pasteur witnessed this "cure" as a boy of nine. Fifty years later he developed and tested a safe, effective anti-rabies treatment.

Louis Pasteur was born in the village of Dôle in the eastern part of France in the winter of 1822. His father had been a soldier in the French army and, after the collapse of Napoleon, had set up a tannery at Dôle. Soon after Louis' birth the family moved to Arbois, in the heart of the grape country not far from Dôle. Ex-sergeant Jean Joseph Pasteur continued in the tannery and, with his wife, devoted himself to his family. Unschooled but self-educated, he had the greatest respect for intellect and learning. His village associates included the local doctor and a historian, Bousson de Moiret. Jean Joseph Pasteur had what he felt were great aspirations for his son. He wanted

Louis to become a teacher in the secondary school of the province.

From his father and from de Moiret, Louis had obtained a feeling of intense patriotism, a love of France and respect for her great men that was to affect him throughout his career.

There was nothing in Louis Pasteur's early life that foreshadowed a career of scientific discovery. At age fifteen he devoted himself to portrait painting. His paintings were extraordinarily good, and he might be known as a famous artist if he had not turned to science. Many of his paintings have been preserved and hang in the Pasteur Institute in Paris.

The headmaster at the local secondary school saw the imaginative, enthusiastic but deliberate student as a future teacher. Although Louis was admitted to the scientific section of the Ecole Normale Superieure, a teacher's training institution in Paris, he delayed entrance for a year because he felt that he was insufficiently prepared. By this time, his chief interests were mathematics, physics, and chemistry.

Pasteur wanted to become a good teacher; his letters reveal his pride when he successfully passed the practical classroom teaching tests in physics and in chemistry. However, when he received his degree, he turned to research and not to teaching.

While a student at the Ecole, Pasteur had begun work on the study of crystals. He had, in the course of his student days, attended chemistry lectures given by Antoine Jerôme Balard, discoverer of the element bromine.

Balard believed, with Benjamin Franklin, that scientific work could be carried out with simple home-built equipment and had set up a make-shift laboratory at the school. Balard had been greatly impressed with Pasteur's original studies and insights and invited him to act as a laboratory assistant. This opportunity enabled Pasteur to continue his optical studies of crystals of tartaric acid. His findings were brought by Balard to the attention of the noted physicist Jean Baptiste Biot who, in turn, presented them to the French Academy of Science.

In 1848, despite the objections and protests of Professor Balard, Professor Biot, and other members of the French Academy of Science, the Ministry of Education assigned Pasteur to teach elementary physics at a secondary school in Dijon. His friends and sponsors, however, continued their pressure on the ministry and a year later Louis was appointed acting professor of chemistry at the University of Strasbourg.

A few weeks after his arrival, this serious, deliberate young man of science asked the rector of the university for the hand of his daughter. He wrote to the rector.

> I have absolutely no fortune. My only means are good health, some courage, and my position in the university. . . . As to the future, unless my tastes should change completely I shall devote myself entirely to chemical research. I hope to return to Paris when I have acquired some reputation through my scientific studies. . . .
>
> My father will himself come to Strasbourg to make the proposal of marriage. . . .

Louis Pasteur and Marie Laurent were married on May 29, 1849. He was twenty-six; she was twenty-two. Marie Pasteur was an extraordinary wife. Emile Roux, who became Pasteur's assistant in 1876 and director of the Pasteur Institute in 1904, described her as follows:

"From the beginning of their married life, Madame Pasteur understood the man she had married. She did everything to protect him from the difficulties of life, taking to herself the worries of the home, that he might retain the full freedom of his mind for his investigations. During the evenings, she wrote under his dictation. She took a genuine interest in crystalline structure or attenuated viruses. She had become aware that ideas become the clearer for being explained to others and that nothing is more conducive to devising new experiments than describing the ones which have just been completed. Madame Pasteur was more than an incomparable companion for her husband, she was his best collaborator."

There was personal tragedy in the lives of Marie and Louis Pasteur. Their first-born, a daughter Jeanne, died at age nine; two-year-old Camille died in 1865; and twelve-year-old Cecile, stricken with typhoid, died in 1866. Jean Baptiste, twenty-year-old son, was reported missing during the defeat of the French Army by the Germans in 1871. Louis dropped his work and searched the long lines of returning, defeated stragglers.

The disheartening report came that of 1,200 men in Sergeant Pasteur's battalion there were only 300 left. Happily for Marie and Louis they found their only son, wounded but alive, and nursed him back to health. Louis Pasteur never forgave the Germans; years later he refused to accept a medal the German government wished to give him in recognition of his scientific achievements.

Now let's see what Pasteur accomplished. His early experiments were with crystals. The physicist Biot had discovered that the plane of polarized light was rotated (that is, the direction of the light was turned) as it went through a quartz crystal. Other scientists discovered that some crystals had to be dissolved before they would rotate the polarized light.

For example, if polarized light is passed through sugar dissolved in water, the plane of polarization will be rotated as it passes through the sugar solution. A German chemist, Eilhardt Mitscherlich, was working on a problem that had to do with tartaric acid, a product of the wine industry. He reported that there were two types of tartaric acid, called true tartaric acid and paratartaric acid. The true tartaric acid rotated polarized light to the right, but the paratartaric acid had no effect on the polarized light. In all other respects, he reported, they are identical.

The mind of young Pasteur seized upon this statement. He could not accept it. There had to be some discernible difference. Pasteur set to work to find the difference. His long studies of crystals had prepared him for the task. He saw small facets on the crystals of tartaric acid. He prepared a paratartrate of the type that Mitscherlich had reported on, let the crystals form and studied them.

In wonderment he discovered crystal facets of two types, some to the left and some to the right. Paratartaric acid was really two kinds of tartrate, equal mixtures of right crystals and left crystals. This was a brand new discovery.

This was not the end of his study of crystals; it was the beginning. Before he gave up this fascinating study, he formulated a theory of life. He believed that right-sided and left-sided molecules always result when produced by living processes. These right-sided and left-sided aspects are termed asymmetrical. Pasteur thought that he could create life itself under the influence of asymmetrical forces which he would introduce into chemical reactions. Pasteur failed, of course, to create life in the chemistry laboratory, but his efforts prepared his mind for the solution of another problem, that of fermentation.

Fermentation is a term applied to changes that occur in certain materials. Sometimes fermentation is desired, sometimes it is undesirable. Wine is produced by the fermentation of grapes, and wine may turn to vinegar by fermenting into acetic acid. Milk turns sour when the sugar of milk turns into lactic acid. Meat and eggs may spoil by fermentation.

The production of wine was a big industry in France, and the fermentation of the grapes was a matter of serious concern. But the conditions under which fermentation took

*Pasteur in his laboratory.*

place were not understood, and letting nature take its course might result in sour wine or no wine. Pasteur made a detailed study of the wine industry, and as a result developed the germ theory of fermentation which he presented to the Societé des Sciences of Lille. He stated his belief, as a result of careful and extensive investigations, that all changes of materials in nature are caused by various kinds of organisms, too small to be seen except with a microscope. He showed that these microorganisms could be controlled by heat. His experimentation and findings placed the wine industry on a firm scientific basis. The same study presented the world with the vital pasteurization process, a process used to safeguard the milk you drink and to prevent its being a disease carrier.

Several years later, the silk industry of France was threatened with disaster as a result of diseased silkworms. Pasteur was invited to investigate the difficulty. With characteristic thoroughness Pasteur studied every facet of this new problem. He became expert in the raising of silkworms. He developed practical methods for the selection of healthy silkworm eggs and saved the industry from extinction.

Louis Pasteur's accomplishments were a result of a kind of chain reaction in thinking. One thing seemed inevitably to lead to the next. His studies of crystals led him to consider the mysteries of life. The study of life led him into the problem and the solution of fermentation, which he stubbornly and accurately held to be accomplished by microscopic beings – microbes. This study brought him to grips with the advocates of spontaneous generation or the theory that living things arose from inanimate matter. Men had ceased, since the time of the Italian scientist Francisco Redi, to believe in the spontaneous generation of such creatures as grubs, maggots, tapeworms, and mice, but it was still held possible that the microbes came out of inanimate organic materials.

Pasteur established the impossibility of spontaneous generation for even microbe life. His firmly held germ theories enabled him to restore the silkworm industry of France. He studied and conquered anthrax, a disease that threatened to wipe out the livestock of Europe. He made extensive studies of gangrene, blood poisoning, and child-birth fever. All these, too, were shown to be germ diseases and Pasteur showed how to control them.

The scourge of rabies, a fatal disease carried by dogs and transmitted to humans, came into Pasteur's laboratory. Rabies too he conquered – and with a dramatic demonstration of inoculation saved the life of a nine-year-old boy who was too badly bitten to survive the cauterization.

Pasteur died on September 28, 1895. He summed up his philosophy as follows:

*"I am utterly convinced that Science and Peace will triumph over Ignorance and War, that nations will eventually unite not to destroy but to edify, and that the future will belong to those who have done the most for the sake of suffering humanity."*

## JOHANN GREGOR MENDEL

"Out of the simplest things shall ye know the truth."

Johann Gregor Mendel worked patiently and carefully, planting many varieties of peas in his beloved garden. In 1866, at the end of eight years of careful scientific cultivation, observation, and analysis he published his findings. That was, it seemed, the end of that. Nothing happened, nobody recognized his work as a classic in science.

But he had laid the foundation for the study of heredity. In 1900, thirty-one years later and sixteen years after his death, three scientists in different lands, working independently, found Mendel's forgotten work and recognized it for its greatness. The world caught up with another giant of science who was years ahead of his time.

Johann Mendel was born into a family of peasants and gardeners in July, 1822. His birthplace was in Moravia, then part of Austria, now a part of Czechoslovakia.

The boy helped his father on the farm, developing a fondness for all of nature and its works. His farming life, or perhaps his heredity, developed in him a tenacity of purpose (or it could be called stubbornness) that was both to help and to hinder him throughout his life.

He attended the elementary school in the village of Heinzedorf. At the insistence of the Lady of the Heinzedorf Manor, this school included a "frill" of education. Much to the disgust of the school inspector, nature study was taught in the elementary schools. He termed it a "scandal." But, through it, the young Johann developed the realization that nature could be studied and analyzed.

From Heinzedorf, Johann went to the *Gymnasium* (secondary school) at the neighboring town of Troppau. Although the family was not poverty-stricken, there was no money available for further education. Johann worked his way through school but could not manage to satisfy the appetite of a seventeen-year-old boy. Inadequate food resulted in illness and what appeared to be the end of schooling for Johann Mendel.

At this juncture, Anton Mendel, Johann's father, suffered a serious accident and decided to sell the farm. He turned over some of the receipts to Johann and to his sister Theresia. His sister turned over her share of money to Johann and with the combined pittance, Johann managed to spend four years of work, study, and hunger at the Olmutz Institute. Later Johann was to repay his sister by sending her sons through college.

Now Johann was ready for a career. His financial struggle colored his thinking. On the advice of one of his teachers he entered the Augustinian Monastery at Altbrünn so that he could "be spared perpetual anxiety about a means of livelihood." At the age of twenty-one, Johann settled down to the monastic life, taking the name of Gregor.

Gregor Mendel found happiness immediately. He was well fed, and – also important – the monastery possessed a well-stocked botanical garden. This scientifically cultivated plot of ground had been established and developed by a friar who had recently died. And so Gregor found himself in a group of congenial men who were interested in theology, philosophy, science, literature – and in scientific gardening. Meanwhile he studied for the priesthood and was ordained in 1847.

For a time Gregor Mendel left the monastery to serve as a parish priest. Unfortunately, he was so sensitive to suffering that he himself became physically ill when required to visit a sick person or to assuage the grief of a family where someone had died. He was speedily relieved of this assignment and returned to the monastery and his garden.

He applied for a teaching position at the local secondary school. The local board of examiners decided that he did not have sufficient knowledge of science to qualify as a regular teacher but permitted him to serve as a substitute at reduced pay. Later, Mendel took a re-examination; this time the decision was that he was not even capable of teaching the elementary grades. He knew his subject thoroughly, but his answers were not understood by the school board. Mendel insisted on his own technical terminology, stubbornly refusing to use the accepted scientific language of the day.

Mendel continued to teach as a substitute, never gaining permanent status. His classroom was a pleasant place. The students enjoyed this happy teacher – he had grown pleasantly round on the good food of the monastery. He relieved the severity of the classes with anecdotes, mostly

*Mendel in his monastery garden.*

centered about his knowledge of the woods and animals of the area. He praised his students; his gentleness was appreciated by them. He avoided giving failing marks and assisted the less able with additional coaching. But all the while he continued his garden plant experiments and his studies. He had meanwhile published his now famous paper, without causing a stir in the outside world.

Unnoticed by the outside world, but beloved by his fellow monks, he was selected to be the head of the monastery when he was forty-seven. His position as abbot made great demands on his time and he reluctantly gave up his teaching position.

The new abbot was a very popular man. He received a good living and used much of it to entertain friends. Festival days were marked by open house to which the entire village was invited. Christmas was celebrated in memorable manner; food and drink were enjoyed by all. Mendel was known to be charitable although he avoided publicizing his gifts to troubled villagers.

In spite of his gentleness he ended his life in dispute with the government. The legislature had passed a bill in 1874 that called for the taxation of church property in order to increase the salaries of the parish priests.

Mendel agreed that the state needed the money for this purpose and offered to send a voluntary contribution. He regarded the law as repressive, however, and stubbornly refused to concede that the state had any right to tax the church. The government would not accept the voluntary contribution but reasserted its demands. The struggle went on without result until his death, but it embittered Mendel, causing him to turn on anyone who tried to reason that the laws must be obeyed.

The experiment which established Gregor Mendel as an outstanding scientist was the result of careful planning. No one has ever been surprised that a parent with red hair has a child with red hair. The relatives gather around the baby and exclaim, "He looks just like his father!" Mendel was the first to establish the laws which explain how characteristics are passed on to offspring, the laws governing heredity. If you look at your parents and sisters and brothers, you know that you all look different, but at the same time look somewhat alike. This bothered biologists; they didn't know how to separate the different traits. Mendel figured out how to do this, and it sounds simple – *just study one separate trait at a time!*

Mendel turned his attention to the study of heredity in garden pea plants. He saw that some plants were tall, some short; some had pods that looked as if they were blown up; other pods fitted tightly about the peas; in some cases the peas were pale yellow or bright yellow or green. All in all he found seven different traits that could be readily and separately identified. He chose the garden peas because the stigma of the garden pea is usually pollinated by pollen from the same flower. This means that the new plant has in effect one parent.

Mendel knew that if a plant was produced from only one parent then he could get pure plant types. For in-

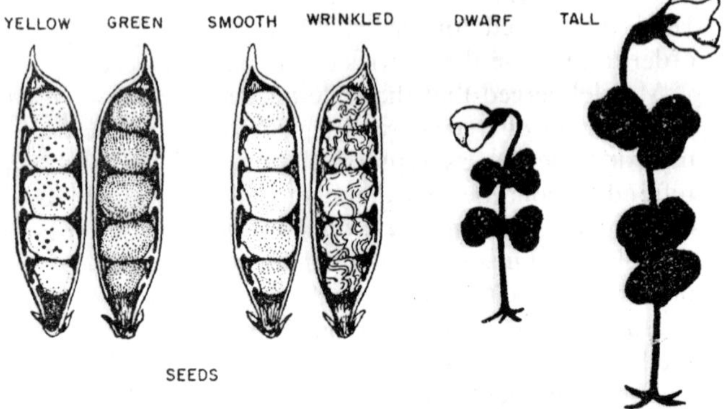


*Some of the traits Mendel studied in pea plants. He found that "in any given pair of contrasting traits, one trait is dominant and the other recessive.'*

stance, a tall plant that reproduces tall plants for generation after generation is "pure" in the trait of being tall. In the same way, a plant that is dwarf for generation after generation is "pure" in the dwarf trait. He carefully produced pure plants in each of the extremes of the seven traits he had decided he would test.

His next step was to keep the plants from pollinating themselves, and to pollinate them from other plants, to cross-pollinate them so that each pea had pure parents but with different traits, for instance, a tall parent and a dwarf parent. He grew hundreds of plants this way and discovered that all the children were tall. This was a puzzle. What happened to the dwarf parent? Didn't it affect the child at all?

More research – this time he crossed many plants each of which had a pure tall parent and a pure dwarf parent. Each of these was a tall plant. The peas from this new union were cultivated. The result: three out of every four of the plants were tall; the fourth was dwarf. The pure dwarf plant *did* affect the offspring after all, but the trait didn't show up until the next generation. The baby might look more like its grandfather than its father!

Mendel figured out that when the *pure* tall and *pure* dwarf produce children, all the children are tall because the tall trait dominate the dwarf trait. The dwarf trait is not destroyed but is hidden. Mendel called this idea the "Law of Dominance." His experiments further showed that some of the children" of parent peas that were not "pure" themselves would become "pure." For instance the children of "pure" dwarf and "pure" tall are mixed or hybrid peas. But if two hybrid plants are crossed, half their children will be hybrids, the rest will be divided equally into pure talls and pure dwarfs. Mendel called this his "Law of Segregation."

Mendel, of course, did not learn all things possible about heredity, and scientists are still working on the problem. His laws, however, have already been of tremendous value to mankind. In Sweden, in the early 1900's wheat production threatened to fail completely. Some kinds of wheat grew wonderfully well, but were too delicate to withstand the cold Swedish climate. Other types, that did not freeze readily, did not grow except in small quantities. Nilsson-Ehle, a Swedish follower of Mendel's work, produced "pure" early-ripening and good-yielding strains of wheat which solved the problem of wheat production in cold countries.

The laws relating to inherited characteristics have also been found to be true of human beings and will be of help in controlling inherited tendencies to certain illnesses.

When Mendel died in 1884 no one realized that a giant of science had passed on.

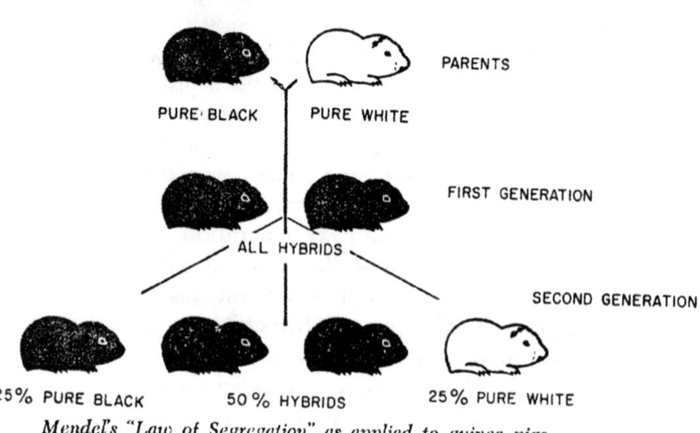


*Mendel's "Law of Segregation" as applied to guinea pigs.*

# JAMES CLERK MAXWELL

Take two thumb tacks and stick them, say, two inches apart, into a piece of paper. Join the pins by fastening a length of thread to them but leave plenty of slack as in the illustration. Now, with a pencil point, stretch the thread taut and draw a line on the paper keeping the string tight.

When he was fourteen, "Dafty" Maxwell invented this method of constructing a perfect ellipse. His father accompanied him to the meeting of the Royal Society of Edinburgh where this mathematical discovery was read by a university professor.

It is not for this ingenious method of drawing an ellipse, but for his scientific and mathematical formulations that we remember James Clerk Maxwell. His treatise *A Dynamical Theory of the Electromagnetic Field* appeared in 1865. This treatise proved to be the key that unlocked the door to radio, television, radar, and all devices that depend upon the generation and control of electromagnetic waves. Maxwell remains enthroned with Newton and with Einstein as a mathematical physicist without superior.

The truly brilliant Maxwell was born on November 13,

1831, in Edinburgh, Scotland. His family was well established and was known, not only for its many accomplished and successful members, but also for their eccentric personalities. James's father, trained for the law, did not care to practice but looked after his small estates and devoted himself to the education of his son. The boy's interest in mechanical devices was encouraged by his father. James early showed his own insatiable curiosity. He wanted to know why, and how, any mechanical contrivance worked. Like many boys of today he made mechanical devices and models. But then there were no hobby shops in which to buy the parts, he had to make his models from the ground up.

James's mother died when he was nine years old. His father, with the help of a maiden aunt, drew closer to the boy in an effort to make up for this great loss. At age ten, James was sent to the Edinburgh Academy, all dressed up in clothes his father had designed for him, even to the square-toed shoes. We may well imagine that Maxwell had a tough time of it. He was someone his schoolmates could pick on, and they did – until his brilliance won them over. Even so, they called him "Dafty."

When James was sixteen he entered the University of Edinburgh. He was already a brilliant mathematician and became absorbed in scientific experiments of all kinds. He liked to write poetry, which he did badly but enjoyed throughout his life.

In 1850 Maxwell left Scotland to study at the University of Cambridge. He was coached in mathematics by William Hopkins in preparation for a competition in which only the best math students competed. Hopkins is quoted as saying of Maxwell, "It appears impossible for him to think incorrectly on physical subjects." But Maxwell took only second place in the competition. Maxwell was promptly elected to the Apostles, a club consisting of the twelve outstanding students at Cambridge.

He must have been a nuisance to his dormitory companions, however. He had some original notions about sleep. He divided each 24 hours into two periods of sleep and wakefulness and he chose to exercise from two to two-thirty in the morning by running up and down the corridors.

Maxwell got his degree in 1854 but decided to stay on to study at Trinity College, Cambridge. His studies led to his invention of a color top to demonstrate that suitable combinations of the three primary colors, red, green, and blue – could produce practically every color imaginable. His scientific paper describing this investigation is the basis for the color in television; all the colors of this modern device are produced by combinations of red, green, and blue. His studies on color won the Rumford Medal of the Royal Society.

His father was ailing and James wished to return to Scotland to be close at hand. He obtained the chair of science at Marischal College in Aberdeen, but unhappily his father died a few days before he was to start this new position.

The average student did not benefit very greatly from Professor Maxwell's instructions; only the bright ones were able to follow his teaching. But Maxwell did profit from his position. He found his wife at Marischal College, the daughter of the head of the college. He wrote to his aunt, "She is not mathematical, but there are other things beside that, and she certainly won't interefer with mathematics." These few lines disclose the basic good humor and pleasantness of this great genius.

Maxwell had done some original and important work on a mathematical analysis of Saturn's rings and on the movements of gases. His mathematical analysis and his physical model of the movement and collisions of particles of gas have stood the test of time and are still in use despite the many changes that modern science has brought. But Maxwell's work in the theory of electricity and magnetism far overshadows his other work.

He was intrigued by Faraday's theory of electromagnetic induction, the production of electricity from magnetism. In his explanation, Faraday had used the term "lines of force" or "tubes of force" to describe the space around a magnet. Maxwell developed, in his mind, a model of the magnetic field. The model consisted essentially of rotating cylinders separated by small spheres like ball bearings. When one cylinder was turned the motion was transmitted through the spheres so that all cylinders would turn. From these models he was able to develop four basic ideas, which look very simple:

A magnetic line of force is a closed line, that is it forms a loop without end.

An electric line of force is also a closed line; it too forms a loop and returns on itself.

A changing magnetic field creates an electric field.

A changing electric field creates a magnetic field.

Faraday had established that a changing magnetic field would produce an electric current in a conductor, but Maxwell had deduced that a changing magnetic field could produce an electric effect in space, and a change in an electric field could produce a magnetic effect. Maxwell went further, his equations showed that it would take *time* for these electric and magnetic effects to travel. He showed they would travel with the speed of light and would travel together.

Ten years after Maxwell's death, Heinrich Hertz proved Maxwell's electromagnetic theory by setting up the first

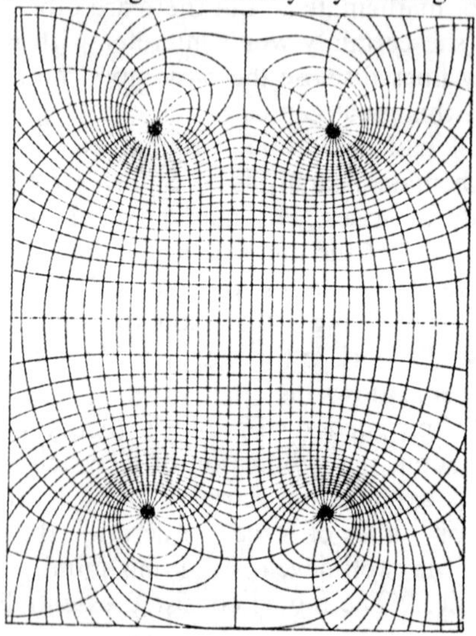

*Maxwell's lines of force.*

radio transmitter and receiver. Seventy-five years after Maxwell's death, electronic engineers and experimenters study Maxwell's equations as the key to the understanding of radar and microwaves. We know now that Maxwell showed that all electromagnetic waves follow the same basic laws, whether the waves are heat or light or radio or X rays or gamma rays.

For a time Maxwell retired to his estate at Glenair to finish his work on electromagnetic theory. He wrote text-books on heat, mathematics, color vision and physics. He was fond of his neighbors, played with their children, went to Cambridge occasionally to act as an examiner, and wrote poetry.

In 1871 pressure was brought to bear on the authorities at Cambridge to set up a chair in experimental physics, so that the new subjects of interest to the times – heat, electricity and magnetism – might be introduced at Cambridge. The Duke of Devonshire, Chancellor of the University and member of the family of Henry Cavendish, contributed the money for the building and furnishing of the Cavendish Laboratory. Maxwell was persuaded to accept the chair of experimental physics, which also entailed supervising the building and equipping of the new laboratory.

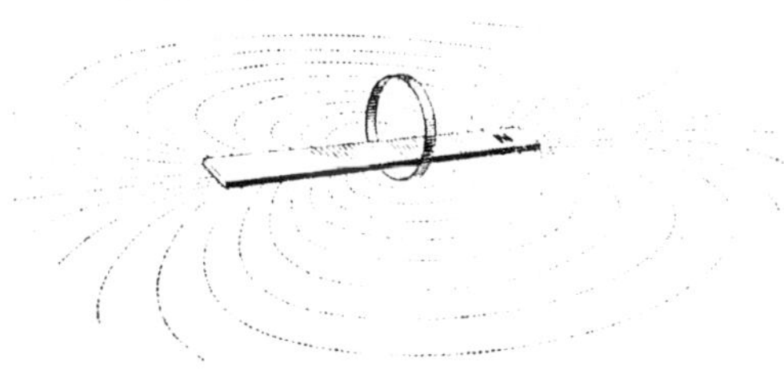

*Maxwell showed how electricity can produce magnetism. A current in the ring produces a magnetic field around the bar.*

Maxwell continued to write on various subjects. He also did a monumental job of editing the papers of Henry Cavendish, thus belatedly giving Cavendish credit for important work in electricity.

The last two years of Maxwell's life were devoted to caring for his invalid wife, although he too was ailing. Aware of the fatal nature of his illness, cancer, he did not consult doctors or tell his friends of his condition for some time. A patient, kindly, selfless man, his wit and humor were soon lost in suffering. He died on November 5, 1879, before he was forty-eight years old.

Mankind has still not exhausted all that his imagination and mathematics foresaw. Many still undiscovered inventions will owe much to the genius of James Clerk Maxwell. His equations had predicted the discovery of the radio spectrum, and X rays and gamma rays which led to an understanding of the atom.

## DIMITRI MENDELEEV

Have you ever tried to fit a jig-saw puzzle together? At first it looks hopeless – hundreds of different pieces, all shapes, all colors, all sizes. But as you study the piece, the puzzle begins almost to solve itself, and as the parts fall into the proper place the picture becomes clear. Before we start a jig-saw puzzle, we know that all the pieces will fit, and that when we finish we will have a complete picture.

By 1869 the world of chemistry had a large number of "jig-saw" pieces of formation. Sixty-three chemical elements had been discovered. Chemists had recognized similarities in the properties of the elements. For instance, sodium and potassium were soft, silvery metals; chlorine, bromine and iodine were colored corrosive materials. Unlike a jig-saw puzzle fan, the scientists couldn't be sure whether there was a complete system, or even what factors should be examined – and they knew they didn't even have all the pieces.

Nevertheless the problem was to take all the thousands upon thousands of pieces of chemical information and put them together so that there would be order and classification.

Many chemists had worked on this problem, but it fell to a Russian genius to succeed where others had failed. Dimitri Mendeleev arranged the chemical elements in the order of their atomic weights and the "Periodic Table of Elements" was presented to the world.

Dimitri Mendeleev is one of the revered scientists of the Soviet Union despite the fact that he lived during the Czarist regime. Mendeleev was born on February 1, 1834, in Tobolsk, eastern Siberia, a desolate spot. He was the seventeenth and youngest child of the director of the local high school. His family had been pioneers in Tobolsk. His grandfather had started the first printing press there in 1787 and followed it with the first newspaper in Siberia. His mother, a Tartar beauty, was also of a pioneer family. Her family had established the first glass factory in Siberia.

Soon after Dimitri's birth, his father went blind and had to give up his job. His mother reopened her family's abandoned glass factory to help support the family. Tobolsk was a center to which Russian political exiles were taken and one of Dimitri's sisters married a prisoner of the revolt of December, 1825. This exile, a man of learning, taught Dimitri natural science. Fire destroyed the glass factory and Dimitri's mother decided to move to Moscow so that her youngest son, an avid student, might attend the university there.

Dimitri was seventeen years old at the time and, knowing only the dialect of Siberia, failed to meet the entrance requirements. His determined mother moved to St. Petersburg where the boy learned Russian and was then admitted to the school intended for the training of high-school teachers. He specialized in mathematics, physics, and chemistry. Mendeleev had little patience for literature or for foreign languages. Nevertheless, he was graduated from the institute at the head of his class.

He was in poor health: he suffered from lung trouble, and his mother's death at this time completely unnerved him. Doctors gave him six months to live and he went south to the warm climate of the Crimea where he obtained a position as a science teacher. The Crimean War forced him back to Odessa, then to St. Petersburg. There, at the university he got a license as a *privat-docent,* which meant that he had permission to teach students and receive part of the fees they paid as his salary.

There was little opportunity for advanced science study in Russia, so Mendeleev obtained governmental permission to study in France and Germany. In Paris he worked with Henri Reynault, a chemical experimenter, and in Heidelberg he set up his own small laboratory. There he met and worked with Robert Bunsen, famous for the Bunsen burner, and Gustav Kirchhof. Together they were developing the spectroscope.

The spectroscope is an instrument for examining the makeup of a ray of light and is useful in chemical analysis. While studying in Germany, Mendeleev attended the Congress of Karlsruhe, where Stanislao Cannizarro made his historic appeal for the molecular theory of Avogadro. Cannizarro's table of atomic weights was later used by Mendeleev when he arranged his "Periodic Table of Elements."

Mendeleev returned to St. Petersburg, married, and wrote a textbook on organic chemistry in sixty days. He gained his doctorate in chemistry with a treatise on "The Union of Alcohol with Water." In 1865, when Mendeleev

*Mendeleev in his laboratory.*

was only thirty-one years old, he was given a full professorship at the University of St. Petersburg in recognition of his scientific genius and of his gift for teaching. His lecture room was always filled. A powerfully built man with piercing blue eyes and unkempt hair he presented a rather bizarre but interesting appearance.

In 1869, after years of collecting and studying chemical data, Mendeleev was ready to devise the table of elements. By that date, there were sixty-three known chemical elements. These elements had different physical properties; some were light metals, some heavy, some were liquid under normal conditions solid at other times, some were light gases, some heavy. Some were so active it was dangerous to handle them without protection, others remained unchanged for years.

Mendeleev knew that he was after some basic harmonious system that would help relate the elements to each other. He arranged the sixty-three elements in the order of increasing atomic weights, starting with hydrogen and ending with uranium.

Mendeleev discovered that by arranging his elements in seven groups according to physical and chemical properties a remarkable order prevailed. The same properties repeated themselves after each seven elements. The table could be used to make predictions about the chemical behavior of elements, simply by examining the position of the elements on the chart.

Mendeleev had solved the jig-saw puzzle, although he had only about two-thirds of the pieces! And now he was to use the Periodic Table to predict how additional elements would be found. He foretold the atomic weights and the chemical properties of several of the missing elements. These elements, silicon, gallium, germanium, scandium, were later discovered; and they had the properties Mendeleev had envisioned. The Periodic Table has since been revised. The elements are now listed in the order of atomic number. The atomic number is equal to the number of protons in the atom of the element. With a few exceptions the atomic number is in the same order as the atomic weight.

Dimitri Mendeleev, who had expected to live only six

months when he was twenty-one, died of pneumonia in 1907 at the age of seventy-three. By the time of his death there were eighty-six elements listed, most of them found because the jig-saw puzzle Mendeleev had devised showed there had to be missing pieces. The Periodic Table is complete. All ninety-two natural elements have been discovered. However, man has learned to create new elements by bombarding atoms. Element Number 101 is called mendelevium.

*Mendeleev's table of the elements.*

| PERIODS | GROUPS | | | | | | | | |
|---|---|---|---|---|---|---|---|---|---|
| | 0 | A 1 B | A 2 B | B 3 A | B 4 A | B 5 A | B 6 A | B 7 A | 8 |
| I | | HYDROGEN 1 | | | | | | | |
| II | HELIUM 2 | LITHIUM 3 | BERYLLIUM 4 | BORON 5 | CARBON 6 | NITROGEN 7 | OXYGEN 8 | FLUORINE 9 | |
| III | NEON 10 | SODIUM 11 | MAGNESIUM 12 | ALUMINUM 13 | SILICON 14 | PHOSPHORUS 15 | SULPHUR 16 | CHLORINE 17 | |
| IV SERIES 1 SERIES 2 | ARGON 18 | POTASSIUM 19 COPPER 29 | CALCIUM 20 ZINC 30 | SCANDIUM 21 GALLIUM 31 | TITANIUM 22 GERMANIUM 32 | VANADIUM 23 ARSENIC 33 | CHROMIUM 24 SELENIUM 34 | MANGANESE 25 BROMINE 35 | IRON 26 COBALT 28 NICKEL 27 |
| V SERIES 1 SERIES 2 | KRYPTON 36 | RUBIDIUM 37 SILVER 47 | STRONTIUM 38 CADMIUM 48 | YTTRIUM 39 INDIUM 49 | ZIRCONIUM 40 TIN 50 | COLUMBIUM 41 ANTIMONY 51 | MOLYBDENUM 42 TELLURIUM 52 | TECHNETIUM 43 IODINE 53 | RUTHENIUM 44 RHODIUM 46 PALLADIUM 45 |
| VI SERIES 1 SERIES 2 | XENON 54 | CESIUM 55 GOLD 79 | BARIUM 56 MERCURY 80 | LANTHANUM* 57–71 THALLIUM 81 | HAFNIUM 72 LEAD 82 | TANTALUM 73 BISMUTH 83 | TUNGSTEN 74 POLONIUM 84 | RHENIUM 75 ASTATINE 85 | OSMIUM 76 IRIDIUM 78 PLATINUM 77 |
| VII | RADON 86 | FRANCIUM 87 | RADIUM 88 | ACTINIUM 89–98 | | | | | |

* FOLLOWING LANTHANUM ARE 14 ELEMENTS KNOWN AS THE RARE EARTH METALS

## WILHELM KONRAD ROENTGEN

A far-reaching scientific, medical and technological revolution was started on a cold December evening in 1895. A fifty-year-old German professor of physics demonstrated his discovery at a quiet meeting of the Wurzburg Physical and Medical Society. Wilhelm Konrad Roentgen had learned how to make shadow pictures. As we may imagine, these were shadow pictures of a very special kind.

Wilhelm Roentgen was born on March 27, 1845, in Lennep, Prussia. His father was a German farmer, his mother was Dutch. He received his early education in Holland and attended the University of Zurich in Switzerland where he studied under the famous Professor Rudolf Clausius. Roentgen was interested in electricity, light, heat and elasticity.

He received a Doctor of Philosophy degree in Physics and went to Germany as an assistant at Wurzburg. He served on the faculty of a number of universities in Germany, at Strasbourg, Hohenheim and Gneissen, but returned to the University at Wurzburg in 1885 as Professor of Physics.

Sir William Crookes, an English scientist, was interested in following up some of Michael Faraday's work. Faraday had passed electricity through liquids, solids, gases – anything and everything he could find. He tried to pass electricity through an empty space, a vacuum. However, the vacuum pumps of his time were not very effective and there the matter rested.

Crookes, however, had more advanced equipment and was able to produce a fairly good vacuum. He also had an assistant who was a highly skilled glassblower and who made tubes containing various devices.

The tube which Crookes devised was essentially a glass container into which two electrodes were sealed and from which the air had been removed. A high voltage was connected to the electrodes, and a "ray" was created inside the tube. The ray originated at the negative end. A little paddlewheel placed in the tube turned when struck with the rays which showed the ray had substance; other objects cast shadows. The ray could be deflected by a magnet and by an electrically-charged plate. When the ray struck the glass a greenish glow appeared. This type of glow is called fluorescence.

By this time you may realize that Crookes had invented the grandfather of the television picture tube, but of course television was not to be invented for more than fifty years. Later on scientists realized that Crookes' "cathode ray" was really a stream of electrons. His tube was one of the devices that led to the discovery of the electron.

In his laboratories at the university, Professor Roentgen was experimenting with a Crookes type of tube. He had placed a black cardboard cover over the tube and had darkened the room. He then discharged the tube, that is, passed an electric current through it. A piece of paper which he had coated with a barium-platinum compound was seen to glow, to fluoresce. Here *was* a discovery. Here was a new kind of ray. This was not the cathode ray. A cathode ray cannot pass through glass. This new kind of unknown ray passed through glass and through paper. This ray could not be deflected with a magnet or with an electric field. In further experiments the rays passed through sheet aluminum, through tinfoil, through rubber, through most materials.

A packet of photographic film, wrapped carefully in black paper, was found to be exposed. These new rays could expose carefully concealed photographic plates. Roentgen called these unknown rays X rays, because he didn't really know what they were.

X rays occur when the electrons that leave the negative terminal, as in a Crookes' tube, strike the positive terminal. In an X-ray machine the positive end is called a target. The electrons inside the atoms of the target are forced out of position and then fall back into place. The electrons oscillate into and out of position very rapidly and in that way produce an electromagnetic wave of about 1,000,000,000,000 cycles per second.

Roentgen was delighted to find that his X rays – or Roentgen rays as they were named by his scientific colleagues – could penetrate flesh. He placed his hand on a photographic plate (wrapped in dark paper) and turned on his X-ray machine. When he developed the photo he found a shadow picture ("not without charm" he said) of the bones of his hand.

In 1896, in tribute to his momentous discovery, Roentgen received the Royal Society's Rumford Medal. In 1900, he was appointed professor of physics at the University of Munich, a post he held until three years before his death in 1923. The Nobel Prize in physics was awarded to him in 1901.

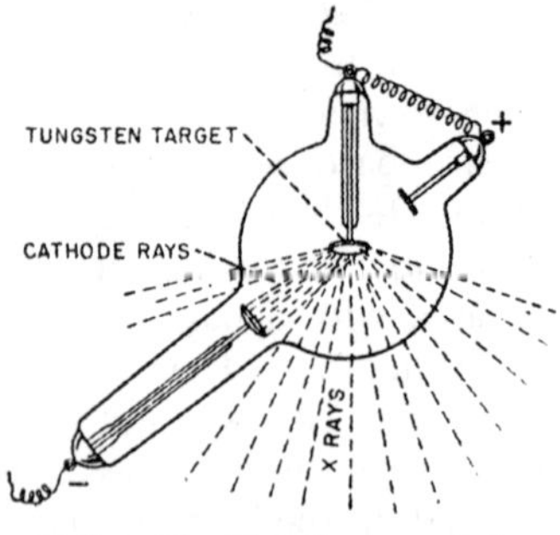

*An X-ray tube. When the stream of electrons hits the piece of metal called a target, X-rays are given off.*

Roentgen's was the first in a long series of discoveries in radioactivity – discoveries that include the work of Becquerel, the Curies, Rutherford, Planck, Thomson, Einstein, and Fermi. In his own lifetime Roentgen saw his rays used in medicine, in such conditions as fractures, tuberculosis and for surgical diagnosis of all kinds. Physicists used X rays to analyze the nature of crystalline structure. Industry uses X rays to examine the structure of metal parts which must operate efficiently in war and peace.

When the dentist places a small piece of paper-covered film in your mouth and turns on his X-ray machine, be thankful that Roentgen discovered these wonderful rays. He might be saving you from an awful toothache.

*Roentgen discovers X-rays.*

## IVAN PAVLOV

Bang! It was only a truck backfiring. Why did you jump? Actually you didn't think there was any danger; you didn't even think. There was no time to think; you just jumped. When there is a sudden loud noise our whole body jumps. When a speck of dirt approaches the eye, we blink. If a little bit of dust gets into one's nose, he sneezes. Suppose some food gets into the windpipe; we cough until the food is driven out.

All of these actions are called reflex actions, or reflexes. We don't have to learn how to do these things; a newborn baby responds in the same way that a grownup does. All of us are born with the ability to perform reflex actions – and fortunately, too, because these reflex actions enable us to stay alive.

Reflexes are actions without the need for thinking, but scientists have done a great deal of thinking about reflexes. Perhaps the greatest and best-known of the scientists in this field was the Russian genius, Ivan Pavlov. He was born on September 14, 1849, the son of the village priest in the small town of Ryazan in central Russia. His parents encouraged him to seek higher education and at the same time gave him the freedom to choose his own field of activity. He attended a religious seminary where he was fortunate to come under the influence of a teacher-priest who awakened Ivan's interest in science.

Pavlov went from the seminary to the School of Natural Sciences at St. Petersburg University. A book entitled *The Reflexes of the Brain,* which explored the connection between our physical actions and our psychological actions, finally decided Pavlov's choice of a career. He would study to be a doctor, so that he could be a professor of physiology. Pavlov completed his medical course in 1879, graduating from the Military Medical Academy. True to his early inspiration he devoted his time to physiological research, establishing a laboratory at a clinic in St. Petersburg.

The laboratory was primitive in the extreme. Pavlov had no regular assistants and had to pay for much of his material out of his own meager salary. But he worked steadily and purposefully and gained local recognition for his achievements. At the age of forty-one he was appointed Professor of Pharmacology at the Medical Academy and a year later was placed in charge of the newly established physiological laboratory at the St. Petersburg Institute of Experimental Method.

Pavlov's work on the function of the digestive system first brought him to international prominence; he was awarded the Nobel Prize in 1904. Pavlov showed the relation of the nervous system to the digestive system. He believed that all the functions of the body were controlled by the nervous system. It wasn't until some time later that scientists began to learn about the part that hormones play in the digestive process.

Pavlov had infinite patience, boundless enthusiasm and confidence. In his experiments on the digestive system – for which he used dogs – his objective was to disturb the normal functions of the dog as little as possible. To this end he devised an operation that would enable him to see what happened inside a dog's stomach. The first thirty tests on dogs failed, but he would not accept the idea that he could not succeed. The thirty-first trial succeeded, and Pavlov gave vent to his happiness, as usual, with an enthusisatically joyful dance.

His work on the digestive system brought Pavlov the Nobel Prize, but it was his work on "conditioned reflexes" that brought Pavlov world-wide popular fame. While he was working on the dog's digestive system, Pavlov became curious about the dog's reaction to food. He noticed that the dog's mouth watered not only when given food, but also even if he only saw the food. Scientists knew that the saliva in the dog's mouth was needed for digestion of the food (as indeed is the saliva in human mouths), and they believed that the saliva was produced as a purely physical or physiological result. But why did the dog's mouth water when shown the food?

Pavlov made the then revolutionary scientific guess that this result could be based on the dog's past experiences, that is, it could be psychological (in the mind), not merely physical.

Pavlov set about to test this idea with his famous experiment. He placed a dog in a small empty room. A bell was sounded and then food was placed before the dog; saliva began to flow. This was repeated many times. Soon the saliva began to flow whenever the bell was sounded – even if no food was brought! Pavlov had changed a reflex; he had conditioned the dog to respond to a bell as if it were responding to food.

In another interesting experiment, Pavlov accompanied the food with a circular light. An elliptical light would also be presented, but at such times the dog would not get food. Soon the dog learned when to expect food – when the circular light came into view. Gradually the ellipse was made more circular until the poor dog could not tell the difference between the circle and the ellipse and so could not tell whether he was going to be fed. This confusion drove the dog into such a nervous condition that he ran about in circles and howled. Fortunately for the dog (and for humans) Pavlov found he could decondition the dog and cure him of his nervous breakdown.

Modern psychologists have learned much from Pavlov's

experiments with dogs. They have transferred some of Pavlov's ideas to the training of humans. A child may be conditioned just as readily as a puppy. Let a parent show fear of a dog or lightning or the ocean, and a young child will acquire these fears. If the parent is obviously unafraid, the child, too, is likely to remain unafraid. In the same way a child will learn how to condition his parents. If throwing a tantrum gets the results the child desires – such as attention – he will continue to throw tantrums. However, Pavlov proved that it is almost as easy to recondition dogs as to condition them. This may hold too for human beings.

The Soviet government, under Lenin, gave Pavlov considerable financial support. Perhaps they saw his experiments as the means to train and control vast numbers of human beings.

Ivan Pavlov died in 1936 at the age of eighty-seven. When he rang the bells for the dogs, he got a response that set psychologists on the path to a new understanding of human behavior.

## ALBERT ABRAHAM MICHELSON

In 1869, the seventeen-year-old son of a German immigrant made a long, uncomfortable trip from Nevada to visit Ulysses S. Grant, the President of the United States. The visit was for the purpose of obtaining one of the ten presidential appointments to the United States Naval Academy at Annapolis.

Albert Abraham Michelson had been foremost in the qualifying examination set by his congressman for an appointment to the Academy but lost the prize to a boy who had superior influence. And now his visit to Grant was apparently too late; all presidential nominations had been made. But the President sent him to see the commandant of the Naval Academy. An "illegal" eleventh appointment was somehow made.

Albert Michelson repaid his adopted country well for its investment in his education. His fifty years of study of the problems of light brought him world-wide fame, brought prestige to the United States, advanced the study of science, and resulted in the first Nobel Prize award to an American.

Albert Michelson was born in Strelno, Prussia, on December 19, 1852, the son of German-Jewish parents. In 1848 the liberals of Germany – those who believed that laws and taxes should apply to all men equally and that freedom of speech should be guaranteed – thought that they had a chance to gain control of the government. Unfortunately they failed. In the next few years many such liberals emigrated to the United States. When Albert was two years old, the Michelson family arrived in New York City.

After a short stay in the East, the immigrants decided to join a relative who had gone to California in the Gold Rush of forty-nine. They took a ship to Panama, thence over the Isthmus to the Pacific and completed the voyage to the west coast by ship.

Albert's father, Samuel Michelson, opened a dry goods store in the Sierra Nevada mountain range in a town called Murphy's in Calaveras County, California. Albert was educated in the local school but was sent to San Francisco when he reached high-school age. He showed remarkable ability in mathematics and in science and was extremely talented mechanically. He received a three-dollar salary for taking care of the school's science instruments – three dollars a month.

When he was sixteen the family moved to Virginia City, Nevada, then a flourishing silver mining community. A year later his brother Charles was born and the following year his sister Miriam. Charles Michelson achieved considerable notice during the Franklin D. Roosevelt administration as the publicity director for the Democratic Party.

Michelson was graduated from the Naval Academy in 1873 and, after serving two years as an ensign in the United States Navy, was recalled to the Academy to teach physics and chemistry. While teaching at the Academy he became fascinated by the problem of measuring the velocity of light, a fascination that remained with him all his life. Using Foucault's rotating mirror technique, he built equipment at a cost of about ten dollars, plus some lenses he had available in the physics lecture room. This material enabled him to measure the speed of light, over a five-hundred-foot measured distance, with extreme accuracy. His first published paper "On a Method of Measuring the Velocity of Light" appeared in the American Journal of Science in 1878. The value he obtained was 186,508 miles per second.

Blowing soap bubbles is quite amusing. Children, and grownups too, derive considerable pleasure from watching the filmy elastic spheres float through the air, but what gives them the beautiful colors? The scientific explanation has to do with an idea called interference. The skin of the bubble, like anything else we can see that is not in itself a source of light, reflects light. The outside of the film reflects light and the inside of the film reflects light. The film is very thin and some light waves actually are reflected in such a way that these waves are wiped out. The waves of particular colors cancel themselves out when the bubble is of a thickness equal to half a wave length. When two waves meet head on, they are both knocked out. This is called wave interference or simply interference. Since white light has many colors in it, when some waves interfere, we are able to see the colors that are left. Sir Isaac Newton knew about colors in bubbles, but he was baffled by it, because he did not believe in the wave idea.

The wave lengths of light could be measured if we knew the thickness of the soap bubbles, but that is pretty difficult to measure. Michelson devised an instrument called the interferometer which used the principle of direct and reflected waves and was able to measure the wave length of light. A sketch of the instrument is shown and its operation is explained in the caption.

This instrument was devised by Michelson in 1887 and brought him world-wide acclaim. The instrument is mainly successful in measuring a single wave length of light at a time. For instance, if electricity passes through cadmium vapor – similar to the passage of electricity through a neon sign – it will produce a red light of a single frequency. Michelson measured the length of this light wave and found it to be .000064384696 centimeters long. This number is expressed by scientists as 6438.4696 angstrom units.

A submarine traveling under water is able to hear the

engines of another ship; the sound waves travel through the water. If a ringing bell is placed inside a glass container, we can hear the bell; the sound travels through the air to our ears. If the air is removed from the container, we can hear no sound; the sound vibrations will not travel through the empty space. But we can still see the bell; the light vibrations travel through the vacuum.

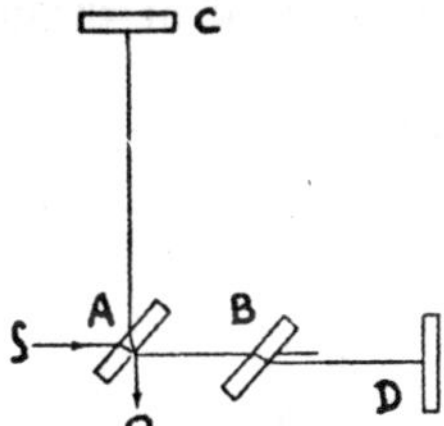


*A simplified diagram shows how Michelson's interferometer breaks a light beam into two beams, sends them in different directions, and brings them back to the same point. The waves from different directions interfere and produce an observable effect called a "fringe" from which wave lengths can be measured. Light from the source S strikes the coated back of glass plate A. Some light is reflected to the mirror C and back, while some goes through plate A to mirror D and back. Both reach the observer O together. The glass plate B is added so that the beam to and from D will go through glass three times, as does the beam to and from C.*

The problem that bothered scientists had to do with the possibility of waves traveling through nothing – from the sun to the earth, from the stars billions of miles away. But all waves that were known about travel through something. To overcome the problem of having light travel through nothing, it was decided to make up a material and give it a name. Scientists called it ether. For a long time scientists accepted the idea of ether, just as they had accepted the idea of phlogiston and caloric. While they talked about ether, scientists tried to find out if the ether really existed. The idea is simple: if the ether exists, then the earth must travel through it, just as an airplane travels through the air. There should be some kind of "ether wind" just as there is a wind along the body of the moving airplane.

Michelson devised an experiment to find out if there was an ether wind. He took a light source that gave him a single wave length and split it into two parts. He sent one wave north and the other west. These waves were reflected back and reunited. The race was even. The waves came back at the same instant. Michelson could tell because his interferometer showed that the two waves returned in the same time no matter which way they were headed, into the "ether wind" or at right angles to it. Perhaps the diagram will help explain just how the experiment works.

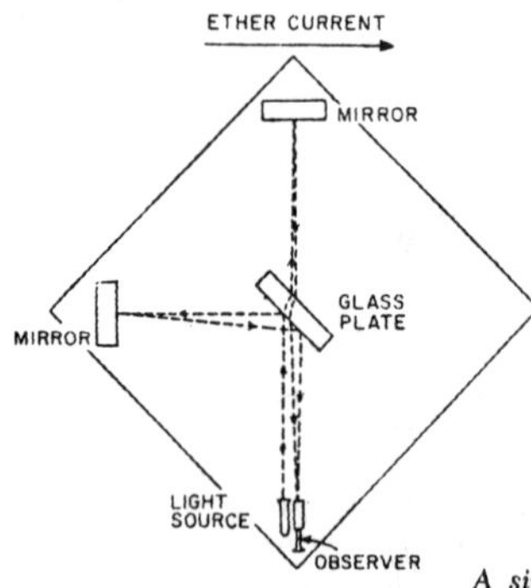


*A simplified diagram of the experiment by which Michelson disproved the existence of an "ether drift." The beam from the light source is broken into two beams in opposite directions and brought back to the observer.*

Michelson and his associate, E. W. Morley, made many observations, day and night, spring and fall, but could detect nothing. The experiment *failed to prove the existence of the ether.* It would seem that the experiment proved nothing, yet the result obtained by Michelson was the starting point for Einstein's theory of relativity.

Albert Michelson had conducted his ether wind experiments while he was Professor of Physics at the Case School of Applied Science in Cleveland. From Case, Michelson moved to Clark University and in 1892 he was appointed head of the Physics Department at the University of Chicago. He had only a few classes there and devoted himself to research.

His students found him a little forbidding. A dark-haired, dark-eyed man of military carriage, he expected a great deal of his graduate students but did not trust them to assist him in his research work. A single-minded perfectionist, he did not have the outward warmth of an Einstein or a Fleming. However, like them, he was interested in the arts. He was a good violinist and taught his own children (of whom he had six in two marriages) how to play. He was also an excellent painter. His own feeling was that "art found its highest expression in science."

Honors piled up on Michelson from all over the Western World. He had eleven honorary degrees, received the Rumford Medal of the Royal Society, the Grand Prize of Paris and of the Exposition of Rome. In 1892 he was made a member of the International Bureau of Weights and Measures of Paris.

He used his interferometer to define the standard meter in terms of the wave length of cadmium vapor light. Up to then the standard meter was defined as the distance between two scratches on a piece of precious metal kept in a vault in Paris. In 1907, Michelson became the first American scientist to receive the Nobel Prize for Physics.

In 1926, Michelson conducted his most famous experiment to determine the velocity of light. His measurement was again based on the rotating mirror principle of Foucault. A laboratory was built atop Mount Wilson in California. A mirror was set up on Mount San Antonio, twenty-two miles away. The distance between the two points was measured by the United States Coast and Geodetic Survey with astounding accuracy; the measurement is within two inches of being absolutely correct. The light waves started at Mount Wilson were converted into pulses by means of the rotating mirror and were directed at the mirror at Mount San Antonio. Those pulses were reflected by the receiving mirror to the observer, but only if the revolving mirror had time to reach the precise next position. The speed of the mirror told the tale. The time for the light to travel round trip to the San Antonio mirror was exactly equal to the time it took for the rotating mirror to make one sixth of a revolution.

Michelson was ill during these experiments but persisted

with his work until the end. He died of a cerebral hemorrhage on May 9, 1931, aged seventy-nine.

His last paper bears the same title as his first published work, "On a Method of Measuring the Velocity of Light."

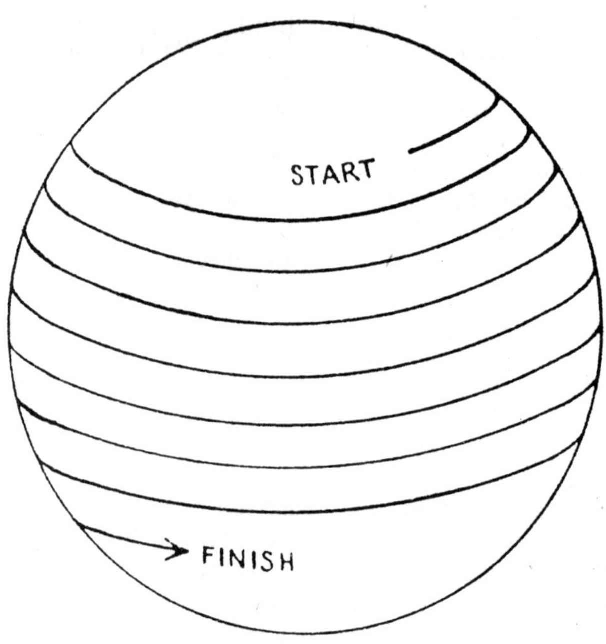


*If light could travel in a circle it would go 7½ times around the earth in one second.*

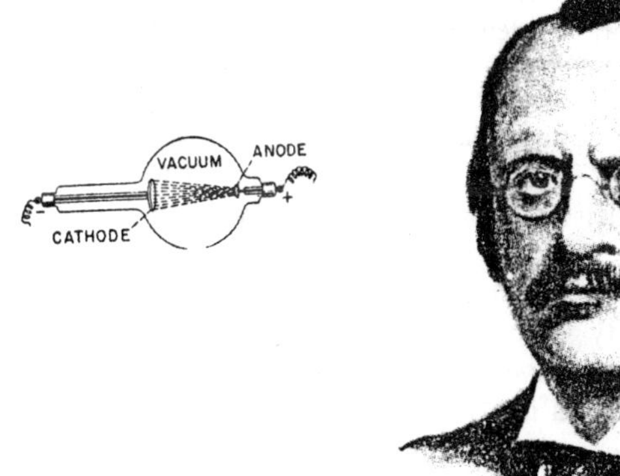


# JOSEPH JOHN THOMSON

One measure of a man's excellence is the receipt of the Nobel Prize. Joseph John Thomson received this award in 1906, but even if he had not been a great scientist in his own right, he would deserve an award as an outstanding teacher. He provided inspiration and leadership to countless scientists the world over. No less than eight of his students became Nobel Prize winners.

J. J. Thomson was born on December 18, 1856, near Manchester, in England. His father dealt in rare and antique books, a business that had been a family tradition. There was some little science background in the family – an uncle had been interested in weather study and in botany but there was no particular family drive in this direction.

Joseph was an avid reader and a good student and the family felt that engineering would be an appropriate profession. He was sent to Owens College, now the Victoria University of Manchester, at the age of fourteen. When his father died two years later, friends made it possible for "J. J." to remain at college. A scholarship fund in honor of John Dalton was fortunately available and helped keep Joseph in school.

Thomson completed his engineering course when he was nineteen, and went direct to Trinity College at Cambridge University where he had obtained a scholarship. The big thing for the science and mathematics students at Cambridge was the competitive examination known as the Mathematical Tripos. Thomson acquitted himself well. He came in second, just as James Maxwell had done some years before.

And as James Maxwell had done, Thomson turned his mathematical ability to a study of theoretical physics. Thomson was not an expert experimenter; he was clumsy with his hands and had nearly blinded himself some years earlier in the chemistry laboratories. He appreciated, however, that theoretical physics has no meaning unless there is experimental confirmation.

In 1881 Thomson wrote a scientific paper that was the forerunner of the Einstein Theory. In it he showed that mass and energy are equivalent. He was then only twenty-four.

Upon receiving his degree, Thomson was awarded a fellowship to Trinity College and turned to research at the Cavendish Laboratories. In 1884 the head of the laboratory, Lord Rayleigh, decided to resign. He named as his successor the twenty-eight-year-old Thomson. This appointment created quite an uproar; no one doubted Thomson's abilities, but his youth was held to be too great a handicap. Lord Rayleigh's choice was a wise one. Thomson held the position of Cavendish professor for thirty-four years, and guided the laboratories into the position of being the foremost scientific institution in the world.

Thomson not only found his life work at the Cavendish labs but found his life partner as well. He did not quite believe that women were able to handle science. He once wrote about the first young lady who attended his advanced lectures, "I am afraid she does not understand a word and my theory is that she is attending my lectures on the supposition that they are on Divinity and she has not yet found out her mistake." In 1890, however, he married

Miss Rose Paget who had been attending his advanced lectures. A son George Paget Thomson was born in 1892.

In 1897, J. J. Thomson became the "father of the electron." He discovered this tiny particle and thus established the theory of the electrical nature of matter. The makeup of the cathode ray was a matter of interest then. This is the "ray" that Crookes had discovered when he passed a high voltage discharge through a glass tube from which the air had been removed. The Crookes tube is the same that Roentgen had used when he discovered the X ray.

There were two theories in existence, both of which had strong supporters. Thomson believed that the cathode rays were electrified particles. The opposite view held that the cathode rays and the electrified particles were different. Although the cathode rays produced a glow when they struck the glass, the electrons, of course, couldn't be seen.

Thomson used a device similar to that shown in the diagram. The cathode rays originate at the cathode, marked K. They pass through a narrow slit connected to A and so form a narrow area of phosphorescence in the glass tube. He took a magnet and brought it near the tube; the phosphorescent spot moved, proving the rays were bent. The magnet was manipulated so that the rays were bent and aimed at the slot on the shield. When they poured through the slot an electroscope connected to the receiver electrode showed a marked deflection. This showed, said Thomson, that the cathode ray is really negative electricity.

The opposition was not satisfied. True, they said, the cathode rays could be deflected by a magnet, but they had not been deflected by an electrostatic field. An electrostatic field is the same kind of field that causes a hard rubber rod (such as a comb or fountain pen barrel of hard rubber) to attract bits of paper when it is rubbed against a piece of woolen cloth. Heinrich Hertz had tried but failed to deflect the ray electrostatically. There was one possible answer – perhaps the vacuum was not great enough; maybe there was enough gas left in the tube to permit a current flow between these flat plates. That would spoil the electrostatic field. Exhaust the tube still more and try again.

This time the cathode ray was deflected. Thomson had

showed that cathode ray is deflected by means of a magnetic field and that it is deflected by means of an electric field. There could be only one meaning: the cathode ray is not a ray at all but is a stream of electrically charged particles.

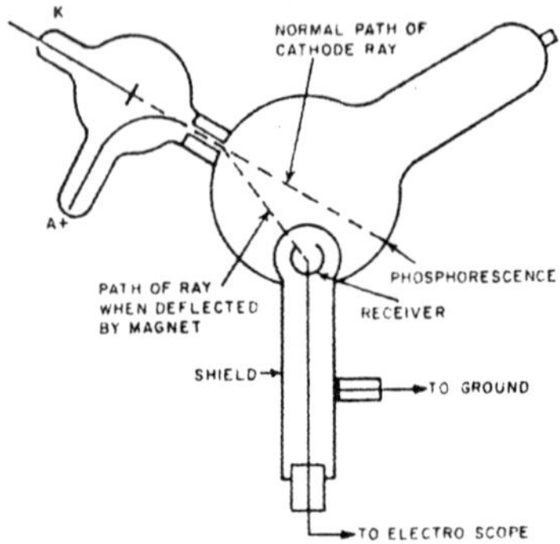


*Diagram of how Thomson showed that cathode rays act like electric particles.*

Thomson went on to measure the relative mass of the negatively charged particle, which we now call the electron. He found it to be approximately $\frac{2000}{1}$ the mass of the hydrogen atom. At the same time he calculated the velocity of the electron and found it to be about 160,000 miles per second.

Of course we are familiar with electrons these days, much of the pioneer theoretical work that J. J. Thomson had done is represented in that wonderful electronic toy, the television set. In fact the picture tube is a cathode ray tube in which the electric particles are deflected rapidly to produce a picture. The deflection is done exactly as Thomson did it, with electrostatic fields and with the magnetic fields.

But in 1897 there was some reluctance to accept the idea of these particles, so Thomson suggested that they photograph them. How? How can we photograph a particle that is the two-thousandth part of a hydrogen atom and is moving at a speed of 160,000 miles per second?

This was the problem that Professor Thomson proposed to student Charles T. R. Wilson. Wilson had done some research into the causes of fog. It is well known that warm air can hold more moisture than cold air. If moisture laden warm air is cooled suddenly, there is a formation of tiny drops of water. But inside each drop of water there is a dust particle. If there is no dust present then the water will not condense and there will be no fog.

Wilson applied this idea to tracking the elusive particle of Thomson's. He built a device in which he could readily produce moisture and in which he could readily produce atomic particles. He worked on it for many years and finally perfected his cloud chamber in 1911. When the atomic particles are shot through the chamber, millions of air molecules are ionized and water vapor collects on these ions. (An ion is an atom or molecule that has lost one or more of its electrons.) These cloud chamber trails, like the vapor trails of a jet airplane, can be photographed and the particle identified by the tracks it makes. The Wilson cloud chamber is still used for the identification of the various atomic particles. Wilson received the Nobel Prize some sixteen years later for this contribution.

The job was complete; the negative particle that Thomson discovered had been weighed, had its speed measured, and, in a sense, had its picture taken. By this time it had been named the electron. Upon it is based the whole science of electronics.

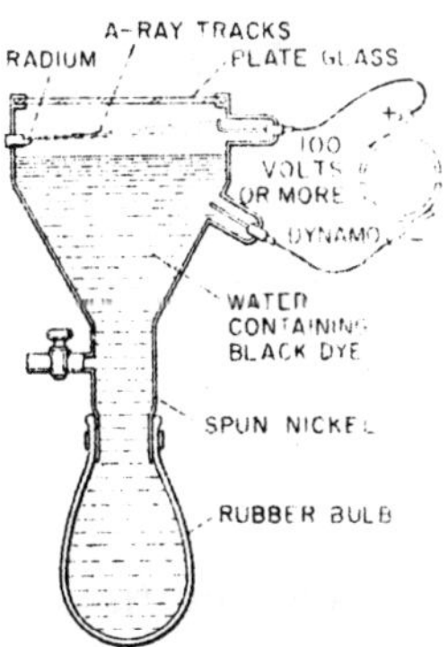


*The Wilson cloud chamber*

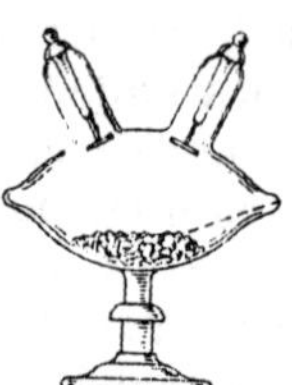

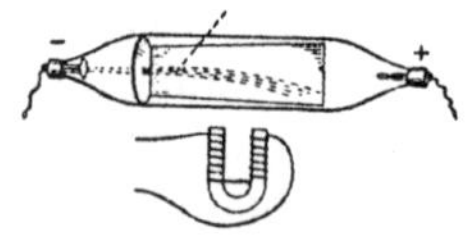

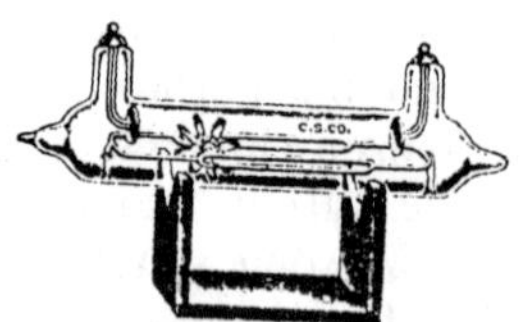


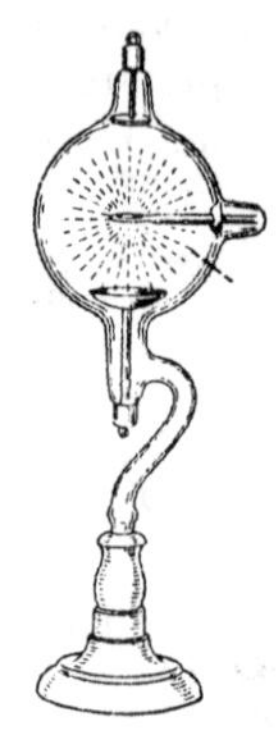

*Cathode ray tubes.*

At the close of World War I, Sir J. J. Thomson retired from the Cavendish laboratories to head Trinity College. Ernest Rutherford, Thomson's former student and a Nobel Prize winner for investigations into the chemistry of radioactive substances, was recommended for the position as head of the laboratories. To this satisfaction of Thomson's was added the happiness of seeing the 1937 Nobel Prize in Physics awarded to son George Paget Thomson for his work on the diffraction of electrons by crystals.

J. J. Thomson died in 1940 at the age of eighty-four. He was a genius whose theory of the electrical nature of all matter destroyed the idea of the immutability of the atom. He was a great human being whose interest in people inspired them to heroic efforts. He was a great teacher and left a legacy of textbooks in physics, mathematics and chemistry.

HEINRICH HERTZ

Radar operates much like a searchlight, except that the searchlight sends out a beam of light energy, and radar uses high-frequency radio energy. When the light from a searchlight strikes an object, some of the energy is reflected back to the observer who sees the object. In the same way, when a radar beam strikes an object, some of the beam is reflected back to the radar receiver which "sees" the object.

Radar is used to detect the approach of an aircraft; it is used to follow the movements of storms; it is used in navigation, both on water and in the air to assist in piloting ships or planes. Radar altimeters measure the true distance to the earth without depending on barometric pressure or a knowledge of the mountain heights over which a plane may be flying.

During World War II radar did much to offset the advantage of enemy aircraft by locating their movements in time to allow defending planes to move into battle.

Radar was a jealously guarded discovery in 1940, but in 1888, about fifty years before, Heinrich Hertz had investigated the theoretical basis for this World War II secret. Not only that, but long before there was an indication of its need or practical use, Hertz had designed and built the kind of antenna used for television transmission and reception, the Hertz dipole.

Heinrich Hertz was born in Germany, at the North Sea seaport of Hamburg on February 22, 1857. The Hertz family was influential and well-to-do. Heinrich set out to study architecture and engineering but soon discovered that he was interested in pure science and research. Hermann Von Helmholtz was currently the professor at the University of Berlin, and it was there that Hertz went to study. Helmholtz was an extraordinarily versatile genius; he held professorships in physiology, anatomy, physics and mathematics. His discoveries included the measurement of the velocity of a nerve impulse; the analysis of beats and wave motion in sound; a theory of musical harmony, based on his physical discoveries; a statement of the law of conservation of energy; a theory of color vision; and the invention of the opthalmoscope, an instrument still used by physicians for the examination of eye defects.

Hertz gained much from his association with this master scientist and Helmholtz realized that he had a rare and unusual student. Upon his graduation in 1880, Hertz became an assistant in physics to Helmholtz.

In 1883, Hertz went to Kiel as an instructor and began his studies of Maxwell's electromagnetic theory. This cornerstone of modern theory had been published in 1865. Hertz was to find his life work and everlasting fame as a result. He set out to find experimental proof of Maxwell's mathematical prophecy, that there were "waves of electric or magnetic force capable of being propagated in the manner of light waves." In performing the epoch-making experiments, Heinrich Hertz, by then professor of physics in Karlsruhe Polytechnic, built a radio transmitter and a radio receiver, the first such units ever constructed. He laid the foundation for all the radio, television and radar that we now have at our service.

One of the first things he set for himself to accomplish was to prove that electric waves and magnetic waves – or more simply electromagnetic waves – take time to travel, as indeed they do. But how to measure this time? We now know that the waves travel at the speed of 300,000,000 meters per second. Experimenters had tried to measure the time between the transmission of a wave and its reception, but if the room in which they worked was as much as 10 meters (about 33 feet) long it would take only one three hundred millionth part of a second for the wave to travel from one end to the other. This is such an incredibly short time that the mind staggers at the idea that it can be measured.

Heinrich Hertz throught that he might be able to use the discharge of the Leyden jar as a timer. The rapid discharge of electricity from the Leyden jar actually involves the shifting of the charge back and forth, the way a pendulum swings, gradually coming to rest. And each period for a single oscillation of electric charge, like the period or time of a single oscillation of a pendulum, is the same. "Why not use the single oscillation of the Leyden jar as a timing device?" thought Hertz. But even this took too long, the time was a whole millionth of a second. This is long enough for the wave to travel 1,000 feet, and Hertz couldn't send waves out that far. He had no amplifying tubes to help him produce a strong signal.

Hertz discovered that a spark could be obtained from the discharge of any kind of a conductor; a Leyden jar was not needed. The discharge of a conductor gives rise to oscillations of between a hundred million and a thousand million cycles per second – modern electronics would say between a hundred megacycles per second and a kilomegacycle per second. The time for a single oscillation is thus between one-one hundredth of a microsecond and one-one thousandth of a microsecond. A microsecond is a millionth of a second. Hertz was experimenting in the realms of the high frequencies used in modern radar and microwave communication.

Hertz devised an indicator so that he could receive the signals. "This can be done," he explained, "by very simple means. At the spot where we wish to detect the force, we place a straight wire which is interrupted in the middle by a small spark gap. The rapidly alternating force sets the electricity of the conductor in motion and produces a spark at the gap." The spark gap of Hertz's "receiver" was ridiculously small, scarcely the thickness of the paper in this book. Remarkably enough, Hertz was able to detect the spark. The room had to be perfectly dark and the eyes of the observer had to become accustomed to the dark.

Hertz had shown that he could send and receive waves, but how did he prove that waves take time to travel. For this he turned to the knowledge of the theory of sound and the studies of Helmholtz. According to the theory of wave interference, two waves reaching a spot from the same source but by means of different paths will either add to each other or will tend to cancel out. As the receiver is moved along from spot to spot, positions of silence follow positions of reception. The distance between silent spots is the length of half a wave.

So Hertz set up his microwave transmitter and receiver and side reflector and gradually moved his receiver away – sure enough he had a succession of regions where he could not receive a signal. He had found the wave length. He knew the frequency of the oscillations and now had all the needed data. The frequency multiplied by the wave length revealed the speed. And the speed of electromagnetic waves was found to be the same as the speed of light: 300,000,000 meters per second.

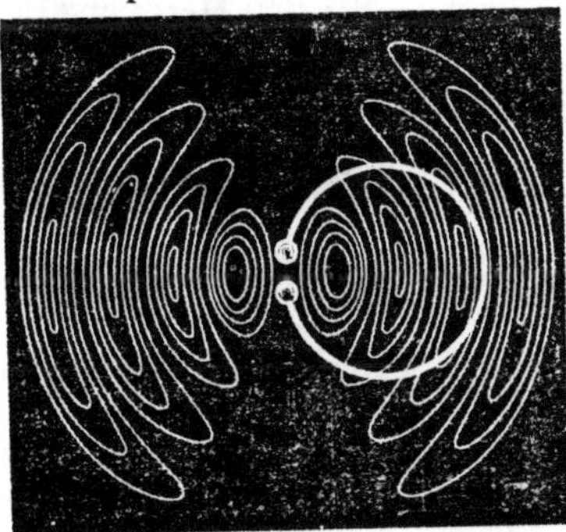

*Electromagnetic waves. Hertz discovered that this pattern of waves was produced around an electric spark. The spark is produced in the gap in the ring-shaped object, called a resonator.*

Heinrich Hertz wasn't finished with the experiments. He had to find out more about the behavior of these waves. He armed his transmitter and receiver with reflectors, large concave "mirrors" and discovered that he could focus his electromagnetic rays in the same way as light waves could be concentrated. He set up reflectors on the side, bounced the waves off these reflectors, found he could focus the waves with "lenses." He discovered that the waves were "polarized." (Notice that your television antenna has its arms in a horizontal position; it won't work so well if the arms are vertical.) The waves did everything that light waves do. He had proved a good deal of Maxwell's theory.

Hertz had performed experiments of incalculable ingenuity and importance. His own statement of his discoveries was: "They mark a brilliant victory for Maxwell's theory." This was an enormous underassessment of his own accomplishments.

In 1889, following the discussion of his experiments and findings at the meeting of the German Association for the Advancement of Natural Science at Heidelberg, he was appointed Professor of Physics at Bonn University. He was but thirty-two years old.

His name was to be immortalized by the term "hertz" to designate "cycle per second" but the designation never became popular, although it is used in Germany. However, every time you see a television antenna with its arms horizontal you may remember that Hertz first devised it. Every time you see a "ghost" on the TV screen, you know it is a result of a reflected wave reaching the screen a little late; and you can recall that Hertz was the first man to prove that it takes time for an electromagnetic wave to travel.

Hertz died in 1894; he was only thirty-seven. What further progress he might have made can only be supposed. His place in the history of science is secure. He gave us radio.

## MAX PLANCK

You have undoubtedly seen doors that open as if by magic. Look closely and you may see a light beam stretched across the doorway. When the light beam is interrupted a motor opens the door. This is but one use for the electric eye. The electric eye – and the television camera too – makes use of a very interesting and very important principle: the principle of photoelectricity. When light strikes a piece of metal, electrons are released. Electricity is thereby produced by light; hence it is called photoelectricity.

Photoelectricity was destined to turn the scientific world into a turmoil and to reopen a controversy that had apparently been settled by Maxwell and by Hertz. Light, these scientists proved, consisted of electromagnetic waves. Light followed all the laws that governed waves and so light must be waves. In 1889 Heinrich Hertz declared "The wave theory of light is, from the point of view of human beings, a certainty." This was a well known fact – or was it really a fact?

Only eleven years later, Max Planck proposed the idea that light consists of bits of energy. Newton, two hundred years before, had said that light consisted of minute particles. Science had apparently buried this theory. Now Professor Planck had made some calculations that convinced him that energy really came in pieces; they were very little pieces, but still they were distinct pieces. Modern science has a name for these pieces of light energy: they are called photons. Planck called the pieces of energy "quanta," and single-handedly founded the quantum theory, a theory of vast importance in modern physics.

Max Planck was born of German parents in the then Danish seaport of Kiel on the Baltic Sea on April 23, 1858. He died in Germany in 1947, his final years filled with personal bitterness and agony. Planck's father was a university professor, a specialist in jurisprudence. Max Planck came from a distinguished, educated family which numbered many judges, public officials, scientists and theologians among its members. When Max was nine, the family moved to Munich so that Professor Planck could assume a post in the university. At Munich, Max attended the Maxmillian Gymnasium, a high school, where he had the good fortune to come under the influence of a thoughtful and devoted physics teacher. This association set him on his life work as a physicist. His family also encouraged him to study music and he was a competent pianist, playing for pleasure and relaxation throughout his long life.

He attended the Universities of Munich and Berlin where he studied under the great physicists Hermann Helmholtz and Gustav Kirchhof. Planck received his doctorate for his thesis on an experiment in the diffusion of hydrogen through palladium. It is said that this was the only experiment he ever performed. He was a mathematical rather than an experimental scientist.

His brilliance was recognized quickly, and in rapid succession he became an assistant professor at Munich, and then a professor of physics at Kiel University. In 1889, at the young age of thirty-one, Planck was appointed to the chair of physics at the University of Berlin.

Planck was a specialist in the theory of thermodynamics, which is the science of heat. Light and heat are related to each other, as you can tell if you touch an electric light bulb. As a matter of fact, the color of light is a basis for measuring temperatures that are too high for usual thermometer measurements. The color inside a furnace is compared with a known standard and the temperature is deduced from this information. The device used is called an optical pyrometer. The closer to white light, the higher the temperature. At low temperatures the radiation consists of the invisible infra-red rays; at about 1,000 degrees Fahrenheit the red becomes visible. At 2,500° F. there will be a nice bright light. The temperature of an electric light filament is about 5,000° F. You can see that light and heat are related and that they are both forms of energy. So Planck extended his study of thermodynamics into a study of light.

While engaged in the study of the radiation of light, Planck ran head on into a theoretical difficulty. When he tried to calculate what happens on the basis of the known theories, he found that even a little bit of heat should produce a very bright light. Since everything has some heat, the calculations proved that we should all be white hot. Since there was nothing wrong with his calculations, there must be something wrong with the known theory. Planck had the courage to say so.

He also had the brilliance to figure out a new theory. That was when he thought of the quantum, or package of energy. The packages of energy, said Planck, come in different sizes to suit the occasion. A big package is needed to increase the energy level of the high frequencies of light, but only a small package is needed to increase the energy level of the low frequencies. Planck reported this quantum idea to the German Academy of Science. And if you have trouble figuring out what the theory is about, do not feel too bad; the scientists who listened to him in December 1900 weren't too sure either. Besides, this quantum theory re-established the corpuscular theory of light, and scientists weren't yet ready for that; the wave theory still worked in most cases they knew of.

Einstein, working on his relativity theory in Switzerland, saw that the quantum effect could explain some of the mysteries of photoelectricity. When these quanta of light struck a piece of metal, electrons were bounced out of the metal. If more light struck the metal, more electrons were bounced out. If the wave theory were correct then an increase in light should increase the speed of the electrons but not the number.

Slowly the scientific world began to take note of the idea of "packages of energy" – of Planck's quantum theory. Eighteen years after his discovery, he received the recognition of the world in general with the award of the Nobel Prize.

In 1913 Einstein, who had done much to advance Planck's quantum theory, came to Berlin. The two men became fast friends. They shared interests in mathematical physics and music. Berlin, with Planck and Einstein, was the undisputed world center of physics study.

After the death of his first wife in 1909, Planck remarried and added three children to his first four. Sadly, none of the seven children survived him. His eldest son Karl was killed in 1916 during World War I. His twin daughters died in childbirth within a year of each other.

The Nazi regime in Germany forced his friends Einstein and Erwin Schrodinger to leave Germany. Planck himself was one of Hitler's defeats. Time and again he refused to sign a loyalty oath to the Nazi Party. The proud, stubborn Prussian could not accept the barbarities of the Goebbels and Hitlers. In 1944 the Nazis came to this eighty-six-year-old man, this time with a hostage. Sign a loyalty pledge, they said, and we will release your son who is guilty of conspiring against Hitler. Again he refused, and his last surviving child, Erwin Planck, was executed. After this blow, it probably mattered not too greatly that his home and library were destroyed in the bombings of Germany.

Postwar Germany planned a mammoth celebration on the occasion of Max Planck's 90th birthday, but this was not to be. Planck died on October 4, 1947, a few months before he was to become ninety years old. In tribute, the Kaiser Wilhelm Academy of Science was renamed the Max Planck Academy. The foremost scientific award in Germany became the Max Planck medal.

What did Planck contribute to science? The famous Dutch scientist, Hendrik A. Lorentz, said, "We have now advanced so far that Planck's constant not only furnishes the basis for explaining the intensity of radiation and the wave length for which it represents a maximum, but also for interpreting the qualitative relations existing . . . in specific heat of solids, the photochemical effects of light, the orbits of electrons in the atom, the wave lengths of the lines of the spectrum, the frequency of Roentgen rays which are produced by the impact of electrons of given velocity, the velocity with which gas molecules can rotate and also the distances between the particles which make up a crystal."

In short Planck's theory is at the base of all modern atomic particle physics.

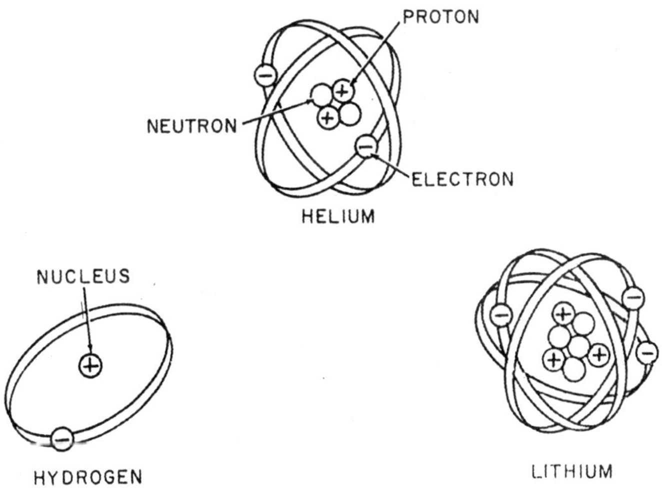


*Diagrams of the three simplest atoms. The number of protons in the nucleus equals the number of electrons moving around the nucleus. The neutrons add to the atomic weight, but have no electrical charge.*

## MARIE CURIE

"I mean to say farewell to this contemptible world. The loss will be small . . ." a lovesick seventeen-year-old wrote to her cousin. But, fortunately for science, the pretty young lady forgot her unhappy love affair and became one of the foremost scientists of all time.

Manya Sklodowska was born on November 7, 1867, in Warsaw, Poland. Her mother and father came from the Polish peasant class but had left the farm for educational pursuits. Her father was a physics and mathematics teacher at the Warsaw High School, and her mother was an accomplished pianist. Sadness came early to Manya: When she was ten years old, her mother died, a victim of consumption.

Poland was, in those days, a part of Czarist Russia. The government at Petrograd imposed restrictions on the Poles in retaliation for their attempts at revolt. Manya's father lost his job at the school because he was outspoken in advocating independence for Poland. In order to support his four remaining children (one had died of typhus) he opened a boarding school. This venture was not a great success, but somehow the family was maintained.

In 1883 Manya won the gold medal upon completion of her high school course. This was an old habit of the Sklodowskas; hers was the third gold medal in the family. Professor Sklodowska, financially unsuccessful, found happiness and satisfaction in the superior mentality of all his children. After her high school graduation Manya was sent to the country for a year. The fear of consumption was uppermost in her father's mind. Her vacation might well have been good physical training for her future work. The Polish country dances took stamina. They started at sunset, continued all night, the following day, and again through the night – and Manya liked to dance.

Her vacation over, she returned to Warsaw. Plans for her future were discussed, but how could she go to the Sorbonne at Paris without funds? Long discussion with older sister Bronya resulted in a plan. Manya would get a job and help Bronya through the University. Bronya then would support Manya while she studied. And so to work.

Manya got a job as a governess and teacher in the home of a Russian nobleman. This did not last long because her mistress was intolerant and vulgar. Fortunately Manya found another position in a more intelligent atmosphere. The eldest son of the family was a student at the University of Warsaw. When he came home on vacation, he quickly fell in love with the pretty governess who danced like a sprite and spoke like a scholar. The lonely Manya returned his love. Marriage was blocked by his mother, who would not permit her son to marry a governess. It was then that Manya wrote the note at the beginning of this story.

Manya continued to teach and to send money to her sister Bronya at the Sorbonne. At last it was Manya's turn; her older sister had not only gained a medical degree at Paris but had married a fellow medical student.

When she was twenty-three, her long awaited dream was to begin. Marie – she had taken the French spelling – registered at the Sorbonne at the Faculty of Science. For four years she worked and studied. Rightfully, she should have fallen prey to all manner of illnesses. She lived in an attic apartment with virtually no heat; her budget for food was so meager that her meals were mainly bread, butter, and tea. For one twenty-four hour period she lived on cherries and radishes. Meat and eggs rarely, if ever, entered her diet.

But she survived and she studied mathematics and poetry, chemistry and music, physics and astronomy. In between, she washed bottles in the chemistry laboratory. At graduation she ranked first in the examination for the Master's degree in Physics and the next year she ranked second in the examination for the Master's degree in Mathematics. Marie was now twenty-seven and her first unhappy experience in love had remained with her. Pretty, blonde, lithe of figure, she had nevertheless kept to herself.

At twenty-two, Pierre Curie had written, "Women of genius are rare, and the average woman is a positive hindrance to a serious-minded scientist." Pierre was now thirty-five, and contact with life had strengthened rather than weakened this attitude. He was engaged in electrical and magnetic research. He worked with his brother Jacques in the laboratory of Professor Paul Schutzenberger. Pierre Curie had become a Bachelor of Science at age sixteen and a Master of Physics two years later. He was already a leader in science, having discovered the principle of piezo-electricity. Piezo-electricity is involved in the crystal pickup of your record player. When a crystal is "squeezed" it produces a little bit of electricity.

Pierre and Marie first met in the home of Professor Kovalski, a Polish physicist who was visiting Paris. The conversation was of science and Pierre asked to see Marie again. To talk only of science? Marie obtained permission to work in Professor Schutzenberger's laboratory – next to Pierre. Manya Sklodowska became Marie Curie a year later.

Pierre had written, "Women of genius are rare." He found the rare woman; his wife *was* a genius. Marie happily continued to work in the laboratory next to her husband on problems in magnetism and electricity.

In Germany Wilhelm Roentgen had discovered a ray of great penetrating power. In January, 1896, he had described these rays to the world of science. He called them

X-rays and showed that they would penetrate solid objects. In France, Professor Henri Becquerel was working on the problem of phosphorescence – the way that certain substances shine in the dark after having been exposed to sunlight. His experiments led him to believe that pitchblende, the uranium ore, contained some element in addition to uranium.

Professor Becquerel had long been impressed with the experimental skill of Marie Curie. It was to her he brought the problem. Marie and Pierre discussed the matter. The substance they were looking for could not be one of the known elements; it must be something new. The Curies stopped all other work; this was more intriguing.

Pitchblende was an expensive ore and not available except in Austria. How to get some without money? They reasoned that if the pitchblende contained this unknown substance, it must still be in the ore even after the uranium was taken out. The Austrian Government was willing to send them the residue of pitchblende just for the cost of transportation.

Tons of pitchblende residue – dirt – were shipped to the leaky-roofed woodshed that was to be their laboratory. Now began one of the most back-breaking feats of research in the history of science. The Curies began to purify the ore; they boiled it in great vats atop a cast iron stove. They stirred the thick liquids and they filtered them. They jealously guarded each drop of liquid. When the fumes became impossible to bear, they moved their operations to the back yard. But they continued; the winter of 1896 found the couple laboring away at their dirt cookery. Marie took to her bed with pneumonia. Pierre kept the dirt boiling. Marie returned to the kettles and caldrons after three months of illness.

In September, 1897, still refining, still purifying the dirt, Marie had to take time off again. This time to give birth to a child, a daughter Irene. In a week Marie was back in the laboratory to test out something that she had thought of while lying in bed. It seemed, though, that Marie might have to suspend activity to take care of baby Irene. But Grandpa Curie, having just lost his wife, came to live with

Pierre and Marie and found happiness in watching over the baby.

Marie went back to purifying pitchblende. Two years of drudgery and they had for their labors a small amount of bismuth compound. But this bismuth compound was 300 times as active as uranium. It acted on photographic film in an amazing manner. The bismuth compound *must* have something in addition to the known elements. Marie went back to the laboratory to find the something else.

In July 1898 she announced the discovery of a new element, which she named polonium after the beloved country of her birth. But the Curies were not satisfied, because the rest of the material, after polonium was extracted, was much more potent than the polonium.

Something else remained, and purification and crystallization continued. At last there was another new element, a few crystals of it in compound. The new element was called radium.

*Pierre and Marie Curie at work in their laboratory.*

Radium was a strange element. It is about a million times as radioactive as uranium, the material that sent Marie Curie on her quest. Radium readily affects the light-sensitive material on a photographic film, even when the film is wrapped in lightproof paper. Radium ionizes the molecules of the gases in the air, that is, it enables gases to carry electricity. Radium compounds produce fluorescence when mixed with other compounds. The luminous hands on your watch probably contain a small quantity of radium. Radium radiations can prevent seeds from growing, can kill bacteria, and even small animals.

The radiation can destroy tissue and, therefore has been used in the treatment of cancer and certain skin diseases. It emits heat continuously, gives off enough heat to melt about one and a half times its own weight in ice every hour. This energy is given off at its own expense, that is, the radium disintegrates into simpler atoms as it gives off energy. Radium is truly a remarkable material.

The Curies, although bombarded with offers from all over the world, refused to make money on their discovery. With Becquerel they received the Nobel Prize for this accomplishment and used the money to pay off the debts they had incurred during their long years of purifying pitchblende.

Pierre Curie was appointed to the Sorbonne, to a Professorship and to a well-equipped laboratory.

A second daughter, Eve, was born to the Curies in 1904. They were more comfortable and happier than they had ever been when a senseless accident destroyed this happiness. On April 19, 1906, Pierre Curie, on his way home from a meeting, was knocked down in the street by a horsedrawn cab and run over by a heavy van coming from the opposite direction. He died instantly.

The heartbroken, now silent Marie sought solace by working in her laboratory. At night she wrote letters to her dead husband, describing the work she had done that day. The French, breaking all precedent, offered Marie the chair of physics left vacant by Pierre.

Anguished cries went up from some scientists. A woman? unthinkable! Besides, they said, it was Pierre who was the great one, Marie had only helped a little.

Marie Curie now proved that alone she was at least as great a scientist as her husband. In 1910 she succeeded in isolating radium in a pure state. She passed an electric current through molten radium chloride (a salt of the element) and noticed an amalgam at the negative mercury electrode. She boiled off the mercury and the free element radium was left. For this work she received a second Nobel Prize.

This remarkable woman died on July 4, 1934. Her vital organs had been destroyed as a result of years of exposure to radiation. The radium she had discovered had conquered her.

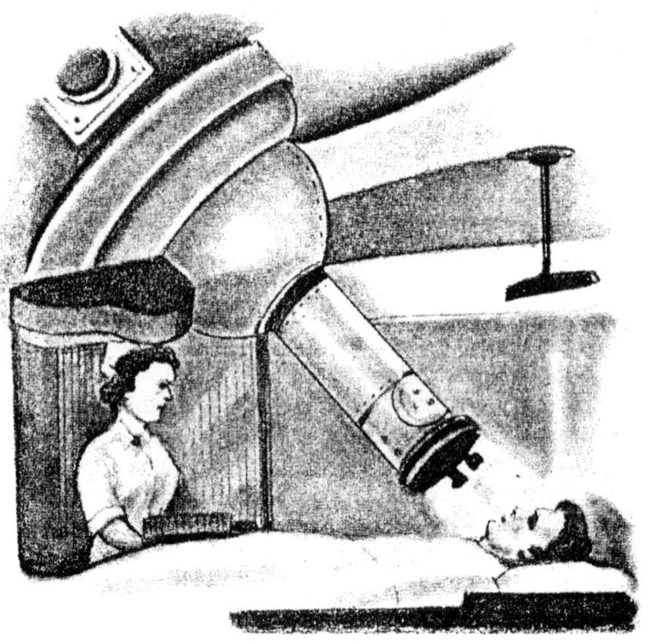

*Treatment of cancer by the radiation from radium.*

## HUMPHRY DAVY

"If the Nation could purchase a potential Watt, Davy, or a Faraday at the cost of a hundred thousand pounds, it would be dirt cheap." Thomas Huxley, an outstanding English scientist, made this statement in 1900 in a plea for government aid in the training of scientists. Humphry Davy, because of his work in electro-chemistry, is responsible for the establishment of industries involving billions of dollars annually. A Davy at a hundred thousand pounds would indeed be cheap.

It is interesting to note that Humphry Davy and his protégé Faraday worked in the Royal Institution in England, which was established by Count Rumford. The Royal Institution had as one of its objectives the education and training of young scientists. The Royal Institution still provides opportunities for scientists and holds annual Christmas lectures designed to interest children. For among young people – perhaps one who reads this book – there will be a "Watt, a Davy or a Faraday."

Humphry Davy was born in December, 1778, the son of a poor woodcarver, in the English seacoast town of

Penzance. The young Humphry attended the schools of Penzance and of nearby Truro but showed no special interest in science. He completed the elementary school and was apprenticed to a pharmacist. This apothecary had an extensive library, and Humphry Davy read widely in his spare time.

His readings included accounts of the experiments of William Nicholson, who used electricity to decompose water into hydrogen and oxygen; and of Antoine Lavoisier, the famous French chemist. Davy turned to chemistry as his life work.

His experiments brought him into contact with James Watt, Jr., the son of the famous engineer, who introduced him to Dr. Gilbert, the president of the Royal Society. Davy's brilliance impressed Dr. Gilbert, who recommended him to the founder of the just-established Medical Pneumatic Institution. This scientific institution was set up to investigate the medicinal properties of various gases. By the time he was twenty, Davy was in charge of the institution.

In April of 1799, this ungainly, even ugly, young man, a self-taught scientist, made a discovery that made him famous throughout England. He produced some nitrous oxide and inhaled a quantity of this gas. It made him happy and "drunk," but most important it made him immune to pain. Davy suggested that it could be valuable in minor surgery. However, it was not used until 1844 when an American dentist, Horace Wells, used it on himself when having a tooth extracted. The effect it had on Davy (it made him hysterical) gave nitrous oxide the popular name "laughing gas."

Count Rumford, an American, was engaged in establishing the Royal Institution in London. He asked Davy to lecture in chemistry. Davy was easily the most popular lecturer of the Institution. In spite of his lack of formal education he was soon made a full professor. His lectures on the chemical principles concerning leather tanning were so successful that the Board of Agriculture of the Royal Institution urged him to concentrate on agricultural problems.

For the next ten years he gave the course in agricultural chemistry and he was responsible for many improvements in chemical fertilizers. It was Davy who instituted the annaul science lectures for children during Christmas week.

Water had been decomposed electrically by Nicholson and his associates but it was Davy who established the practice of electro-chemistry. In a few short years he performed the experiments that place him in the forefront of the great scientists of all times.

Davy placed a piece of moist sodium hydroxide (the common name for this is caustic soda or lye) in a platinum cup. He then connected one terminal of a large electric cell to the cup and the other terminal to a platinum wire which he touched to the sodium hydroxide. The sodium hydroxide melted. Davy could see tiny globules of molten metal float to the top, where they promptly burned up.

Sodium is manufactured today by means of the electric process, but it is now made from sodium chloride. Sodium is silvery white and shiny but it tarnishes within a minute or two after being exposed to air. It is very soft and so light it floats on water. Sodium has to be stored under oil since it will combine with the moisture in the air to produce a dangerous reaction. It is useful in making Ethyl fluid for high test gasoline. Some highways are lighted with yellow lamps that contain sodium vapor.

Davy used the same electro-chemical technique in producing the element potassium. As a matter of fact, Davy discovered more elements than any other chemist. He used his electro-chemical method to isolate sodium, potassium, magnesium, strontium, calcium, chlorine, and barium. He failed, however, to produce aluminum. Charles Martin Hall, using the same method that Davy pioneered, electrolytically liberated aluminum from aluminum oxide in 1886.

For his discovery of sodium and potassium, the Emperor Napoleon presented Davy with the Medal of the French Institute. Although France and England were at war, the medal was presented to the scientist in Paris. Davy was only about thirty years old at the time.

As an outgrowth of his experiments in electro-chemistry Humphry Davy discovered the arc light, which he demonstrated before the Royal Institution in 1809. He connected two pieces of charcoal to his enormous battery. He touched the charcoals together until there was a red hot spot. Then he slowly drew the charcoals apart. A brilliant arc of light formed a path between the lumps of charcoal. Man-made illumination as bright as this had never been seen. However, the world of science and industry was not ready to provide for this kind of a light. The electric generators needed to run the arc lamps for any length of time were not yet invented. Years later the carbon arc lamp was used for many special lighting jobs – in military searchlights and in moving picture projectors, as well as in street lighting.

In 1812 a twenty-one year old young man by the name of Michael Faraday presented himself – and a handwritten set of notes – to Humphry Davy. The notes were taken while Faraday attended Davy's lectures. Davy hired this young man, and he became another of the "giants of science."

*An early arc light, called a Davy lamp. From an early engraving.*

In the same year Davy was knighted by the king, and in the following year married a widowed heiress. He and his bride, accompanied by his secretary, Faraday, went on a tour of the scientific capitals of the world. In Paris he was made a member of the French Institute. At Genoa, Italy, he investigated the electricity produced by the torpedo fish. In Florence, Italy, he used his electric arc to burn a diamond – to verify that the diamond was pure carbon. In Sweden he visited the chemist Berzelius and discussed the matter of chlorine with him.

Davy argued that chlorine was an element, not a compound as had been thought. Berzelius, who had held that chlorine was a compound, soon became convinced that Davy was correct, but he was very annoyed with Davy as a man. Sir Humphry Davy was possessed of a great deal of arrogance and vanity. He did not get along with the sensitive Swedish scientist. Davy completed his tour with a visit to the Germans.

Upon his return to England in 1815 he was presented with a new problem. The coal mines of Newcastle were disrupted by a series of accidents stemming from the coal miners' lamps. These lamps were nothing more than open torches which frequently touched off fires and explosions. The problem was to devise a lamp that would not cause an explosion. This was before the day of the electric lamp.

Sir Humphry Davy's solution was brilliant and simple. He merely wrapped the lantern flame in a metal gauze. The explosive gases couldn't get through the gauze to the heat of the flame. The gauze itself did not get hot enough to explode the gases. If any gas did get to the flame it burned up inside the gauze. The lamps was safe, and mine explosions were greatly reduced.

Davy refused to apply for a patent on this device; he gave it without charge to the miners. The grateful mine owners presented Davy with a complete silver dinner service. By the terms of his will, this silverware was melted down and sold. The proceeds went to establish the Davy Medal which is awarded annually for the most important chemical discovery in Europe and America.

In 1818 Davy was given a baronetcy, and two years

later elected President of the Royal Society. An erratic personality, he was not a success in this position. He was frequently tactless and irritating and alienated the members of the society.

Davy wrote poetry as a hobby. His contemporary, Samuel Taylor Coleridge, author of the "Rime of the Ancient Mariner," said of him, "If he were not the first chemist he would have been the first poet of his age."

Sir Humphry Davy died at the relatively early age of fifty in 1826. He had been a poor boy without a formal education who had risen to become a baronet of England. He was the savior of mineworkers, the discoverer of six chemical elements, the father of electro-chemistry.

ALBERT EINSTEIN

"Dear Mr. President," wrote the world-famous scientist Albert Einstein. "Some recent work by E. Fermi and L. Szilard which has been communicated to me in manuscript leads me to believe that the element uranium may be turned into a new and important source of energy in the immediate future. A single bomb of this type exploded in a port might very well destroy the whole port together with the surrounding territory."

This letter was written to President Franklin D. Roosevelt in the fall of 1939. Six years later on August 6, 1945, a "single bomb of this type" was dropped on the Japanese city of Hiroshima. Sixty thousand persons were killed, one hundred thousand were injured, two hundred thousand were left homeless. The atomic bomb had devastated about six hundred city blocks. A few days later a similar bomb was dropped on the city of Nagasaki. The Japanese government surrendered; World War II was over.

The atomic bomb was based on a conclusion, reached by Einstein in 1905, that mass (matter) could be changed into energy, and energy could be changed into matter.

Previous scientific theory held that matter could neither be created nor destroyed. His calculations led him to the simple-looking alebra equation:

$$E = mc^2$$

This means energy equals mass times the velocity of light times the velocity of light. Since the velocity of light is such a very large number, 186,000 miles per second or 60,000,000,000 feet per minute, the energy obtained from even a small amount of matter is very large. In fact, if one pound of material, say coal, could be converted entirely into energy the result would be more than ten billion kilowatt hours of energy. *Thus ten pounds of matter could supply the entire world with electricity for a whole month.*

Albert Einstein was born on March 14, 1879, in the southern German city of Ulm. A year after he was born the family moved to the suburbs of the city of Munich. Albert's father owned and operated a small electrochemical factory. Albert's bachelor uncle, who was trained as an engineer, assisted in this enterprise and lived with the Einstein family. Einstein's mother was interested in music, Beethoven in particular.

This interest in music resulted in violin lessons for the boy from the age of six. At first he resented the lessons. However, he acquired skill and especially liked to play Mozart's sonatas. This early musical training stayed with him throughout his entire life, providing him with hours of relaxation and enjoyment.

Albert was far from being a child prodigy. He was so long in learning how to speak that his parents began to fear that he was dull. From early childhood he separated himself from children of his own age and spent his time in daydreaming and "doing nothing." He avoided any strenuous physical exertions, did not play active games, and particularly hated to play soldier. The streets of Munich were frequently the scene of German army parades, an exciting view for most youngsters. But Albert grew uneasy at the parades. He disliked the machine-like movements of humans, turned into automatons.

Munich did not have a system of public education; the elementary schools were run by the various religious denominations. Although Einstein's parents were Jewish, they were not interested in any religion and sent Albert to the nearest school, which was a Catholic elementary school. At the age of ten he was sent to a "secondary" school, called a *Gymnasium,* which prepared students to enter the universities. He was not happy or successful in school. The students were required to learn by rote. Lacking was the informal discussion of subject matter which leads to deeper understanding.

While in the *Gymnasium,* Einstein received instruction in the Jewish religion. He had learned about Catholicism in elementary school. As a result he gained a lasting respect for the ethical values of religion but felt that all religious rituals were superstitions designed to prevent man from thinking independently. After his graduation from the *Gymnasium* he gave up membership in his religious group, but returned to the Jewish community when the Germans, during the Hitler-Nazi regime, engaged in the persecution and mass murder of the Jews.

Einstein's uncle, the engineer, enlivened the study of mathematics. He showed Albert how algebra could reduce the amount of work needed in solving a problem. He appealed to the boy's sense of humor saying, "It is a merry science; when the animal we are hunting cannot be caught, we call it 'x' temporarily and continue to hunt it until it is bagged." The study of geometry made a deep impression on the young Einstein. He was thrilled with the methods used – the clean cut, precise language, the "proof" that must be given for each statement, the sequential logic involved in each formal proof and the opportunity to reason out the solutions to problems. Einstein has said that the two most important events of his youth were the gift of a magnetic compass when he was five and the study of Euclid's geometry when he was twelve. He said, "Any one who was not transported by this book in youth was not born to be a theoretical searcher."

When Einstein was fifteen it became necessary for his father to liquidate his electrical business in Munich. He moved to Milan, Italy, to start a new enterprise. Albert was still in the *Gymnasium,* and it was arranged for him to stay in Munich to earn his diploma. The school was becoming increasingly intolerable to Einstein; he was far advanced in mathematics but did poorly in other subjects which were taught by constant drill. He was dismissed from the *Gymnasium* because he did not display the blind respect for his teachers that was demanded of the students, and went to join his father in Italy.

After a short time in Italy and a chance to think about his future, he decided that he would devote his life to a study of mathematical physics. Accordingly, he took the entrance examination to the famous Swiss Federal Polytechnic School in Zurich, Switzerland. He failed; his mathematical knowledge was outstanding, but he was weak in languages and in biology. The director of the Polytechnic was amazed at his mathematical ability and arranged for him to complete his entrance requirements in Switzerland. Here Einstein was overjoyed to find the schools conducted in an altogether different manner from those at Munich. There was no drilling, the students were expected to think for themselves, the teachers were able and willing to discuss matters with the students. Einstein found school enjoyable for the first time in his life. He completed the course and was admitted to the Federal Polytechnic School in Zurich.

While at Zurich he decided to become a physics teacher, and took the courses leading to that objective. He became, also for that reason, a Swiss citizen. His life at Zurich was not easy from a financial point of view; his father, unsuccessful in business, could not help Albert at all. Fortunately, a wealthy relative was able to help him through the university.

In spite of the fact that he was an outstanding student, and in spite of the fine letters of recommendation he obtained from his professors, Einstein was unable to obtain a teaching position. Faced with the necessity of making a living, he obtained employment as an examiner in the Swiss Patent Office in Berne.

In 1905, while employed in the patent office, Einstein formulated the special theory of relativity which led ultimately to the atomic bomb. Up to that time all physics had been based on Newton's laws of motion which had been formulated some two hundred years before and which gave the answers to most of the problems in physics. But some difficulties were beginning to develop. For instance if a rocket is launched from an airplane in the direction of travel, the rocket will have a speed equal to its own plus that of the airplane. If Newton's laws are applied to light, then the speed of light should be greater if the source of light moves towards the observer; if the source moves away, then the speed of the light should be reduced. However, A. A. Michelson, an American scientist and a teacher at the United States Naval Academy in Annapolis, performed some experiments that showed that the speed of light did not follow Newton's laws.

Einstein based his thinking on Michelson's results and formulated a statement somewhat as follows: No matter what the velocity of the source may be, light is emitted with the same velocity relative to all observers, no matter how they may be moving. This statement is called the principle of the constancy of the speed of light.

This statement may not seem to be very great or unusual but it is the mark of Einstein's genius that he was able to develop it into some very wonderful and unbelievable, ideas which are nevertheless true. One of these ideas is that a traveling clock runs slower than a clock that is at rest. This has nothing to do with the mechanism of the clock. The theory has been tested experimentally and found to be true. When the problem of interplanetary travel in atom-propelled space ships is solved, a traveller may come back from a journey that took only a month (by the space ship clock) to find that his baby son is twenty years older than the father!

From the same principle of the constancy of the speed of light, Einstein was able to produce his famous transformation of matter-into-energy law, told about before in connection with the atomic bomb. This law explains, for the first time, the source of the sun's energy. If the sun operated by burning its fuel, it should have cooled off long ago, but by converting matter into energy as Einstein has shown by his famous formula $E = mc^2$, the sun has been able to radiate for a long time and will continue to do so for millions of years to come.

Not long after the publication of his theories as well as the experimental proof that began to come from the laboratories and observatories of the world, Einstein's worth was recognized.

He was Professor Extraordinary at the University of Zurich in 1909 and went from there to the German University at Prague, then back to Zurich and then to the Kaiser Wilhelm Institute in Berlin.

He was a professor at the University of Berlin, but fortunately on a lecture tour of England and the United States when the Nazis came to power in 1933. These barbarians stripped him of his property, university position, and the Honorary Citizenship the German republic had awarded him. He came to the United States as director of the School of Mathematics in the new Institute for Advanced Study at Princeton, New Jersey. He became an ardent supporter of the State of Israel and an advocate of World Government. However when he was invited to become President of Israel he declined, saying, "Scientific problems are familiar to me, but I have neither the natural capacity nor the necessary experience to handle human beings."

Einstein received the Nobel Prize for his work on photons and the quantum theory. In 1950 he published his unified field theory. In twenty-four pages of mathematics he combined the physical laws of gravitation and electromagnetism.

Albert Einstein regretted the atomic bomb. He had hoped that its force would be demonstrated to representatives of the Japanese Government, without the necessity of dropping this deadly device on the Japanese people – but this was not to be. He hoped that atomic power would be used for the benefit of mankind.

Einstein died on April 18, 1955, still trying to make mathematical simplicity out of the laws governing the Universe. "God" he said, "does not play at dice."

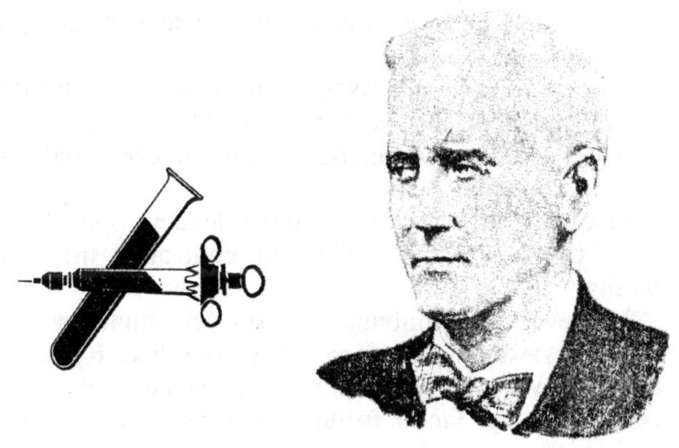

## ALEXANDER FLEMING

"Before you can notice any strange happenings you have got to be a good workman, you have got to be a master of your craft." Sir Alexander Fleming discovered penicillin because he was an extraordinarily good workman and a master of his craft. Modestly, he would have us believe that he was lucky. "The very first stage in the discovery of penicillin" he said, "was due to a stroke of good fortune." Perhaps the first stage of discovery was fortunate, but Alexander Fleming was ready; his was the "mind prepared."

Alexander Fleming was born on Lochfield Farm in southwestern Scotland on August 6, 1881, the youngest of the eight children of Hugh Fleming. His father died when he was only seven, but his mother, a cheerful woman of great character, supervised the running of the farm. She maintained the affection of her large family; her four step-children were devoted to her, as were her own four children.

Until he was ten, Alexander attended the nearby Loudoun Moor School. He was then transferred to Darvel

School, which he attended with his brothers. Alexander learned a good deal about nature during that four-mile downhill hike to school and the four-mile uphill return trip. He was a quick student, and at twelve, the age limit prescribed for Darvel School, he was sent to Kilmarnock Academy.

Two years later he joined his brothers John and Robert at the home of his elder brother Thomas, who was to become a successful oculist in London. John and Robert became opticians, and ultimately started a business of their own, which they built into a leading optical laboratory. The business is still in the control of the Fleming family.

However, the economic success of the family was yet to be, and Alexander was forced to leave school for economic reasons. When he was sixteen he obtained a job in a shipping company. Good fortune, however, was on his side and on the side of humanity. In 1901 he received a share in a legacy which made it possible for him to return to school. He decided to study medicine.

While still working for the shipping company, Alexander, along with his brothers John and Robert, had joined the London Scotttish Volunteers. He was a member of the regimental swimming and water-polo team. This team had taken part in a contest with St. Mary's Medical School. And so Alexander Fleming chose to attend a particular school for the inconsequential reason that he had played water polo against its team. He couldn't know that Almroth Wright was to join the faculty as a teacher of bacteriology.

Fleming was an honor student at St. Mary's. The records of the medical school show that he led his class in every phase of medical study: in physiology, in pharmacology, in pathology. He won virtually all the prizes offered, but he was not a grind. His excellence was not due to total devotion to his studies. He was a member of the rifle team, he was on the swimming team and played water polo. He found time to take part in amateur theatrical productions. His studies came easy to him.

Upon his graduation from St. Mary's in 1906 at twenty-five, Dr. Alexander Fleming joined Almroth Wright to do medical research. Wright was more than a teacher of bacteriology; he was famous for his work on phagocytes, a part of the blood.

Pasteur had discovered microbes, and had demonstrated that they were all about us and could not fail to be with us in our bodies at all times. The scientists realized that bacteria can enter our bodies with the air we breathe, with the food we eat and drink, through cuts or breaks in the skin. Why then are we not all destroyed by the bacteria? Elie Metchnikoff, at work in the Pasteur Institute in Paris, found part of the answer. He discovered that the white corpuscle in the blood – called the phagocyte – was a living cell that swallowed up and digested the microbe. Robert Koch on the other hand had decided, based on his observed evidence, that the blood fluid itself had the power to kill bacteria.

This controversy was settled by Wright's research. He discovered that it was not enough for the phagocytes to meet the microbes in order to engulf them. The microbes had to be prepared by the blood fluid before the phagocytes could engulf them. This property of the blood fluid Wright called opsonin.

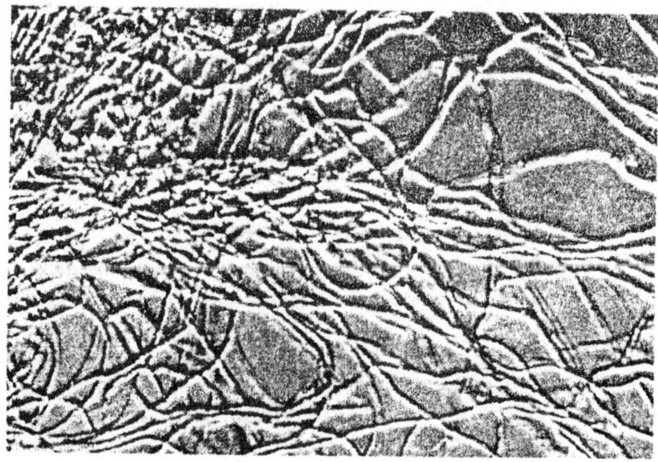

*The mold that produces penicillin, seen through a microscope.*

This discovery was a starting point for a new type of medicine. Up to now the doctor had to diagnose illness mainly by touching the patient or listening to his heart and lungs. But now the microscope could come into use; the blood could be examined. The opsonic power of a patient could be examined by testing a blood sample under the microscope. This sample could be compared with the blood of healthy people to find out how well the phagocytes digest the bacteria. If the blood and phagocytes couldn't do the job then a vaccine could be injected into the patient to produce antibodies and help destroy the bacteria.

This was Wright's thesis, and he felt that the solution to the problem of bacteria-caused diseases was in sight. It was to this research that he had recruited the brilliant Fleming. Wright insisted that the bacteriologists stay in touch with practical medicine, that they work with the hospital patients. It was a severe grind, laboratory and hospital work around the clock if need be, but it was preparation for the great discovery.

During this period Fleming became a close friend of the artist Ronald Gray, whom he successfully treated for a tubercular knee. Through Gray, Fleming was elected a member of the Chelsea Arts Group. Gray had him submit a picture of the Children's Ward at St. Mary's to a gallery exhibit. This picture was painted in the "modern-art" style. When the critics praised the painting, Gray felt that he had proved his point that modern art was not to be taken seriously, but perhaps Fleming was a good artist. Fleming continued to amuse himself by painting "bacterial" pictures. He used vividly colored germ cultures as his pigments.

During World War I, Wright's laboratory team moved to Boulogne in France. Here Fleming formed a strong opinion opposing the use of chemical antiseptics. An antiseptic is a substance which has the power to destroy bacteria. Research had proved to Fleming that although the strong chemical antiseptics did destroy some of the microbes invading a wound, they also destroyed the natural defenses of the body, the white blood corpuscles which fought the harmful microbes. Fleming was convinced that the "most important antibacterial agents in the body are the cells themselves" and that research should find out how these natural powers perform.

On February 13, 1922, the Royal Society of London received a paper *On a Remarkable Bacteriolytic Element found in Tissues and Secretions.* This paper contained a description of Fleming's discovery of a natural material which he called lysozyme.

Fleming was suffering from an inflammation of the nasal passages which was accompanied by a running nose. He began to investigate by growing a culture of the secretions. After four days he saw a large bright yellow microbe colony. He treated the colony by adding a small amount of diluted nasal mucus. He was astonished to find that a single drop of diluted mucus had caused a cubic centimeter of the microbes to disappear. He investigated further and found that lysozyme could be found in tears, in sputum, and in a very large number of tissues and organs of the body. Blood, too, contains this marvelous material. Where else could lysozyme be found? Fleming examined chicken eggs and found it in the white of the egg. Cow's milk and mother's milk contained quantities of lysozyme. Fleming wrote, "Lysozyme is a widely distributed anti-bacterial ferment which is probably inherent in all animal cells and constitutes a primary method of destroying bacteria." Nature thus provides its own antiseptics.

In the cold damp summer of 1928 in his dingy laboratory in St. Mary's Hospital the now 47-year-old Alexander Fleming opened a Petri dish in which he had a staphylococcus growth – a grapelike cluster of bacteria which causes pimples and boils. He discovered that the culture had been contaminated by a bluish mold. Apparently a wind-borne mold spore had come through an open window and had come to rest on the momentarily opened culture dish. The spore had grown into a whole colony.

Something about this colony caught the observant eye of Dr. Fleming. The mold was in the dish, the microbe culture was in the dish, *but there was a microbe-free ring around the mold.* The mold had dissolved the bacteria, the mold had the power to destroy bacteria!

The bluish bacteria-destroying mold was brushlike in appearance and hence is given the name of penicillium.

Fleming began a scientific, systematic investigation of penicillium mold. He planted some spores on a nutrient material and allowed them to grow for several days. Next he deposited various kinds of bacteria on the plate, right up to the mold. When he examined the result, some of the bacteria had grown up to the mold while others had stopped short. The mold had produced a material that destroyed certain microbes.

The investigation continued. Fleming grew his mold in a liquid medium. The fluid could destroy bacteria. More tests were made. He discovered that the material – now called penicillin – produced by the mold could prevent bacteria from growing, could kill bacteria, and could dissolve bacteria. The penicillin could kill bacteria in a Petri dish. Would it harm the body cells? Was it poisonous? More tests – this time on rabbits and white mice. The results were excellent. Fleming said, "It was this non-toxicity . . . that convinced me that some day it would come into its own as a therapeutic agent."

Fleming went as far as he could with his small staff in the discovery and investigation of penicillin. He publicized its powers as best he could, but research had to stop; there were no funds.

Meanwhile Professor H. W. Hovey and Dr. E. B. Chain at Oxford had completed research on lysozyme and were casting about for a new field of investigation. This was in 1937. They read Fleming's report on penicillin and decided to check into the chemistry of this material. They produced some small quantities of it and met with enormous success in experiments with animals.

They decided the time was ripe to try it on humans. The first patient on whom anything new is tried is a hopeless case, having failed to respond to any known treatment. The first patient treated with penicillin was on his way to recovery when their stock of material ran out. Nevertheless Chain and Hovey had seen enough to realize the tremendous potential of this new material.

In 1941, with Britain at war, Hovey came to the United

States to interest American manufacturers in its production. Penicillin was produced so that it was ready for the war. It saved countless lives. In peacetime penicillin has saved countless more.

Seventeen years after he discovered the value of penicillin, Fleming was awarded the Nobel Prize. He was knighted by a grateful British monarch in 1944. Until his death in 1955, he continued his research on the field of bacteriology.

Sir Alexander Fleming had opened up a whole new world of research. In the United States, Dr. Selman A. Waksman of Rutgers University developed streptomycin. Aureomycin and terramycin have become household words for other antibiotics. Each of these controls a particular group of bacteria.

And so one discovery leads to another. Sir Alexander Fleming said:

*"It is the glory of a good bit of work that it opens the way for better things and thus rapidly leads to its own eclipse. The object of research is the advancement . . . of knowledge."*

## NIELS BOHR

The courtly old gentleman rose from his seat, swept his hat off his head, and bowed low. The lady, the wife of an American physicist, had mentioned that her husband was studying at the Institute for Theoretical Physics at the University of Copenhagen. The scene took place on a streetcar, and the deep bow was not so much for the lady, or for her husband, but for Denmark's great scientist. It is said that the Danish people are proudest of their shipping industry, dairy products, Hans Christian Andersen, and Niels Bohr.

Niels Bohr was born on October 7, 1885, the son of Ellen Adler and of Christian Bohr, professor of physiology at the University of Copenhagen. He saw the light of day at his maternal grandmother's home, called King Georg's Palace, still held to be the most beautiful private residence in Copenhagen. Niels, a brilliant student, studied at the University of Copenhagen. At the age of twenty-two he was awarded the gold medal of the Danish Scientific Society for original studies of surface tension. He and his brother Harold, who was to become an outstanding mathematician, were already known throughout the Scandinavian countries as superb soccer players, members of the All-Danish team.

Bohr received his Ph.D. in 1911 and headed for the Cavendish Laboratory at Cambridge, England, to study under the father of the electron, the great J. J. Thomson. He worked with Sir Ernest Rutherford, and the two scientists became lifelong friends – Bohr named his son Ernest. He carefully did not use the Danish equivalent, Ernst, but spelled it in exactly the same way as did Rutherford.

In 1913 Niels Bohr published his basic theory on the structure of the atom. This theory has since been extended and modified, but the original Bohr model of the makeup of the atom led to greater understanding of chemistry and electricity and ultimately to the development of atomic energy.

The atom is accepted as the smallest particle of matter that can be identified as a distinct material. There can be atoms of copper, for example, or of neon or of uranium or of any *element*. Theoretically these materials can be divided and divided into smaller and smaller pieces; but no matter how small the pieces get – even down to the single atom – they can still be recognized as copper or neon or uranium or whatever element. *But divide the atom and the material is no longer the same element but something else.*

The atom itself is made up of two main parts. A central portion is called the *nucleus*. Separated from this are particles called electrons. In the Bohr conception of the atom, the nucleus is at the center and the electrons move about the nucleus in circular paths. This scheme is likened to the solar system in which the planets move about the sun as the center or nucleus.

The atom is incredibly small; five hundred million average size atoms wouldn't quite make it across this page. The atom, small as it is, is mostly empty space. The nucleus of the atom is only about one one-hundred thousandth as large in diameter as the atom itself. The electrons revolve about so fast that all the space seems to be taken up.

The electrons, and they are much, much smaller than

the nucleus, don't fly around haphazardly but stick to fixed orbits. The orbits shift slightly each revolution and so the electron doesn't stay in a ring, but forms a "shell."

The simplest atom is that of hydrogen, the lightest element. The hydrogen nucleus consists of one proton. A proton has an electrical charge that is equal and opposite to that of the electron, but the proton weighs almost two thousand times as much as the electron. There will normally be one electron circling about the hydrogen nucleus. The next simplest atom is that of helium–the well-known non-explosive light gas. The nucleus of helium consists of two neutrons and two protons. This element has two electrons flying about in orbit. Uranium, that earth shaking element, has 92 electrons racing about the nucleus, all neatly spaced in seven shells. In every element the nucleus consists of different numbers of protons and neutrons – and the electrons travel about in "shells."

It is well known that an electrical discharge through a gas causes it to glow. When electricity flows through neon gas you see a beautiful orange-red light. Every element has a kind of a fingerprint, or rather light print of its own, and scientists can identify the makeup of a material just by analyzing the kind of light that is produced when an electric arc is produced in the material.

Bohr used his atomic model and Planck's quantum theory to explain this, and to predict the color and kind of light that would be produced by different materials. He advanced the idea that electrons race about the nucleus in fixed orbits or raceways, but when electricity passes through the atom, the electrons jump to the next larger raceway and then go back to their usual path. As the electrons jump from orbit to orbit, light is produced. Bohr was able to predict the wave lengths of the light from the makeup of the atom, and the jump from electron orbit to electron orbit.

Like many other scientific innovations, the Bohr atom was not fully appreciated except by a small group of people. It took nine years, until 1922, for the Nobel Prize committee to get around to noticing. And in spite of the delay, Niels Bohr at thirty-seven was the youngest Nobel

Prize winner in physics up to that time. Recognition did not wait for the Nobel Prize, Bohr had already been made head of the Copenhagen Institute for Theoretical Physics.

Soon students and scientists from all over the world came to tiny Denmark to study and work. They were attracted by Bohr's brilliance. Albert Einstein said of him, "Nobody knows how the stand of our knowledge about the atom would be without him. Personally, Bohr is one of the most amiable colleagues I have met. He utters his opinions like one who is perpetually groping, never like one who believes himself to be in the possession of definite truth."

In January of 1939, Lise Meitner, an Austrian Jewish refugee from the Nazi terror, and her nephew Otto Frisch were working at the Institute with Niels Bohr. They read of discoveries of some German scientists and they guessed from the article that it would be possible to split the nucleus of uranium into approximately equal parts. When the nucleus split, and this was the important military consequence, there would be a sudden release of enormous quantities of energy. Bohr came to the United States and met with Einstein and other scientists. He discussed the matter, too, with Enrico Fermi who was working at Columbia University. In a short time the laboratories of the world confirmed the Meitner-Frisch educated guess – and the rest is the history of the atomic bomb.

Bohr returned to Denmark and remained at work at the Institute. In April of 1940, Germany attacked and overran the country in a matter of hours. For almost four years the Germans allowed the Danes to manage their country. The Germans hoped to win the Danish people by a cooperative attitude, but to no avail. Sabotage and strikes plagued the invaders; in September of 1944, the Germans imprisoned the king and disarmed the army. When the Germans attempted to annihilate the 6,000 Danish Jews, they found that 5,000 of them had been secretly shipped by small boats to Sweden – a heroic action by the people of Denmark.

Niels Bohr, son of a Jewish mother, and his wife had made good their escape from the Nazis. They, too, went to Sweden, aboard the *Sea Star,* a small fishing boat. It is said the Nazis searched his home, but overlooked the Nobel Prize Gold Medal. It had been dissolved in a bottle of acid and was to be reclaimed and recast when the war was over.

From Sweden the Bohrs came to the United States and to the atomic project at Los Alamos where they joined their son, Aage, a physicist.

When the war was over, Bohr returned to Copenhagen and to his beloved Institute. His interests are in science and in peace. As soon as the atomic bomb proved successful and devastating, Bohr pleaded for immediate international control, but without success. As Chairman of the Danish Atomic Energy Commission he attended the Atoms for Peace Conference at Geneva in 1955 and was chosen as chairman of this meeting. In October, 1957, Niels Bohr received the Ford Atoms for Peace Award, a $75,000 prize. Bohr has received more awards and prizes than any living scientist, and probably more than any scientist in history.

Bohr has a lively sense of humor; in commenting on a discussion of a theory in particle physics he said, "We are all agreed that the theory is crazy. The question that divides us is whether it is crazy enough to have a chance of being correct. My own feeling is that it is not crazy enough."

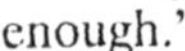

Bohr is a grandfatherly looking man, heavy set, with bushy white eyebrows. He speaks softly and swiftly. An athlete as well as a scientist, he skis, sails a boat, rides a bicycle and displays tremendous physical stamina. At the age of fifty-four, he won a ski race at Oslo, Norway.

Approaching eighty, he considers himself too old for creative scientific work but applies himself to teaching and to working for peace.

We too, like the old gentleman in the street car, take off our hats and bow low to Niels Bohr, a scientific giant who helped change the world with his model of the tiny atom.

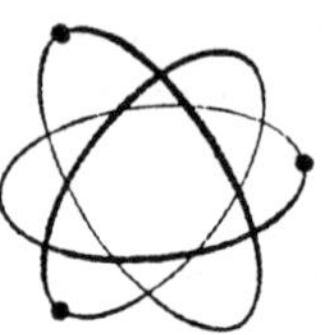

ENRICO FERMI

"The Italian navigator arrived at the shores of the new world and found the natives were friendly. It is a smaller world than he believed."

This message had nothing to do with Columbus arriving in America in 1492. It was part of a telephone conversation between Arthur H. Compton, head of the nuclear fission project at the University of Chicago, and James B. Conant, Director of the National Defense Research Commission. Compton took this means to inform Conant that the first nuclear chain reaction had been achieved. The message was transmitted in 1942. The "smaller world" referred to the amount of uranium needed, the "friendly natives" meant the reaction could be controlled and the "Italian navigator" was scientist Enrico Fermi.

As to the "new world," that was prophetic. The world has been changed irrevocably by that first nuclear chain reaction on the deserted squash court underneath the stadium at the University of Chicago. That first experimental chain reactor was the key to the atomic bomb, and the key to peaceful uses of atomic energy.

Enrico Fermi was born on September 29, 1901, in Rome, Italy. His father, with very little formal schooling, had worked his way up to head a division of the railroad. His mother was an elementary schoolteacher. Caring for three children only three years apart in age was too much for his mother's health, so Enrico, the youngest, was sent to the country to live, away from his family for almost three years. When he did get to know his brother, a year older than he, they became inseparable companions. They spent a good deal of time making model electric motors and model planes. Unhappily his brother died when Enrico was but fourteen, and his mother never seemed to recover from this shock. Luckily for Enrico, a shy retiring child, his grief and loneliness was softened somewhat by his brother's classmate, Enrico Persico. The two Enricos found much to do together; they found play in scientific study. They plotted the earth's local magnetic field and worked out the theory of the gyroscope for themselves.

In 1918 Fermi went to college in Pisa. There he wrote a paper on vibrating strings which gained him a fellowship for continued study; and in 1922 he earned a Doctor of Physics degree for experimental work with X rays. Fermi continued his studies at the University of Gottingen in Germany under the famous Max Born. These studies were made possible by a grant from the Italian Ministry of Public Instruction. By 1926, only twenty-five years old, Enrico Fermi was a full professor at the University of Rome.

When a charged particle moves through the air, there are sparks, and these can be recorded on a photograph. But when a neutron moves there is no trace of its path. Scientists know that a neutron is loose only when the neutron hits the nucleus of an atom. The collision changes the path of the nucleus. It is as if two balls collided in midair, one ball (the neutron) invisible and the other (the nucleus) visible. The change in path of the visible ball would tell us about the presence of the invisible ball.

Enrico Fermi decided that neutrons would be able to penetrate the nucleus of the atom. The electron wouldn't penetrate because it was so light and didn't go fast enough to make up for its small weight. The proton, although it was heavy, would be repelled by the nucleus, since they both have positive charges. The neutron, on the other hand, was as large as the proton but since it doesn't have a charge it would not be repelled. Fermi acted on his analysis, and in 1934 he bombarded uranium with neutrons. The nucleus of the uranium atom captured the neutron! The nucleus of the atom was therefore changed: the uranium was no longer uranium but became a new element, Neptunium. The uranium had 92 protons in the nucleus, neptunium has 93 protons. The extra proton came into being when the nucleus emitted an electron after capturing the neutron.

Atomic scientists the world over were working to find out more of what happens when atoms are bombarded. The break came in 1939. Other scientists followed Fermi's lead and bombarded the uranium with neutrons; and they succeeded in splitting the nucleus. With the split, some of the material disappeared and in place of it out came enormous amounts of energy. Matter was converted into energy, exactly as Einstein had predicted.

Lise Meitner and Otto Frisch, working with Niels Bohr in Denmark, realized the military significance of this atomic fission or splitting of the atom. Niels Bohr visited Einstein in the United States, and slowly American scientists, and a host of foreign scientists working in the United States, came to understand the military importance of the problem. Einstein transmitted their urgent concern to the United States government. Enrico Fermi, working at Columbia, verified the actual split of the atom and the "Manhattan Project," the name given by the War Department to the Atomic Bomb Project, was under way.

Fermi's job in the Manhattan Project was to find out whether a chain reaction was possible. A chain reaction is the sort of thing that happens when paper burns. Ignite one end and the end catches fire, the heat from this piece ignites the area next to it and so on until the whole sheet is ablaze.

Fermi met his future wife while she was a science student at the university. They were introduced by a mutual friend. Enrico's courtship was rapid; he married Laura Capon in 1928.

By this time Enrico had published some thirty papers on molecules, electrons, radiation, and the behavior of gases, and was elected to the Royal Academy. With this honor came an impressive uniform of silver-striped trousers, embroidered jacket and cloak, a feathered hat and a sword, the title His Excellency, and very important, a considerable annual income. The Fermis did some traveling to the new world. In 1930 he lectured at the University of Michigan and in 1934 he gave a series of lectures in Brazil and Argentina.

1938: Hitler and Mussolini, the brown-shirted Nazis, and the black-shirted Fascists marched arm-in-arm through the streets of Rome. Italian Fascism now took on an additional sinister note. Placards appeared in Rome: "Jews do not belong to the Italian race," "Down with the Jews." Enrico Fermi had always been lukewarm, at most, toward the Fascists; now he had an immediate pressing fear – Laura Capon Fermi was Jewish.

In December 1938, Enrico Fermi, his wife, their two children and their nurse got permission to visit Sweden in order for him to accept the Nobel Prize in Physics. The family did not return to Italy but came to New York City where Enrico Fermi had arranged for a position at Columbia University. His Nobel Prize was, among all its other advantages, a passport to freedom. The prize was awarded to Fermi for the identification of new radioactive elements and the discovery of nuclear reactions effected by slow neutrons.

Niels Bohr, in his model of the atom, spoke of protons in the nucleus and electrons around it. James Chadwick performed a series of experiments, and in 1932 showed that yet another particle, the neutron, was bound up inside the nucleus of the atom. The neutron is a heavy particle, as atomic particles go. It weighs about as much as a proton and about 2,000 times as much as the electron. Unlike either the electron which has a negative charge or the proton which has a positive charge, the neutron has no charge at all. Charged particles can be controlled readily by magnets or by electric fields, but a neutron cannot be detected or controlled in this manner.

The chain reaction with the splitting of the atom is about as follows: First a source of neutrons splits a uranium atom. There is energy given off, but in this case that is not what keeps the chain going. The important thing is that when the uranium atom is split it sends out more neutrons. These neutrons in turn split more atoms which give out more neutrons, which split more atoms and so on, until all the uranium is split. When the uranium atoms split, they give off the enormous amounts of energy that make the explosion so terrible.

The problem was to find out how, if it was possible at all, to produce a chain reaction. Fermi suggested that if the uranium was mixed with graphite (the "lead" in a pencil), the graphite would slow down the neutrons so that they would not shoot past the uranium atoms but would hit them. It was known that a slow moving neutron has a much greater chance of scoring a hit because when it gets near the nucleus, the neutron will be attracted by a kind of gravitational force. A high-speed neutron doesn't hit a nucleus very often; it usually flies right past, just as a golf ball hit too hard rolls right over the cup.

Fermi, with the help of many other scientific workers, succeeded in constructing an atomic pile, a pile of graphite and lumps of uranium and uranium oxide. About six tons of metal were used. Strips of cadmium, another metal, were inserted in the pile. Cadmium absorbs neutrons thus preventing too rapid a chain reaction. The pile was first operated on December 2, 1942. It was on that occasion that Arthur Compton advised James Conant that "The Italian navigator arrived" – the atomic age was a reality.

Enrico Fermi was awarded a $25,000 prize by the United States Atomic Energy Commission in November, 1954, in recognition of his contributions toward the development of the atomic bomb. Twelve days later he died of cancer, a disease that may one day be wiped out by scientists using atomic products pioneered by the work of Enrico Fermi.

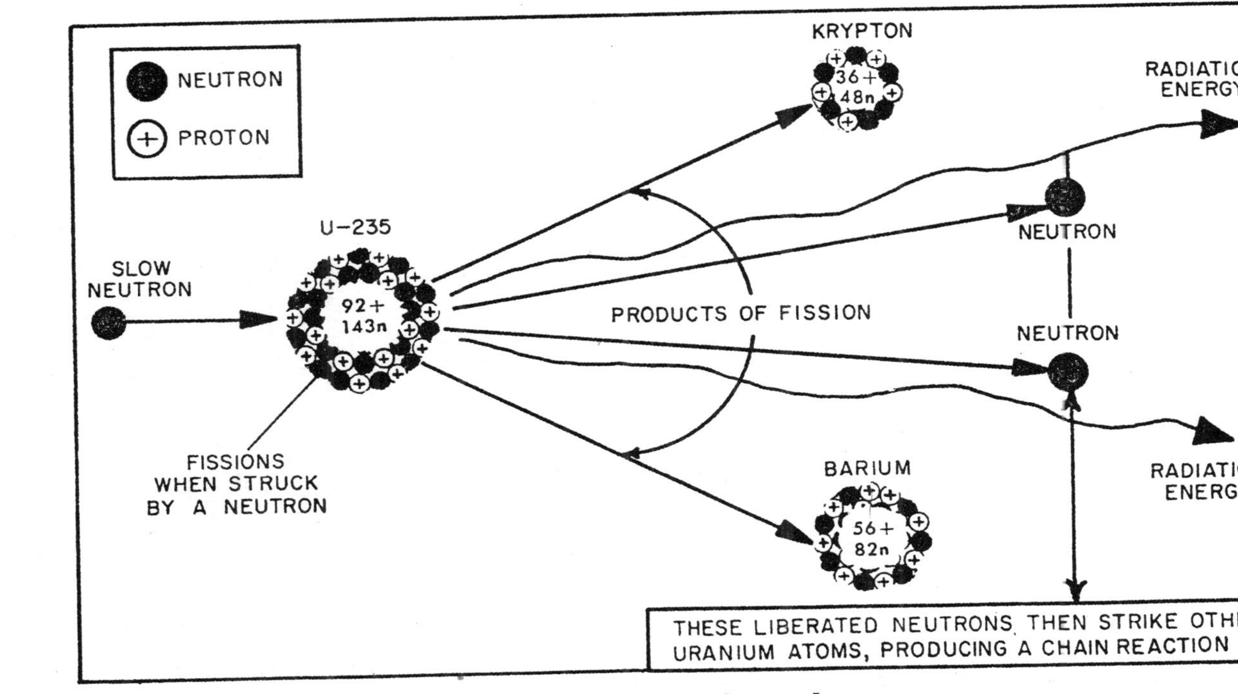


*How energy is released from the atom.*

# INDEX